PROJECT MIND CONTROL

ALSO BY JOHN LISLE   *The Dirty Tricks Department:*
Stanley Lovell, the OSS, and the
Masterminds of World War II
Secret Warfare

To Osiris

PROJECT MIND CONTROL

Sidney Gottlieb,
the CIA, and the
Tragedy of
MKULTRA

John Lisle

ST. MARTIN'S PRESS ≋ NEW YORK

First published in the United States by St. Martin's Press,
an imprint of St. Martin's Publishing Group

PROJECT MIND CONTROL. Copyright © 2025 by John Lisle.
All rights reserved. Printed in the United States of America.
For information, address St. Martin's Publishing Group,
120 Broadway, New York, NY 10271.

www.stmartins.com

The Library of Congress Cataloging-in-Publication Data is available upon request.

ISBN 978-1-250-33874-7 (hardcover)
ISBN 978-1-250-33875-4 (ebook)

Our books may be purchased in bulk for promotional, educational,
or business use. Please contact your local bookseller or the
Macmillan Corporate and Premium Sales Department at 1-800-221-7945,
extension 5442, or by email at MacmillanSpecialMarkets@macmillan.com.

First Edition: 2025

10 9 8 7 6 5 4 3 2 1

Once secrecy becomes sacrosanct, it invites abuse.

—SENATOR MIKE MANSFIELD

Security is like liberty in that many are the crimes committed in its name.

—JUSTICE ROBERT JACKSON

CONTENTS

Prologue

On September 25, 1980, Rosanna Del Guidice arrived thirty minutes early to an office building in downtown Boston. Inside were cubicles, a small dining area, and, most importantly, a conference room where the depositions occurred. Rosanna was a court reporter. By typing on a stenograph machine, she converted the spoken word into written text as fast as her clients could talk.

Rosanna had always dreamed of being a teacher, but when she learned that teachers made "garbage money," as she said in a later interview, she changed career plans. She briefly worked as a legal secretary making $1.63 an hour. On seeing an ad for a court reporting school offering its graduates six times as much, she enrolled against her father's advice, graduated in 1972, and became one of the few female court reporters in New England.

The work was overwhelming, at least in the beginning. Rosanna cried after her first deposition because she couldn't keep pace with the attorney's relentless questions. "I didn't know anything about the setup," she said. "I didn't know what the hell I was doing. That's how it all started." For the rest of the year, "I prayed my way through half of the depositions."

Pretty soon, however, she gained enough confidence to become one of the fastest and most trusted court reporters in the industry, despite the discrimination that she faced as a woman. Attorneys would often ask her to do clerical work, something that they never asked of the male court reporters. "I don't make copies," she would tell them with a straight face. "Get your secretary in here." In fact, she often earned twice as much money as the attorneys did for the day's work.

In 1978, Rosanna experienced one of her most memorable days on the job. The case involved a group of photofinishers—the people who develop photographic film—who were suing the Kodak film company because their customers kept returning photos with red-eye. The photofinishers maintained that the problem was with Kodak's equipment, and therefore Kodak should be held financially responsible. Kodak maintained that the problem was with the photofinishers' development process, not the equipment, and therefore the photofinishers should be held financially responsible. Millions of dollars were on the line.

A Kodak attorney had told the company's scientists to keep their mouths shut during their depositions, but one elderly scientist slipped up and accidentally revealed that he had known about a problem with Kodak's equipment. On hearing this, the attorney demanded to adjourn the deposition, an obvious attempt to silence the scientist. The photofinishers' attorney yelled, "You're not taking a break now, we're in the middle of questioning!" Each side began shouting obscenities back and forth. In the heat of the moment, the Kodak attorney grabbed his counterpart by the necktie and dragged him across the conference table, leading to an all-out brawl. Rosanna, caught in the middle of it, clutched her stenograph machine and ran out to the hallway. "I'll never forget it to the day I die," she said. "The old scientist blew the case, all because he told the truth!"

Rosanna had arrived at the Boston office building thirty minutes early to arrange the conference room just how she liked it. She positioned herself at the head of the heavy wooden table. To her left would sit the attorney asking the questions; she wanted him as close to her ear as possible. To her right would sit the deponent, Sidney Gottlieb, whom she would turn to face. "I can't tell you how much I learned to read lips. You can't miss a beat."

At 10:00 A.M., Gottlieb entered the conference room. Small in stature and with stark white hair, he didn't want to be there, but he had no choice. Weeks earlier, a U.S. marshal had handed him a subpoena requiring him to provide a deposition in an ongoing case. Seven prisoners from the Atlanta Federal Penitentiary were suing the government for using them as guinea pigs in secret drug experiments. One prisoner described his experience in Atlanta as involving "horrible periods of living nightmares." Another tried to kill himself by hanging, burning, and chewing off his own arm.

Once the attorneys arrived, everyone sat in their respective seats. Rosanna swore in Gottlieb and the deposition began. Attorney Thomas Maddox initiated the direct examination.

"Dr. Gottlieb, you understand I represent Mr. Don Roderick Scott, who was an inmate at the Atlanta Federal Penitentiary in the late 1950s; is that correct, sir?"

Gottlieb, a stutterer whose condition worsened when he was nervous, shook his head up and down.

Maddox intervened, "You need to answer something verbal, so this young lady—she can't record nods."

"I do," Gottlieb said. "I am trying to say yes."

Maddox next asked Gottlieb to describe his educational background.

"Well, my PhD was from Cal. Tech. . . . in something called bio-organic chemistry."

Maddox then skipped to the crux of the issue: "When did you first begin your association with the Central Intelligence Agency?"

Over the next three years, Gottlieb sat for four additional depositions conducted by legendary civil rights attorney Joseph Rauh and his young law partner James Turner. All four took place in Culpeper, Virginia—one at a Holiday Inn, the other three at the Boxwood House Motel. The five total depositions lasted a combined twenty-five hours and consist of 823 pages of material. Many of Gottlieb's colleagues sat for depositions of their own, as did many of their victims, constituting thousands more pages.

These depositions, which I discovered tucked away in the Library of Congress, provide a window into Gottlieb's and his colleagues' inner thoughts about their participation in some of the most controversial projects ever undertaken in the history of the CIA, projects that involved sex, drugs, torture, hypnotism, electric shocks, chemical comas, sensory deprivation, and assassination attempts. In short, the depositions represent a foray into the minds of those who perpetrated, as well as those who suffered, these infamous acts.

Upon rereading the transcript of Gottlieb's first deposition, Rosanna said that he had revealed "a lot more than I would have expected." While most people tend to conveniently forget their memories whenever they have an incentive to do so, Gottlieb, to her surprise, "was pretty open. His answers were so long. I was fascinated."

Paul Figley, an attorney for the Department of Justice, had been present at another of Gottlieb's depositions and reached a similar conclusion. In an interview, he said that Gottlieb "was going to tell the story that he wanted to tell. He had retired at that point and was going to do whatever he wanted to do, maybe what he had done his whole life."

When asked whether Gottlieb had provided more information than was advisable from the perspective of a defense attorney, Figley took a long pause. "He was not as—" Another pause. "I didn't have as much control over him as I would have liked." He continued:

> In a deposition setting, what you really want if you're defending is for your client to tell the truth, the whole truth, and nothing but the truth about the question that is asked, and not to then go on and say, "This might be of interest to you" or "When I did that I thought . . ." It just opens up more areas and will lead to more rocks that people will have to turn over and see what's underneath. He was not the kind of witness that if you're defending a case you want to have because you don't know what he's going to say.

From the defense's perspective, Gottlieb's depositions were a disaster. From the historian's perspective, they're a gold mine.

1

The Outsider

Sidney Gottlieb had a number of unusual quirks. Most noticeably, he walked with an awkward limp, the result of two clubfeet. He also talked with a stutter. It wasn't too pronounced—unless he was nervous—but when he was young, it gave his classmates yet another reason to tease him. From an early age, Gottlieb felt like an outsider.

His other quirks were self-inflicted. Throughout his life, he was known to drink goat milk, tinker with gadgets, and perform unusual dances to folk music.

Born in New York City on August 3, 1918, to Orthodox Jewish immigrants from Hungary, Gottlieb was an extremely bright child. When his older brother, David, built a makeshift laboratory in the basement of their brick house, Sidney developed a lasting love for science. He attended elementary and high schools in the Bronx, then jumped between colleges— City College of New York, Arkansas Polytechnic College, the University of Wisconsin—where for once in his life he apparently fit in. The Arkansas yearbook called him "a Yankee who pleases the southerners."

At the University of Wisconsin, Gottlieb studied under the renowned bacteriologist Ira Baldwin. "Mr. Gottlieb is a very high type of Jewish boy," Baldwin wrote in a glowing letter of recommendation. "He has a brilliant mind, is thoroughly honest and reliable, and is modest and unassuming." Baldwin also mentioned that Gottlieb had "a slight speech impediment."

After earning a bachelor's degree in chemistry in 1940, Gottlieb enrolled in graduate school at the California Institute of Technology. Young, trim, and talented, he not only excelled in his coursework but also met the love of his life, Margaret Moore, who was studying preschool education at nearby

Whittier College. Margaret had grown up in India, where her father was a Presbyterian missionary. To her father's chagrin, she was a freethinker who questioned the morality of missionaries as well as the claims of Christianity.

Although Gottlieb and Margaret had been raised in completely different cultures on completely different continents, they shared the same eccentric spirit. In 1942, they married in a small civil ceremony. Margaret's mother, accustomed to her daughter's rebellious ways, wrote to her relatives, "If they have Each Other, they are indeed fortunate in this world full of sorrow."

The United States had just entered World War II, and like many young American men, Sidney Gottlieb felt a sense of patriotic duty to fight for the country that had given his immigrant parents a second start at life. As soon as he earned a PhD in biochemistry in 1943, he tried to enlist in the Army. His limp, however, disqualified him from service. "I wanted to do my share in the war effort," he later said, "yet I couldn't convince anyone that I would not be hampered in my performance." The rejection was one of the major disappointments of his life because it seemed to legitimize his long-held belief that he was an outsider. Gottlieb may have been unconventional by nature, but he nevertheless craved acceptance.

Over the next eight years, Gottlieb worked brief stints at the Department of Agriculture, the Food and Drug Administration, the National Research Council, and the University of Maryland, mostly developing tests to detect drugs in the human body. The jobs, he said, "became repetitive and sometimes pretty monotonous. I needed more of a challenge."

Meanwhile, his personal life was full of excitement. He and Margaret soon had their first two children, both girls. The family of four (eventually six with two more little boys) moved into a remodeled former slave cabin in Virginia that had no water, electricity, "or any of that fancy stuff," Margaret wrote in an autobiographical essay. "It sat under three very magnificent oak trees, and when I saw it, I said, 'This will be my home.' Sid, having grown up in New York City, thought I was nuts, but I persuaded him that I knew how to live this way." Despite his initial skepticism, Gottlieb quickly adjusted to the primitive lifestyle. "Sid is pitching in more than he ever has before and he's wonderful. I feel guilty sleeping when he has to milk the goats."

Once his family was settled, Gottlieb began looking for a new job that

PROJECT MIND CONTROL

was both intellectually stimulating and of service to his country. He might have been prevented from fighting in World War II, but his sense of patriotism was as strong as ever, especially at the outset of the Cold War.

The United States and the Soviet Union had shared an uneasy alliance during World War II. After the war, their alliance crumbled, prompting the onset of the Cold War, a decades-long period of geopolitical tension between the two countries. Contributing to the tension was the fact that many aspects of Soviet society—atheism, communism, slave-labor gulags, the dissolution of democratic institutions—seemed incompatible with American values.

Several other important world events further heightened the sense of tension. For one, the Soviets blockaded West Berlin in an attempt to extend their control over Germany. They also detonated their first atomic bomb, ending the American nuclear monopoly. Moreover, Mao Zedong and the Chinese Communist Party defeated the Chinese Nationalists in their civil war, and Communist North Korea invaded South Korea, initiating the Korean War.

Many Americans feared that Communists would next try to overthrow the government of the United States. As a result of this "Red Scare," blacklists, loyalty oaths, and book bans spread across the country. (The children's story Robin Hood was a notable target because it glorified stealing from the rich to help the poor.) Congress even passed anti-Communist legislation, such as the McCarran Internal Security Act, which barred suspect individuals from obtaining citizenship, holding passports, working in government jobs, and, in some cases, traveling to and from the country. At the state level, the Texas legislature made Communist Party membership a felony punishable by twenty years in prison. Governor Allan Shivers hesitated to sign the bill because of the punishment; he thought that the death penalty was more appropriate.

Conservative politicians capitalized on the Red Scare. In a gambit of political theater known as McCarthyism, they would accuse anyone with even the most tenuous connection to left-leaning causes of being a card-carrying Communist. The sensational nature of the accusations, regardless of whether they were true, generated fear, which generated press coverage, which generated votes for the politicians on Election Day. Journalist George Reedy joked that the eponymous Wisconsin politician Joseph McCarthy "couldn't find a Communist in Red Square. He didn't know Karl

Marx from Groucho Marx." Nevertheless, McCarthy recognized an opportunity to advance his political career when he saw one, even if it meant that he had to invent an enemy to fight.

Politicians weren't the only ones exploiting the Red Scare. If the Navy wanted new ships, it exaggerated the threat of Soviet ships. If the Air Force wanted new bombers, it exaggerated the threat of Soviet bombers. The CIA once bought thousands of subscriptions to *The Daily Worker,* a Communist Party mouthpiece, in an effort to inflate the apparent circulation of the newspaper. If the Soviet Union was seen as powerful, the logic went, then Congress would give the military and the intelligence community more money to help defend the United States. And it worked.

A good portion of the Red Scare was manufactured for the benefit of a few individuals, companies, and organizations, but there still existed many people, for many good reasons, who believed that the Soviet Union represented an existential threat to the United States. Sidney Gottlieb was one of them.

At the height of the Red Scare, Gottlieb's patriotism drove him to apply for a job at the CIA, where he thought that his scientific expertise would compensate for his physical shortcomings. The CIA had been created in 1947 to coordinate American efforts to gather and analyze intelligence. President Harry Truman noted that the original CIA "was not intended as a 'Cloak & Dagger Outfit'" that engaged in sabotage, assassinations, and other covert operations. Rather, it was "intended merely as a center for keeping the President informed on what was going on in the world," though that would soon change.

Enabling the change was a series of laws that gave the CIA an unprecedented lack of oversight. Most notably, the Central Intelligence Agency Act of 1949 gave the CIA the ability to spend unvouchered funds and freed it from disclosing to Congress who its employees were and what they did. In other words, CIA personnel were emboldened to engage in covert operations because nobody was looking over their shoulders.

During the Red Scare, it was easy for those personnel to rationalize the need for covert operations. A government report on the CIA from the 1950s best summarizes their philosophy: "It is now clear that we are facing an implacable enemy whose avowed objective is world domination by whatever means and at whatever cost. There are no rules in such a game.

Hitherto acceptable norms of human conduct do not apply." Put simply, desperate times call for desperate measures.

Later, reflecting on the trajectory of the CIA, Truman lamented, "For some time I have been disturbed by the way [the] CIA has been diverted from its original assignment. It has become an operational and at times a policy-making arm of the Government. This has led to trouble and may have compounded our difficulties in several explosive areas." In time, nobody would become more intimately acquainted with troublesome CIA operations in explosive areas than Sidney Gottlieb.

But in the summer of 1951, Gottlieb didn't know much about the CIA. All he knew was that it was a place where he might repay the debt that he felt that he owed to his country. And to his good fortune, the CIA was looking to hire brilliant scientists like himself. The development of atomic bombs had shown that science was now an integral part of national security. The CIA needed someone like Gottlieb to explore the frontiers of knowledge and find new ways to win the Cold War, no matter how odd or esoteric.

Gottlieb was culturally, but not religiously, Jewish. Like so much else about his life, he would try to keep his beliefs shrouded in mystery. Margaret, on the other hand, was more forthcoming about her and her husband's New Age sense of spirituality:

> I am impatient when I hear people equate being "good" or "religious" with being Christian. There are many "goods" and many religions, and a Muslim's way to God is very similar to ours, and so is a Hindu's or a Buddhist's, and I can't see that Christianity is more full of love or less full of fears and superstitions. . . . Is there a God? There is certainly a Force or a Source that all mankind (and maybe animals too) feels. It amazes and delights me that peoples who have not known of each other's existence on the earth have come to very similar questions and to similar answers down through the ages since our very beginnings. There is Something that we all sense and are familiar with. Please let us not say, "My way is the only way."

Given Gottlieb's unique background and unorthodox beliefs, he once again felt like an outsider at the CIA, an organization whose workforce of affluent Ivy League graduates was often summarized as pale, male, and

Yale. Gottlieb spent his first two years in the CIA working as a chemist for what was then called the Office of Policy Coordination, the division responsible for conducting covert operations abroad. While reminiscing in his depositions about this early work, he said that he had been involved in the "more classical application of chemistry to the intelligence field, things like secret writing, the use of chemistry in the printing process, areas like that."

In 1953, he became the head of the Chemical Branch of the CIA's Technical Services Staff (TSS). What did the TSS do? During one of Gottlieb's depositions, attorney Thomas Maddox asked him, "Did [it] produce the gadgets and things we have associated with James Bond?"

"That's the right idea," Gottlieb said. "You are in the right ballpark."

But both Maddox and Gottlieb knew that the TSS did much more than produce clever gadgets. Under Gottlieb's influence, it conducted some of the most notorious projects in American history.

Throughout his depositions, Gottlieb stressed that in order to understand his work, it was necessary to understand the context in which it was done. At the beginning of the Cold War, the CIA had feared that Communist powers like the Soviet Union and China possessed methods of mind control powerful enough to manipulate a person's beliefs and behaviors. One reason why the CIA feared such a thing was because Russian scientists had pioneered the field of behavioral conditioning. Back in 1897, Russian physiologist Ivan Pavlov had shown that by ringing a bell every time that a dog ate, he could condition the dog to salivate at the sound of the bell alone. Surely the Soviets had since extended Pavlov's work to include human subjects.

Another reason was because in the 1930s, Soviet leader Joseph Stalin had held a series of show trials in Moscow to remove his political opponents from power. Strangely, many of the defendants begged to be found guilty of the false charges levied against them. Yuri Pyatakov even prostrated before Stalin and asked for the honor of shooting his fellow defendants. (Perhaps his plea fell on deaf ears because his ex-wife was among the group.) Why were the defendants behaving so bizarrely? Had they been drugged? Had they been hypnotized? Had they been subjected to some other form of mind control?

Then, in 1948, Cardinal József Mindszenty, leader of the Catholic Church in Hungary and a vocal critic of the country's new Communist regime, was arrested on charges of treason. Again, the charges were obviously false. The

Communists were simply trying to silence one of their most influential crit-ics. But at a show trial six weeks after his arrest, Mindszenty had somehow changed. He wasn't his fearless, outspoken self. Instead, he appeared cold and unemotional. He didn't even recognize his own mother when she came to visit him. Strangest of all, he confessed to the false charges. The image of this downtrodden priest, once so full of conviction, confessing to crimes that he didn't commit caused many CIA personnel to wonder whether he had been subjected to mind control. "Somehow they took his soul apart," said one intelligence officer.

In reality, Mindszenty confessed because he had been subjected to the more traditional methods of coercion: fatigue, hunger, torture, and isolation. Yet nobody in the CIA knew this for sure. Out of an abundance of cau-tion, they assumed the worst. Maybe the Communists had perfected mind control. The recent success of dystopian novels like Aldous Huxley's *Brave New World* and George Orwell's *Nineteen Eighty-Four* certainly made it seem possible.

The Communist threat of mind control was considered so real that a CIA memo from the early 1950s recommended that all overseas employees based near the Iron Curtain avoid hospitalization, medical attention, and psychiat-ric treatment of any kind unless conducted by "fully authorized and trusted institutions and doctors." The enemy might strike at any unguarded moment.

Such a fear wasn't as strange as it sounds, and Gottlieb knew that it sounded strange. "All of this might seem farfetched now," he said in his depositions. "But I would beg you to try to live in another context, namely that of 30 years ago, when it was—" He paused. "Things were thought possible then."

2

Bluebird and Artichoke

A year before Sidney Gottlieb joined the CIA, Sheffield Edwards, head of the CIA's Office of Security, created a new research project called Bluebird. Its stated goal was to "utilize the polygraph, drugs, and hypnotism to attain the greatest results in interrogation techniques." Edwards essentially wanted to develop the equivalent of a truth serum, something to make a captured spy "sing like a bird," hence the name Bluebird. This was the CIA's first foray into the business of mind control.

Morse Allen, a domineering polygraph expert in the CIA's Office of Scientific Intelligence, took command of Bluebird. He posed four main questions for the project to answer:

> Can accurate information be obtained from willing or unwilling individuals?
>
> Can agency personnel . . . be conditioned to prevent any outside power from obtaining information from them by any known means?
>
> Can we obtain control of the future activities (physical and mental) of any given individual, willing or unwilling?
>
> Can we prevent any outside power from gaining control of future activities (physical and mental) of agency personnel by any known means?

Beyond these four main questions, Allen posed other subsidiary questions, which, he said, "can only be resolved by experiment, testing and research." Among them:

Can we create by post-H[ypnotic] control an action contrary to an individual's basic moral principles?

Could we seize a subject and in the space of an hour or two by post-H[ypnotic] control have him crash an airplane, wreck a train, etc.?

Can we . . . force a subject (unwilling or otherwise) to travel long distances, commit specified acts and return to us or bring documents or materials?

Can we guarantee total amnesia under any and all conditions?

Can we "alter" a person's personality? How long will it hold?

Seeking answers, Allen contacted a well-known stage hypnotist for guidance. If anyone knew how to control human behavior, surely it was him.

The hypnotist was six feet tall, wore horn-rimmed glasses, and, according to Allen, "has a strong, aggressive look, and, physically, is quite impressive." It was almost certainly George Estabrooks, who in 1950 had written a magazine article claiming that it was possible to "hypnotize a man—without his knowledge or consent—into committing treason against the United States." The article continues, "A small corps of carefully trained hypnotists attached to an armed force could wreak more far-reaching havoc than an atom bomb." He also claimed to have created "hypnotic couriers" for the Allies during World War II, soldiers in whose subconscious minds he would implant secret messages for delivery.

Allen interviewed Estabrooks about whether hypnotism could be used to gain control of a person's actions. Estabrooks assured him that it could. As proof, he regaled Allen with sordid stories of how he had hypnotized various women into having sex with him. In a summary of their conversation, Allen wrote that an unnamed orchestral performer "was forced to engage in sexual intercourse with [redacted] while under the influence of hypnotism." Allen further noted that "many times while going home on [redacted] he would use hypnotic suggestion to have a girl turn around and talk to him and suggest sexual intercourse." Estabrooks "spent approximately five nights a week away from home engaged in sexual intercourse."

Allen bit the bait. Hypnotism, it seemed, offered him a way to take Bluebird beyond what he called the "mental claustrophobia of book and lecture hall knowledge." It would revolutionize the CIA—if it worked.

To give his colleagues a sense of his vision for Bluebird, Allen paid for the production of a short film called *The Black Art*. The opening scene of the film shows an American agent placing an Asian diplomat in a hypnotic trance. The next day, the Asian diplomat walks into his embassy, opens a safe, steals classified documents, and brings them to the American agent. As the film fades to black, a narrator speaks, "Could what you have just seen [be] accomplished without the individual's knowledge? Yes! Against the individual's will? Yes! With complete amnesia of performing the act? Yes! How? Through the powers of suggestion and hypnosis."

Morse Allen conducted his first hypnotism experiments on the female secretaries working in his office. Unlike Estabrooks, he was principled enough not to trick them into sleeping with him. Instead, during one experiment, he placed a secretary in a hypnotic trance and told her that when she woke up, she wouldn't be able to see the person sitting in front of her. According to the summary of the experiment, "She was asked to count the number of people inside the room (4) including herself. She replied that there were three people." When asked who was sitting in front of her, she said, "There is no one sitting there." Afterward, she exhibited a "complete amnesia" of the events. The results thrilled Allen, who emphasized, *"This test should have operational value."*

But there was one catch. What if the secretary had faked her behavior because she didn't want to disappoint her boss? That seems to have been the case during another experiment in which Allen placed a secretary in a trance and tried to convince her that she was reliving a recent vacation in Florida. When asked where she was, she claimed to be sitting on a surfboard in the Gulf of Mexico. She even proceeded to fall off of the surfboard and swallow a mouthful of imaginary seawater. However, she later admitted that she had never ridden a surfboard in her life.

Allen needed a way to determine whether the secretaries were truly hypnotized or just humoring him. His solution was to hypnotize a secretary and command her to do something that she would never do under any circumstances in real life. If she did it anyway, then surely she was truly hypnotized.

For this new experiment, Allen placed a secretary in a trance and told her to fall asleep until he—and only he—woke her up. He then placed a second secretary in a trance and told her to try as hard as she could to wake her sleeping coworker. If she couldn't do it, per Allen's instructions, "Her rage would be so great that she would not hesitate to kill." A pistol was strategically placed on a nearby table.

The second secretary had previously expressed a fear of guns and didn't know whether the pistol was loaded (it wasn't). Nevertheless, when she couldn't wake her sleeping coworker, she went into a blind rage, grabbed the pistol, pointed it at her coworker, and pulled the trigger. Both secretaries "were awakened and expressed complete amnesia for the entire sequence," Allen wrote. The second secretary "was again handed the gun, which she refused (in an awakened state) to pick up or accept from the operator." Confronted about what she had done, "she expressed absolute denial that the foregoing sequence had happened."

Yet the question still remained: Did Allen gain control of his secretaries through hypnotism, or did a suggestible young woman suspect that her boss had planted an unloaded pistol in the room? Allen desperately wanted to believe the former, but he feared the latter, especially in light of what other researchers had found.

Some thirty years earlier, French psychologist Pierre Janet had conducted a similar experiment on a young woman. He hypnotized her before an audience of distinguished judges and convinced her to stab them with a rubber dagger, poison them with sugar pills, and commit several other "murders." At the end of the performance, some of Janet's male assistants suggested that she take off her clothes, which immediately caused her to snap out of the "trance."

Moreover, during World War II, psychiatrists Karl and William Menninger had informed the Office of Strategic Services (OSS), the precursor to the CIA, "There is no evidence that supports post-hypnotic acts, especially where the individual's mores and morals produce the slightest conflict within him. A man to whom murder is repugnant and immoral cannot be made to override that personal tabu." Psychiatrist Lawrence Kubie, another consultant to the OSS, similarly concluded that unless someone already had the motivation to commit a specific act, "I am skeptical that [hypnotism] will accomplish anything."

Despite Allen's inconclusive results, and despite the checkered history of hypnotism, the CIA began planning covert operations involving hypnotism. One research team wondered whether it would be possible to hypnotize an unidentified thirty-five-year-old subject into assassinating "a prominent [*redacted*] politician" or even "an American official." Since the subject was a heavy drinker, "it was proposed that the individual could be surreptitiously drugged through the medium of an alcoholic cocktail at a social party." Once he was inebriated, he would be hypnotized into performing the assassination. As for what would happen to him afterward, "it was assumed that the subject would be taken into custody by the [*redacted*] Government and thereby 'disposed of.'" Of course, all of this was just wild speculation. The research team knew that hypnotism wasn't *that* good. At least not yet.

In 1951, the CIA let the Army, Navy, and Air Force join Project Bluebird. A joint program among all of them would spread the financial burden, give each organization access to the results, and eliminate any unnecessary duplication of research. Since the Navy already had a Project Bluebird of its own, the CIA changed the cryptonym of the project to "Artichoke."

The goals of Artichoke were similar to those of Bluebird: learn how to extract information from a subject, how to prevent such extraction from occurring, and how to control a subject's actions "whether they wish it or not," says an early Artichoke memo. The potential areas of study were broadened beyond hypnotism to include drugs, food deprivation, "gases and aerosols," "electro-shock narcosis," "the effects of high and low pressures," "bacteria, plant cultures, fungi, poisons," and, most disturbing of all, "surgical (e.g. lobotomy)."

Regarding lobotomies, one memo says that the CIA contemplated removing parts of a person's brain as a "neutralizing weapon" to render them "harmless from a security point of view." In general, though, the CIA shied away from lobotomies because the procedure was "fraught with very many problems," not least of which was its barbarity. Dr. Walter Freeman, a neurologist who traveled around the country performing lobotomies on thousands of alcoholics, homosexuals, and children as young as four years old, once described the procedure in a letter to his son: "This consists of knocking them out with a shock and while they are under the 'anesthetic' thrusting an ice pick up between the eyeball and the eyelid through the roof of the orbit actually into the frontal lobe of the brain and making a lateral cut by swinging the thing from side to side." Freeman acknowledged that it was "definitely a disagreeable thing to watch." Many of his patients left the operating room worse off than when they had entered. In his most prominent failure, Freeman lobotomized twenty-three-year-old Rosemary Kennedy, President John F. Kennedy's sister, in 1941, leaving her disabled, incontinent, and institutionalized for the rest of her life.

Another memo says that the CIA lost interest in lobotomies for two reasons. First, the CIA didn't want to deal with the inevitable moral objections of the doctors who would be asked to perform the procedure on healthy individuals. Second, the potential for blowback was way too high. If the press ever learned that the CIA had lobotomized people, "its exposure would cause irreparable damage to the reputation of this country and this Agency and to any claims we may have of virtue or high ideals." On a personal level, the anonymous author of the memo (most declassified CIA memos are sanitized of their authors) wrote that he was "morally opposed" to lobotomies.

The only other internal objections to Artichoke appear in two short notes that CIA officers scribbled to their colleagues. One reads, "What in God's name are we proposing here? Does it not strike anyone but a few that these projects may be immoral and unethical, and that they may fly in the face of international laws? What really are we attempting to accomplish? Where does respect for life and human dignity come into play?" The other note says, "Where does this stuff end? The sheer madness of some of these ideas is getting difficult to swallow." However, these objections weren't enough to prevent Artichoke from moving forward. For the few CIA personnel who knew about Bluebird, Artichoke, and other similar projects, it was much easier to nod their heads than shake them.

In his depositions, Sidney Gottlieb said that Artichoke was all about "how you interrogate somebody that is potentially hostile and wants to withhold information, and make it not possible for him [to do that] through a truth serum. . . . Although it had wording which gave it broader missions." Lobotomies may have been intriguing in theory, but for all intents and purposes, Artichoke was mostly concerned with developing drugs and hypnotic techniques to make someone talk during an interrogation.

Little is known about the experiments and operations that were conducted as part of Artichoke, though the few files that survive paint a harrowing picture. In June 1952, two captured foreign spies were taken to a safe house—a secret location for conducting illicit activities—and interrogated with Artichoke methods. CIA officers injected them with sodium pentothal to lower their inhibitions and administered "a highly controlled hypnotic technique," the details of which remain secret. The spies then fell into a "deep hypnotic trance state" and were questioned for nearly two hours.

The next day, one of the spies underwent a second interrogation. This time he received "heavy dosages" of sodium pentothal mixed with the stimulant Desoxyn. The drugs, combined with the hypnotism, produced a "remarkable regression" that was "almost too perfect from an intelligence point of view." Apparently he was deluded into thinking that the interrogator was an old friend. Whenever the interrogator asked a question, the spy would respond, "Why are you asking me this? You know all these things."

A subsequent report on the interrogations notes that both spies talked at "great length" and revealed "extremely valuable" information. The report concludes, "Every success with this method will be pure gravy."

Other Artichoke interrogations occurred at the Camp King military facility near Frankfurt, Germany. Several military personnel have argued that the CIA enlisted the help of former Nazi scientists to turn Camp King into a veritable dungeon where "expendable" prisoners were given a cornucopia of disorienting drugs. Even if this is true, the CIA was about to embark on a new project that would eclipse both Bluebird and Artichoke in depravity.

3

The Origins of MKULTRA

Halfway through the Korean War, in January 1952, pilots Kenneth Enoch and John Quinn of the U.S. Air Force Third Bomb Wing were flying over enemy territory when their B-26 was hit by antiaircraft fire. Two of their crewmates died instantly. Enoch and Quinn managed to parachute from the sputtering bomber, but a group of Chinese soldiers was waiting for them on the ground. Both men were captured as prisoners of war.

Over the next twenty months, Enoch and Quinn were routinely tortured and interrogated. During their interrogations, they confessed to a litany of war crimes, including committing biological warfare against North Korea. Their bomber payloads, they said, had contained anthrax, typhus, cholera, smallpox, malaria, yellow fever, and bubonic plague. Enoch wrote in an open letter, "I am beginning to see very clearly just who is the peace-lover and who is the warmonger responsible for this inhuman war, and I am determined to struggle for peace against Wall Street capitalism, to clear my conscience of my past errors."

Quinn similarly excoriated the United States:

It is very clear from these facts that the Capitalistic Wall Street war mongers in their greed, their ruthless greed, have caused this horrible crime of Bacteriological Warfare to be launched in order to get more money for themselves and in the hope of spreading the war. . . . This is a horrible crime against the people, even the German Nazis would not use it, those people like [Ilse] Koch who would make lamp shades out of human skin would not use it, but I used it for the U.S. imperialist warmongers of Wall Street. . . . My own conscience bothered me a great deal, and it is very good to be rid of this burden, to confess and repent.

If their confessions were true, then the United States had violated the Geneva Conventions and perpetrated major crimes against humanity.

In July 1952, the *China Monthly Review* published a story detailing the different types of biological weapons that the United States had supposedly dropped on North Korea. There were germ bombs, germ dust, bombs containing "germ-laden insects," parachutes carrying "small germ-laden animals," and "germ-laden handbills, fountain pens, clothing and food." Accompanying the story were staged photographs of masked Korean women using chopsticks to catch disease-carrying fleas in the countryside. To further substantiate the story, North Korea's secret police infected two prisoners with cholera and claimed that they had contracted the disease from the bombings.

By the end the war, thirty-eight other American POWs had made confessions similar to those of Enoch and Quinn. One of them, Second Lieutenant Floyd O'Neal, described in stunning detail a lecture that he had supposedly attended before deploying: "If the germ-infected insect bombs contained more than one type of insect, they could be separated by the pasteboard partitions inside the bomb. Then when the bomb touched the ground there would be a small door in each section which would open to release the insects. At this point we were given a 10-minute rest to get a coke."

None of the confessions were true. The United States hadn't engaged in biological warfare. So then why did the POWs confess to something that was false? Once again, many CIA personnel suspected mind control.

As news of the POW confessions reached the United States, several other events contributed to the impression that the Communists possessed methods of mind control. For one, former OSS officer and self-described "propaganda specialist" Edward Hunter published an article in the *Miami Daily News* on how the Chinese used Pavlovian tricks to manipulate people into joining the Communist Party. The article popularized the term "brainwashing," which Hunter said derived from the Chinese word *xinao*, meaning "to cleanse the brain."

Another curious event occurred in September 1952 when a Russian journalist asked U.S. ambassador to the Soviet Union George Kennan about his social life in Moscow. Kennan tersely responded that his isolation in the city was worse than the isolation that he had experienced while interned in Nazi Germany during World War II. The Soviets took offense to the comment and declared Kennan persona non grata. Richard Helms, chief of operations for the CIA's Office of Policy Coordination, later said that he had wondered whether the Soviets had secretly slipped Kennan "some drug that caused him to act in such an aberrant fashion."

In reality, neither the POWs nor Kennan had been manipulated with drugs. The POW "confessions" resulted from months of physical and psychological torture. Psychiatrist Louis "Jolly" West interviewed the POWs upon their return to the United States and concluded, "What we found enabled us to rule out drugs, hypnosis or other mysterious trickery. Just one device was used to confuse, bewilder and torment our men until they were ready to confess to anything. That device was prolonged, chronic loss of sleep." As for Kennan, he had simply been in a bad mood and made an ill-advised comment. He had recently learned that the Soviets were bugging his house and preventing his two-year-old son from playing with the other children at the embassy, prompting him to lash out.

But to the CIA, an organization already interested in mind control, already primed to suspect mind control, it seemed possible that mind control was involved. And even if the odds were against it, few personnel wanted to ignore the topic altogether. The security of the Western Bloc depended upon the United States leading the world in weapons development. Maybe mind control was the next arms race.

The chief of the CIA's medical staff urged his colleagues to take mind control seriously: "It is difficult not to keep from becoming rabid about our apparent laxity." He also urged them to "be cautious . . . because of the havoc that could be wrought by such techniques in unscrupulous hands." The CIA would soon heed his call to study mind control, but it would fail to heed his call for caution.

On April 10, 1953, Director of Central Intelligence Allen Dulles delivered an alarming speech on "Brain Warfare" at a Princeton University alumni conference. Dulles, a suave and sophisticated spymaster, had assumed the top position at the CIA only two months earlier. Inspired by what Richard Helms had told him about mind control, he warned the audience of an ongoing "battle for men's minds." The Soviet Union, he said, was subjecting people "to such a treatment that they are deprived of the ability to state their own thoughts." These "parrot-like" individuals "can merely repeat thoughts which have been implanted in their minds by suggestion from outside. In effect the brain under these circumstances becomes a phonograph playing a disc put on its spindle by an outside genius over which it has no control."

In addition to Pavlov's experiments, the Moscow show trials, the Mindszenty affair, the POW confessions, Hunter's article, and Kennan's outburst, Dulles knew of another reason to believe that the Communists possessed methods of mind control. Several people "have escaped from the ordeal of brainwashing to tell their story." They included a young Bulgarian officer named Mikhail Shipkov, who had been "arrested by the Bulgarian Communists, subjected to the brainwashing technique, miraculously managed to escape, reported on his experiences to the American authorities and then, in attempting to escape from Bulgaria, was tragically caught and liquidated."

Hinting at the CIA's work in progress, Dulles said, "If we are to counter this kind of warfare we must understand the techniques the Soviet is adopting to control men's minds." At the same time, he acknowledged that it would be difficult to close the mind control gap because while the Soviets experimented on political prisoners, "we have no human guinea pigs on which to try out these extraordinary techniques."

Dulles had been remarkably candid and surprisingly forthcoming in the speech. This last statement, however, wasn't quite true.

Three days after his "Brain Warfare" speech, at the urging of Richard Helms, Dulles created a new project that dramatically expanded the CIA's research into mind control. Helms wrote that its purpose was to find ways of "discrediting individuals, eliciting information, and implanting suggestions." In essence, it was a Manhattan Project for the mind.

The project was called MKULTRA. The digraph "MK," allegedly the initials of an administrative secretary, indicated that it fell under the jurisdiction of the CIA's Technical Services Staff. "ULTRA" was an homage to the Allies' code-breaking effort during World War II.

MKULTRA would eventually grow to encompass 149 subprojects, some of which involved dangerous—even deadly—experiments. Given the sensitive nature of MKULTRA, Dulles exempted it from normal reporting require-

ments. And given the CIA's "need-to-know" policy of compartmentalization, whereby personnel were prevented from discussing their work with
anyone other than their immediate colleagues, only about a dozen people
within the CIA even knew that it existed.

Bluebird, Artichoke, MKULTRA, Chemical Branch, Technical Services
Staff, Office of Security, Office of Policy Coordination, Office of Scientific
Intelligence. If it all seems confusing, that's because it was meant to be.
"These things are not bureaucratically neat," Sidney Gottlieb said when
asked why the CIA frequently changed the names of its projects and de-
partments. "You see, in an attempt to make it very hard for memos to be
understood by people who weren't supposed to understand them, these
techniques were used on purpose."

The intelligence community has long embraced obfuscation. Its employees
cloak their writing in euphemisms, both to hide their intent and to avoid complicated legal issues that could arise if they spoke candidly about their work.
Hence torture isn't "torture"; it's "enhanced interrogation." Kidnapping isn't
"kidnapping"; it's "extraordinary rendition." Assassination isn't "assassination"; in the Eisenhower administration it was "elimination," in the Kennedy
administration it was "executive action," in the Reagan administration it was
"pre-emptive neutralization," in the Bush Jr. administration it was "lethal direct action," and in the CIA, at least for a time, it was "health alteration."

The perpetrators of MKULTRA spent lots of time and effort hiding their
actions inside a forest of euphemisms. Fortunately, a trail of breadcrumbs
has since been found.

Sidney Gottlieb, the outsider chemist, was given command of MKULTRA,
partly because of his scientific skill, but also because Dulles, who had similarly been born with a clubfoot, took a liking to him.

During Gottlieb's later depositions, attorney Thomas Maddox asked
him, "What part did you play in its inception, pulling everything together
under MKULTRA?"

Gottlieb cautiously accepted full responsibility. "I think I played the key
role in it," he said. "Was I the principal figure in all of this? . . . You know, the
buck doesn't go beyond me, I think yes. Although," he added defensively, "I
was not sort of the implementing person, really. There were people above me
that very carefully approved each of these projects."

Asked whether he had received any advice on how to conduct MKUL-TRA, Gottlieb replied, "Very vaguely. They weren't quite sure. It was a question of a new unit being organized there."

"What was your understanding of what your function would be?"

"My understanding? I really didn't have much of an understanding in my mind. I decided I would give it a try for six months."

Gottlieb had been put in charge of MKULTRA to research mind control, but he didn't know how to research mind control. The scope of the endeavor went well beyond his expertise. Not knowing where to begin, he turned to history for ideas.

Inside a small meeting room of the Boxwood House Motel in Culpeper, Virginia, attorney James Turner handed Gottlieb a memo from the early days of the CIA and told him to read the names listed on it. Gottlieb spent a silent moment studying the memo.

Turner then asked, "The Lovell referred to is Stanley Lovell?"

"I believe that is who he is."

"Who is he?"

"Stanley Lovell was somebody who was active in World War II in OSS in the technical side."

"What was his connection with the Agency?"

"I don't think he had any formal connection. This memorandum certainly implies contact of some kind. I would describe what relation he had with the Agency as ad hoc contact with whom they would talk every once in a while."

"Did his areas of expertise include the use of drugs and similar techniques?"

"I don't know that I would know all his areas of expertise. They were some of the areas he talked about or wrote about when he was in OSS."

Stanley Lovell was a cunning New England chemist who had led the OSS Research and Development Branch, a secret group of scientists who created the dirty tricks of World War II. If a spy or saboteur needed a forged passport for maintaining cover, an incendiary device for starting fires, a fighting knife for slitting a guard's throat, or a cyanide pill for committing suicide before being captured alive, the scientists in the R&D Branch made it.

Besides creating ingenious weapons and gadgets, Lovell—or "Professor Moriarty," as he was known—oversaw some of the most unusual projects in American history. Under his purview, R&D Branch scientists attached napalm bombs to live bats, concocted a spray that smelled like feces, and painted foxes with glowing radioactive material in an attempt to scare the Japanese into submission. Moreover, they developed poisons to assassinate foreign leaders, truth drugs to interrogate prisoners of war, and chemical and biological weapons to deploy against enemy soldiers.

Incidentally, in 1951, Lovell persuaded Allen Dulles to create a Cold War equivalent of the OSS R&D Branch. Dulles thereafter created the CIA's Technical Services Staff, the division that sponsored Gottlieb's MKULTRA project. But the connection between Lovell and Gottlieb was even more direct. When Gottlieb had started MKULTRA, "I didn't know anything about [mind control]," he said in his depositions. "I was pulling all of the stops I could, looking at World War II Office of Strategic Services records." Searching through those dilapidated boxes of long-forgotten files, he chanced upon Lovell's work: the gadgets, the forgeries, the assassination attempts, the drugs to manipulate human behavior. In those boxes, Gottlieb found the blueprints for his career at the CIA.

4

LSD

Back in 1938, chemist Albert Hofmann began studying compounds derived from the rye fungus ergot. He was hoping to discover one that could stimulate blood flow and lead to the development of new medications, which would earn him and his employer, the Sandoz pharmaceutical company in Switzerland, a handsome profit.

As part of his research, Hofmann synthesized a compound called lysergic acid diethylamide (LSD). Although LSD—and its hallucinogenic effects—would eventually become well-known, it initially attracted little interest from the pharmacologists at Sandoz. The company shelved it for the next five years. Yet during that time, Hofmann held a nagging suspicion that LSD had more to offer. In the spring of 1943, he resynthesized the compound for further examination. During the process, twenty micrograms of LSD, equivalent to the weight of a single eyelash, accidentally contacted his skin and was absorbed into his body. Soon he began to feel unusual sensations.

Three days later, his interest piqued, Hofmann intentionally ingested 250 micrograms of LSD. Within half an hour, he became so dizzy that he had to leave work for the day. Then, while riding his bike home, he began hallucinating. He later recalled, "It was particularly remarkable how every acoustic perception, such as the sound of a door handle or a passing automobile, became transformed into optical perceptions. Every sound generated a vividly changing image, with its own consistent form and color."

When Hofmann got home, he "sank into a not-unpleasant intoxicated-like condition, characterized by an extremely stimulated imagination. In a dreamlike state, with eyes closed (I found the daylight to be unpleasantly glaring), I perceived an uninterrupted stream of fantastic pictures, extraordinary shapes with intense, kaleidoscopic play of colors." He had just experienced the world's first acid trip.

In the late 1940s, Sandoz brought LSD to the United States as a treatment for psychiatric problems. However, government science advisor Vannevar Bush hinted that the drug may have crossed the Atlantic even earlier. Hours into a 1964 interview, he said that whenever Stanley Lovell had encountered a tough problem in the OSS R&D Branch, "he'd come to me about it" for help. One of those problems was "when lysergic acid showed up and it was regarded as a very dangerous thing and put under wraps." It would "give a man symptoms of schizophrenia for some seven or eight hours." Bush added, "At the end of the war, of course, or after the war all this sort of thing went over to the CIA."

The CIA didn't experiment with LSD until 1951, the year that an anonymous consultant warned that hallucinogens such as "Ergot and Lysergic Acid groups" were of "great importance to national security." That same year, a bizarre event occurred in southern France that seemed to prove the consultant right.

On August 16, 1951, dozens of residents of Pont-Saint-Esprit, a sleepy French town dotted with medieval buildings, began experiencing vivid, nightmarish hallucinations. One man jumped into a river because he thought that snakes were eating him alive. Another told a doctor that his heart had fallen out of his chest and begged him to put it back in. Yet another ripped off his clothes and danced naked in the town square. A reporter from Paris noted, "The doctors are beside themselves with work; the rumors are wild and contradictory; fear hangs over the town everywhere. No one knows when it will end." Five people ultimately died.

All of the victims had eaten rye bread that had been contaminated with ergot fungus. No foul play was detected, but the incident forced the CIA to wonder what would happen if, say, the Soviets released a hallucinogen into the water supply of a major American city. Given that an accidental poisoning in France could cause such mayhem, how much more devastating would a coordinated attack be? And how could it be stopped? To learn the answers, the CIA first needed to learn more about hallucinogens.

By the end of 1951, the CIA had procured a batch of LSD from Sandoz. "Tasteless, odorless and capable of easily being concealed," says one declassified memo, a heavy dose of LSD "could rest on the head of a pin." According to another memo, "An infinitesimally small dose will produce mental derangement." As soon as CIA personnel began thinking about the potential uses of LSD in covert operations—controlling, eliciting, discrediting, incapacitating—their eyes grew wide with excitement. One of them remembered, "We had thought at first that this was the secret that was going to unlock the universe."

The CIA wasn't the only governmental organization studying hallucinogens. Luther Greene, the scientific director of the Edgewood Arsenal chemical weapons facility in Maryland, viewed them as the future of warfare. In Greene's vision, the military would use hallucinogens to incapacitate enemy soldiers on the battlefield. "War without death" became a common catchphrase among his workers.

Ironically, Greene had earlier helped the United States develop some of the most lethal substances known to man. He and the other scientists at Edgewood Arsenal created the country's first nerve agents, chemical compounds so dangerous that a fraction of an ounce applied to the skin is fatal. In fact, whenever the scientists would release vapors containing trace amounts of nerve agents into the air for disposal, birds flying overhead died midair and crashed onto the roof of the building.

Beginning in 1948, Greene conducted secret experiments at Edgewood Arsenal in which he gave small doses of nerve agents to Army volunteers. One of the volunteers later said of his experience, "I was not in control. It was incredible. This tiny drop had rendered me helpless." Safety precautions for the experiments were more suggestions than requirements. The chief medical officer at Edgewood Arsenal, Colonel Douglas Lindsey, was so lax that he was known to dip his finger into a beaker containing VX nerve agent, rub it on the back of a shaved rabbit, and, as the rabbit began to convulse in its cage, swirl his finger in a martini to wash the remaining VX off.

Within a year of these experiments, Greene wrote a classified report, *Psychochemical Warfare: A New Concept of War*, arguing for the development of drugs that could produce the same debilitating effects as nerve agents minus the physical harm. "Throughout recorded history," the report begins, "wars have been characterized by death, human misery, and the destruction of property; each major conflict being more catastrophic than the one preceding it. I am convinced that it is possible, by means of the techniques of psychochemical warfare, to conquer an enemy without the wholesale killing of his people or the mass destruction of his property." The plan was to fill bombshells with hallucinogens and drop them onto enemy encampments. Once everyone on the ground became too disoriented to fight, American troops would move in.

In 1952, Greene presented his ideas at an Army Chemical Corps conference. Among those in attendance were Stanley Lovell, Sidney Gottlieb, Gottlieb's young colleague Robert Lashbrook, and Frank Olson and John Schwab from the Camp Detrick biological weapons facility in Maryland. Greene's speech left a lasting impression on Gottlieb, who later said, "I was fascinated by the ideas Greene was advancing. He was convinced that it was possible to actually win a battle or larger engagement without killing anyone or destroying any property."

One year later, Gottlieb took command of MKULTRA. Influenced by Greene's arguments and Lovell's previous wartime drug experiments, he decided to focus on LSD as his first method of mind control.

Not long after the CIA acquired LSD, it received reports that the Soviet Union had, too. An American military attaché in Switzerland claimed that the Soviets had bought five kilograms of LSD from Sandoz, enough to prepare fifty million doses. In response, a panicked CIA pledged to buy the rest of Sandoz's available supply—ten kilograms, according to the military attaché—for $240,000, thus ensuring an American stockpile and depriving the Soviets of theirs. Two CIA officers flew to Switzerland with a bag of cash to make the purchase.

Sandoz's representatives were shocked to learn the quantity of LSD that the officers were attempting to buy. The company had never produced anywhere near ten kilograms of LSD. It only had ten *grams* available. Apparently the military attaché didn't know the difference between grams and kilograms, resulting in a miscalculation by a factor of a thousand.

To assuage the CIA's fears, Sandoz's representatives agreed not to sell any LSD to the Soviets. They also agreed to supply the CIA with one hundred grams of LSD per week for the next two years. Even so, the CIA still thought it prudent to secure a second source of LSD, just in case. Sandoz, after all, was a foreign company; the CIA wanted a domestic backup. On Gottlieb's urging, the Indianapolis-based Eli Lilly pharmaceutical company began synthesizing LSD for the CIA.

Gottlieb and his underlings in the TSS didn't waste any time before they tried LSD for themselves, ostensibly to better understand how they might employ it in covert operations. A handful of them rented a hotel room and took various doses of the drug dissolved in water, "usually with a physician present, not always," Gottlieb said. As for the effects, "I remember . . . kind of having a transparent sheen, like an aura around all the edges of my body." Gottlieb elsewhere described the experience as "an out-of-bodyness, a feeling as though I am in a kind of transparent sausage skin that covers my whole body and it is shimmering, and I have a sense of well-being and euphoria for most of the next hour or two hours, and then it gradually subsides." Not everyone was so lucky. Others had bad trips, known as "bummers," characterized by mood swings, extreme paranoia, and frightening hallucinations.

Now that Gottlieb had personally experienced the mind-altering effects of LSD, he turned his attention to figuring out how to dose others with it without them even knowing.

John Mulholland cut a dashing figure in his three-piece suit, bow tie, and top hat. The outfit, along with his gigantic features, gave him a strange allure that befitted a magician. Mulholland was famous for his spellbinding magic shows, which had included eight performances at the White House for Franklin and Eleanor Roosevelt. A skilled practitioner of sleight-of-hand tricks, he captivated audiences with cards, coins, Chinese rings, and, of course, the occasional rabbit in a hat. Albert Wiggam, editor of *The American Magazine*, raved, "I've seen all the magicians from Herrmann the Great down to the local wag who could do a couple of card tricks. Houdini was a good friend of mine and I knew his stuff from A to Z. But I have never seen any man tie an audience into knots . . . as John Mulholland did."

And then, without warning, Mulholland gave it all up. In 1953, he stopped performing shows. Just as surprising, he stepped down as editor of *The Sphinx*, the country's premier magic magazine, telling its subscribers that the pain from his rheumatic fever prevented him from working. Yet this was another of his deceptions.

Mulholland indeed had rheumatic fever, but he hadn't quit magic because of it. He just needed an excuse to give him more time to complete a secret assignment. For $3,000, Gottlieb had hired him to teach the TSS scientists how to surreptitiously dose someone with drugs. Like other CIA contractors, Mulholland signed an oath never to "divulge, publish, nor reveal either by word, conduct, or by any other means" what he was doing. Gottlieb said of their arrangement, "He was happy to become a contractor with us; he seemed to really relish the work."

Mulholland held six in-person training sessions at New York's Statler Hotel to teach the scientists his sleight-of-hand tricks. He also wrote a secret manual, *Some Operational Applications of the Art of Deception,* comprising his best advice. In it, he emphasizes the importance of staying relaxed and employing misdirection. The hand doesn't have to be faster than the eye, he says. The goal of a trick is to deceive the mind's eye, not the eye itself.

The first trick in the manual is how to spike a drink without being caught. According to Mulholland, the "performer" (perpetrator) should hold a box of matches in his left hand, concealing a pill underneath. Whenever the "spectator" (target) places a cigarette in his mouth, the performer insists on lighting it for him. Once the spectator agrees, the performer strikes a match and slowly lifts it to light the cigarette. The spectator's eyes will naturally fixate on the flame in front of his face. Meanwhile, the performer uses his left hand to stealthily drop the pill into the spectator's drink.

Regarding the covert delivery of powders, Mulholland suggests hiding them inside an inconspicuous container, such as beneath the removable eraser on a pencil, and pouring them into the drink. For liquids, he suggests placing them in a small, flexible container with a tiny hole poked into it, then placing the container in a wallet with a slightly larger hole cut out of it. The performer simply squeezes the wallet and a stream of liquid shoots out.

The TSS scientists were eager to test Mulholland's tricks for themselves. Following each training session, it wasn't unusual for them to spike the office coffee pot with LSD. On one occasion, an unwitting victim drank the coffee and "couldn't pull himself together," said a TSS veteran. The victim left the office and walked across a bridge over the Potomac River. Every time a car passed, "He would huddle down against the parapet, terribly frightened. It was a really horror trip for him. I mean, it was hours of agony. It was like a dream that never stops, with someone chasing you." One anxious colleague resorted to bringing his own bottle of wine to office parties. Things became so cavalier that the CIA's Office of Security had to issue a warning that it would discipline anyone who tried to put LSD in the holiday punch bowl.

Within the CIA, the TSS scientists were well-known for performing these irresponsible pranks. Gottlieb often told a story about a time when he was flying back to Washington, D.C. He walked up the narrow aisle of the plane to ask the stewardess for a martini. As he returned to his seat, a man smoking a pipe stopped him and asked, "Is that LSD you're drinking?" The man was Allen Dulles.

The pranks were partly motivated by legitimate concerns. For instance, the CIA needed to know what would happen if unwitting Americans were dosed with LSD. Would they go crazy? Would they harm themselves or others? By spiking their colleagues' drinks and observing the reactions, the scientists could partially answer these questions. At least that's how they justified their actions to themselves.

Mostly, however, when the scientists dosed their colleagues with LSD, they were—in their own myopic view—just messing around, just trying to have fun. Pretty soon their reckless behavior would prove to have fatal consequences.

5

Deep Creek

Harold Blauer, a professional tennis player undergoing a difficult divorce, checked himself into Bellevue Hospital in New York for a psychiatric evaluation. He was suffering from severe depression on account of his failed marriage. Most days he couldn't eat or sleep, and he worried himself sick thinking about raising his two daughters in a broken home.

While in the hospital, Blauer responded well to the prescribed medication. His spirits soared even higher when his wife, Amy, began visiting him regularly. She had filed for divorce because they had grown apart, but she still cared about him. In fact, seeing him in the hospital seems to have rekindled their lost spark. Family friends thought that the couple was on the verge of reconciliation.

At the end of his five-week treatment program, Blauer was transferred to the New York State Psychiatric Institute where his new doctors, Paul Hoch and James Cattell, asked him to participate in an experimental drug trial. Blauer gave his oral consent, thinking that the drug would speed his recovery. What he didn't know was that it was actually part of an Army Chemical Corps experiment to develop chemical weapons.

Just days before Blauer was scheduled for release, he received five injections of a mescaline derivative that had only ever been tested in mice. Cattell later said, "We didn't know if it was dog piss or what it was we were giving him."

Cattell wrote in his notes that Blauer was "very apprehensive" for the first injection and needed "considerable persuasion" to accept it. Once he did, his head began to hurt and his right leg developed a slight tremor. The doctors nevertheless continued with the next two injections. As the effects took hold,

37

Blauer began shaking uncontrollably. He said that he wanted to stop the treatment, but the doctors insisted that he continue. Within two hours of the fourth injection, he experienced violent body tremors, repeatedly slammed his head against the hospital bed, and told a nurse, "I'm in awful shape. I feel as if something is inside my head. I don't know if I can stand it."

Blauer outright refused the fifth injection, saying, "I'm fine now. I'm going home tomorrow. I don't need to be given anything." The doctors didn't listen.

Blauer's medical records provide a horrifying minute-by-minute account of what transpired. At 9:53 A.M. on January 8, 1953, Cattell administered the fifth and final injection. Blauer began sweating profusely and flailing his arms. At 10:01, his entire body went rigid. He clenched his teeth, began frothing at the mouth, and his pupils stopped responding to light. By 11:17, he was "lapsing into coma." Thirty minutes later, "Quiet. Deep coma." Blauer's heart soon stopped and he died.

Doctors Hoch and Cattell immediately tried to cover up what they had done. They falsely claimed that the drug had activated an undisclosed heart condition that killed Blauer. A friend of theirs in the Chemical Corps stamped Blauer's medical records secret so that nobody could question the official narrative, thus hiding the Army's culpability behind the veil of national security. When Blauer's personal physician requested the records, he was told to mind his own business.

The truth wouldn't emerge for over three decades. Finally, in 1987, U.S. district judge Constance Baker Motley ruled that "the United States negligently caused the death of Harold Blauer" and awarded his family $702,044 in damages. But the money did little to ameliorate the family's pain. Elizabeth Barrett, Blauer's eldest daughter, said in testimony before Congress, "My country destroyed my family, as well as my father, with grossly negligent and purposeful acts by professionals—doctors and lawyers who were supposed to protect us from harm, not cause it. . . . How would you feel if you found out your father died not in Nazi Germany, but in the United States, eight years after we hanged war criminals for the same events?"

Sidney Gottlieb was one of the few people who had known the full details of Blauer's death back in the 1950s. During his depositions, attorney James Turner asked him, "After hearing of that death, did you take any steps to protect the health and well-being of experimental subjects in MKULTRA?"

"Not to my recollection," Gottlieb said.

* * *

Inside the small meeting room of the Boxwood House Motel, attorney Joseph Rauh handed Gottlieb a declassified document and asked him whether he was "identity A," someone who had given LSD to four CIA case officers as an experiment.

Gottlieb conferred with his CIA attorney, Lee Strickland, and said, "Yes, I was identity A."

Rauh then asked about the "adverse results" of the experiment, as described in the document.

"I don't feel I can comment on that," Gottlieb said, his stutter becoming more pronounced.

Rauh pressed him for an answer.

Gottlieb again conferred with Strickland. He finally responded, "I don't remember that incident. I don't remember administering LSD to four case officers. I don't know who said that I did."

Rauh was livid. "First you invoke security, then you talk to Mr. Strickland, and then you don't remember."

Strickland interjected, "I think that is an unfair characterization."

"That is exactly what happened," Rauh snapped.

"We were trying to have him answer the questions," Strickland explained. "You obviously know or have a good guess as to what the secret is in that document and you are trying—"

"What is the secret in that document?" Rauh said in exasperation. "I don't know what the secret is in that document. I want to know."

Strickland shot back, "As long as I am on the case you probably won't, sir."

Rauh took a moment to collect his thoughts, then he started on another line of inquiry. He asked Gottlieb, "Will you please relate the events that occurred in November of 1953 when LSD was put in liquor which was served to a group of scientists from the Agency and Fort Detrick at Deep Creek Lodge?"

Gottlieb winced. He knew where this line of questioning would lead, and he didn't want to go there.

Rauh was asking about a periodic work retreat that Gottlieb had participated in. Throughout the 1950s, two groups of scientists occasionally met at a scenic cabin on Deep Creek Lake in Maryland to discuss their ongoing work, exchange research results, and, if time allowed, try their hand at some fishing. At the specific retreat that Rauh had mentioned, one group of four scientists had come from the CIA's Technical Services Staff (Gottlieb, Robert Lashbrook, Allan Hughes, and Henry Bortner) and another group of seven scientists had come from the nearby Camp Detrick biological weapons facility, which mass-produced anthrax spores, botulinum toxin, and other deadly organisms for the military.

More specifically, the seven scientists from Camp Detrick were part of a secret division called the Special Operation Division (SOD), "a little Detrick within Detrick," said one member. Most people at Camp Detrick "didn't know what was going on in [SOD]. And they got angry because you wouldn't tell 'em what was going on."

Regarding the secret collaboration between the TSS and SOD, Gottlieb said, "We felt that—" He paused. "We had a directive . . . to keep in touch with the state of that art. It was part of U.S. capability to be aware of the possibilities in covert use of biological and chemical weapons." A CIA memo lists some of the projects that the two groups collaborated on throughout the Cold War: "suicide agents for U-2 pilots, L-pills, means for incapacitating guards or guard dogs, material to anesthetize the inhabitants of a building so as to allow its entry, material to dissolve the Berlin Wall, aphrodisiacs for operational use."

On November 18, 1953, ten months after the death of Harold Blauer, the eleven scientists from the TSS and SOD arrived at Deep Creek Lodge for their retreat. The next evening, Gottlieb and his lanky, sandy-haired colleague Robert Lashbrook decided to liven up the affair. Surely, they thought, the scientists from the SOD would enjoy a classic TSS prank. Quickly and quietly, they slipped a small amount of LSD into the Cointreau liquor bottle and started pouring drinks.

Attorney Joseph Rauh started his next question, "Who put the LSD—"

"Dr. Lashbrook," Gottlieb blurted.

"Under your instructions?"

"Yes, under my general instructions. I didn't tell him exactly whose drink to put it in and whose not to."

"How many of these people received LSD?"

"I can't remember, but I would guess seven or eight."

"And Dr. Lashbrook put LSD in the liquor of all seven or eight?"

"Well, I think we didn't sit down and [say] so and so is going to get this and so and so isn't. But I think his point was to not give some people LSD and [to] give some."

"Did you receive LSD at that meeting?"

"I can't remember but I might well have. I really honestly don't remember."

"Did Dr. Lashbrook?"

"I don't remember but I think not. He probably would have not."

"About how many got LSD?"

"As I said, my recollection is that seven or eight did."

"How many of the seven or eight knew they were getting LSD?"

"I don't think—probably none of them did."

Rauh also took Lashbrook's deposition, but only after a struggle. He had initially called Lashbrook on the phone and asked him if he would be willing to travel from his home in California to Washington, D.C., expenses paid, to answer some questions about his past. Lashbrook firmly declined. Rauh wrote in a summary of their conversation, "[Lashbrook] didn't want to come East and I asked him if any particular day in April was more convenient than the rest. He said, 'No. I am not really interested in your bullshit anyway' and he banged down the phone on me." Rauh wasn't one to suffer disrespect. Following the phone call, he got a subpoena forcing Lashbrook to sit for the deposition, though Rauh had to travel to California to conduct it.

To begin the deposition, Rauh asked Lashbrook about an incident that had occurred when the subpoena was served: "Now, you were handed a subpoena sometime after this conversation?"

"Uh-huh," Lashbrook huffed.

"And you threw it back at the subpoena server; is that correct?"

"Yes. Didn't do much good."

"Why were you so anxious not to testify?"

"Because I have very little patience with people who wish to criticize the CIA."

"You have no remorse for what you did?"

"No."

"You have no guilty feelings about what you did?"

"No."

Later on, Lashbrook claimed that Gottlieb *had* informed the SOD scientists that they would be dosed with LSD at some point during the retreat, contrary to what Gottlieb said in his depositions.

Rauh asked, "Now, it is your testimony, and you are under oath, that [Frank] Olson," one of the SOD scientists, "knew this was coming?"

"It was my understanding that this had been discussed with the people at Detrick, yes."

"From whom did you get that understanding?"

"Sid Gottlieb."

"Well," Rauh said with surprise, "if Gottlieb had testified the other way, would that affect your testimony any? Gottlieb never suggested that Olson knew this was coming."

"Are you sure?"

"Yes."

Lashbrook squirmed in his seat. "He definitely told me this before the meeting."

"What did he tell you exactly?"

"That he discussed it with . . . Vincent Ruwet," head of the SOD scientists.

Gottlieb, generally a more reliable deponent, denied ever doing so. Ruwet himself also denied it. Lashbrook, it seems, was lying to save his own skin.

Rauh next asked Lashbrook to explain how he had determined who would and wouldn't get the LSD.

"Okay," Lashbrook said. "There was one of the people at Detrick that was specifically excluded because of a medical problem. . . . I did not take it. I do not believe Sidney took it, because we felt there must be people on hand who would be able to do something if anything was required to be done. So not everyone took it."

Rauh wasn't satisfied. "If the man with the medical problem reached for the Cointreau bottle, what would you do, pull it away? You knew that there was LSD in the Cointreau bottle."

"There were two Cointreau bottles," Lashbrook revealed.

Now the full picture dawned on Rauh. "You shifted them around so only the people—"

"Sure."

"—who you wanted to have it had it?"

Lashbrook nodded his head.

"Is that right?"

"One in your left lapel, one in your right lapel. Yes, of course."

Rauh had a hair-trigger temper, and this last flippant comment set it off. "I don't think it's very funny when somebody dies as a result of something you did. You think it's funny, but I don't."

At 7:30 in the evening, Lashbrook distributed the spiked drinks to the scientists at the Deep Creek retreat. Two men were spared the treatment: Jim Stubbs because of a heart condition and John Malinowski because he was a reformed alcoholic. Twenty minutes later, Gottlieb informed everyone that they had just ingested seventy micrograms of LSD.

The retreat soon turned into a lively affair. Most of the men started laughing uncontrollably. Their conversations became unintelligible. The walls of the cabin began to spin. Ruwet later said, "To me, it was the most frightening experience I ever had or hope to have." At 1:00 in the morning, everyone stumbled to their rooms and went to sleep. Everyone, that is, except for a restless Frank Olson.

Olson was a balding, blue-eyed bacteriologist specializing in aerobiology. He had gotten a job at Camp Detrick through the machinations of Ira Baldwin, his former thesis advisor at the University of Wisconsin (and Gottlieb's former mentor). Within the SOD, Olson studied the airborne distribution of pathogens. His colleague Oliver Fellowes said of their work, "We dried the virus in bulk. Then we sometimes mixed the powder with feathers and, though I never discovered where the tests were carried out, I know the mixture was to be delivered in the same way as leaflets were dropped over enemy territory, in leaflet bombs." Olson had also worked on Operation Sea-Spray, in which the military sprayed harmless strains of bacteria over major American cities to simulate a biological attack and analyze how the bacteria spread via the air currents.

In Olson's personnel file from Camp Detrick, several of his superiors noted that he was a respectable chemist, sociable person, and devoted father of three. Others, however, considered him to be disagreeable, especially because he had sympathized with Nazi Germany before the United States entered World War II. One colleague wrote, "He is extremely tactless and has made many enemies which will probably in later life affect his career." Olson's brother-in-law, Arthur Vidich, called him a bigot and anti-Semite: "I didn't like to be around him when Jewish people were present. I'd leave the room. He could be awful. It was embarrassing." Vidich added, "I always wondered how he was around Gottlieb and Harold Abramson," a physician connected to the CIA. "Abramson was a Norwegian Jew, I think, and I couldn't imagine Frank not saying something to him."

When Olson returned home from Deep Creek, his wife, Alice, remembered him being "a totally different person," almost as if he had experienced a psychotic break. He wouldn't talk to her or their kids, nor would he eat the meal that she had prepared for him that evening. Alice later recalled confronting him, "I said something about the adults in this family not communicating, and he said 'I'll talk to you when you get the children in bed.' I got the children in bed, and he sat there and said, 'I've made a terrible mistake,' and was totally depressed." The foggy weather outside fit the mood perfectly. "We sat in front of the fireplace and held hands. I didn't know what was wrong. . . . And he wouldn't tell me anything that had happened except, 'I'm going to have to resign.'" She asked him if he had broken security or falsified data—two of the most serious offenses at his job—but he denied doing either.

Alice wasn't the only person to notice a change in her husband's demeanor. The next day at work, Olson's boss, Vincent Ruwet, found him to be in an extremely paranoid state: "[Olson] asked me if I should fire him or if he should quit. I was taken aback by this and asked him what was wrong. He stated that in his opinion he had messed up the experiment and did not do well at the meetings." Ruwet spent half an hour trying to calm him down. The next day, they had another frantic conversation. "He appeared to be greatly agitated and in his words, all mixed up. He said he felt that he was not competent, that he had done something wrong," but he couldn't explain what. Ruwet thought that Olson needed psychiatric help.

That evening, Olson walked in the front door of his house with a colleague and told Alice matter-of-factly, "Jim Stubbs wanted to come home with me because he thought I might do you bodily harm."

Alice remembered, "I was standing at the kitchen table and I suddenly had to sit down. My legs buckled underneath me. I couldn't believe what I was hearing."

Later that week, while eating lunch at a restaurant with SOD scientist John Malinowski, Olson leaned over to Alice and whispered, "I can't eat this food. It's poisoned."

"It stopped me cold," she remembered. "This was a rational man who I suddenly realized was not rational."

After they left the restaurant, Malinowski dropped off Olson at a CIA office on the National Mall. Reflecting on the significance of that night, Alice said, "I kissed him goodbye and Malinowski drove me home, and that was the last I ever saw him."

Sidney Gottlieb and Robert Lashbrook, the two men who had distributed the LSD at Deep Creek, likewise knew that something was wrong with Olson. During one of Gottlieb's depositions, attorney Joseph Rauh asked him, "How did Lashbrook describe Olson's condition to you?"

"He told me he was depressed," Gottlieb said.

"That is all he said, one word?"

"He might have said he was acting strangely."

"But you didn't feel any responsibility then?"

"Oh, I did."

"What did you do?"

"I made sure that to the extent we could, we provided medical help for him."

"Did you provide a psychiatrist?"

"We provided somebody who knew more about LSD than anybody we knew."

Concerned about Olson's deteriorating mental condition, Gottlieb sent him to New York to see Dr. Harold Abramson (the "Norwegian Jew"), an expert on LSD and a cleared consultant to the CIA. In fact, Abramson had been the attending physician the first time that Gottlieb had tried LSD.

When Abramson wasn't guiding CIA personnel on their acid trips or treating patients in his private practice, he subjected university students to LSD experiments. Dr. Margaret Ferguson had worked for him in the 1950s and said in an interview, "Once there was a student who came back over the weekend from a Friday experiment. He was shaking, terribly frightened and vomiting. I wasn't sure what to do, so I called Dr. Abramson at home. He told me to tell the boy to come in on Monday. I couldn't do that. I took care of him myself." Abramson's carefree attitude extended to his personal life as well. His palatial home on Long Island was known to be a hub for LSD parties that got "wild and crazy, right along with all the sex and what have you," said one participant. Another participant teased, "You'd be very, very surprised at who attended some of these events. But I'm not the type to kiss and tell."

Ruwet and Lashbrook accompanied Olson to New York. On the flight there, Ruwet noticed that Olson "was very anxious and he had the feeling that someone was out to get him." As soon as they landed, they went straight to Abramson's office in Midtown Manhattan.

The session started well. Abramson and Olson realized that they had already met once before, during World War II. "Many older interests were recalled," Abramson wrote in his notes. "We discussed construction of gas masks, filtration problems, our attitudes toward mutual friends, and many things which were most pertinent at that time." Olson behaved normally, at least until Ruwet and Lashbrook left the room. "As soon as these gentlemen left, he showed greater anxiety about his sense of inadequacy." Olson insisted that his memory was poor "and that he was failing to live up to the expectations of his family and friends." On top of everything else, he felt guilty for having sought a medical discharge from the Army because of a stomach ulcer.

Abramson gave Olson the sedative Nembutal to calm his nerves, but Olson, overcome with extreme paranoia, found this suspicious. Before Olson went to bed that night, he confronted Ruwet in conspiratorial tones, "What's behind all this? Give me the low-down. What are they trying to do with me? Are they checking me for security?" Ruwet had no idea what he was talking about.

The next day, November 25, 1953, Olson had a long session with Abramson. In the evening, he, Ruwet, and Lashbrook saw the musical *Me and Juliet* at the Majestic Theater. Halfway through the show, Olson stood up and left without explanation. When Ruwet caught up to him, Olson said that he was trying to escape from the people outside who were waiting to arrest him. That same night, as Ruwet and Lashbrook slept, Olson snuck out of the hotel, tore up his money, and threw his wallet in a trash bin, apparently in another attempt to elude his imaginary pursuers.

Although Olson's mental state was deteriorating, the three scientists returned to Washington, D.C., in the morning to celebrate Thanksgiving with their families. However, on the drive home from the airport, Olson told Ruwet that he was too ashamed to see his wife. Ruwet didn't know how to respond, so he pulled into the parking lot of a Howard Johnson's to talk.

"What do you want me to do?" he asked.

"Just let me go," Olson said. "Let me go off by myself."

"I can't do that."

"Well, then, turn me over to the police. They're looking for me anyway."

Ruwet, confused and concerned, suggested that Olson immediately return to New York for further treatment. Lashbrook agreed to accompany him—again—while Ruwet stayed behind to notify Alice of the change of plans. Alice would later say that Ruwet "came up to my house and spent the evening talking to me and trying to reassure me that it was going to be okay. . . . That it was probably the pressure of the job that had made Frank irrational. . . . It never occurred to me that he wasn't going to be okay."

Before leaving for New York, Lashbrook invited Gottlieb over to his apartment to assess Olson's condition. What Gottlieb saw disheartened him. He wrote in a subsequent report that Olson "talked about the incompetence of his work, the hopelessness of anybody helping him, and the fact that the best thing to do was to abandon him and not bother about him. . . . It seemed to me that he was very mentally disturbed at this time."

In New York, Olson once again met with Abramson and revealed to him that for some weeks, the CIA had been "giving me dope to keep me awake." Abramson diagnosed Olson as being in a "psychotic state which seemed to have been crystalized by an experiment in which Mr. Olson participated the preceding week," the LSD experiment at Deep Creek. After considerable discussion, Olson agreed to commit himself to the Chestnut Lodge sanitarium in Rockville, Maryland, where he could get round-the-clock treatment. Abramson made the necessary arrangements, but the sanitarium needed an extra day to prepare a room. Olson would have to bide his time until it was ready.

That evening, Olson and Lashbrook ate Thanksgiving dinner together, during which Olson said that he was scared because everyone, including Lashbrook, was plotting to "get" him. The next day, they met with Abramson for two hours, watched television, and checked into room 1018A of the Statler Hotel, across the street from Madison Square Garden. They spent the evening drinking martinis in the cocktail lounge and eating dinner at the Café Rouge. For the first time since the retreat, Olson appeared relaxed and, at least to Lashbrook's eye, cheerful.

Before going to sleep, Olson and Lashbrook discussed what time they needed to wake up to catch the morning flight to Maryland. Olson then called Alice for the first time in three days to say that he would see her soon. In reality, he would be dead before sunrise.

6

The Frank Olson Incident

"Somewhere around 0230 Saturday morning I was awakened by a loud noise," Robert Lashbrook wrote in a report of the incident. "Dr. Olson had crashed through the closed window blind and the closed window and he fell to his death." On the way down, Olson struck a wooden barrier and landed hard on the Seventh Avenue sidewalk. The Statler Hotel's doorman screamed, "We got a jumper, we got a jumper!" He later described Olson's fall as "like the guy was diving, his hands out in front of him, but then his body twisted and he was coming down feet first, his arms grabbing at the air above him."

Armond Pastore, the hotel's night manager, ran outside. He saw Olson lying on his back, arms outstretched, legs twisted unnaturally to one side. A large piece of wood protruded from his chest. Blood trickled from his eyes, nose, and ears. Olson had suffered multiple compound fractures in his feet, legs, pelvis, ribs, shoulder, and skull. "Just hold on, you'll be okay," Pastore said reflexively, even though he knew otherwise. For a brief moment, Olson tried to speak, but his words were unintelligible, mere gurgles in a mouth choked with blood. Pastore remembered, "His right hand clutched my arm and he raised his head slightly, his lips moving. His eyes were wide with desperation. He wanted to tell me something. I leaned down closer to listen, but he took a deep breath and died."

Inside room 1018A, Lashbrook peered out of the broken window. He could see Olson splayed on the ground thirteen stories below. (The first three floors of the hotel were used for special functions, so room 1018A was on the thirteenth floor.) There was no point in going down, he thought. What good would it do? A crowd was already gathering around the body.

Instead, Lashbrook grabbed the telephone and called Sidney Gottlieb to tell him what had happened. Then he asked the hotel's operator to call the police.

Night manager Armond Pastore and a security guard hurried up to room 1018A. When they reached the door, Pastore slid a key in the lock, but on second thought he decided to wait to open it until the police arrived. Twenty minutes later, two officers joined them and asked, "Somebody in there?"

"I'm not sure," Pastore said.

The officers pulled out their revolvers. Pastore opened the door. Inside, the room was dark and the covers of the two twin beds were strewn about the floor. Street noise entered through the shattered window. One of the officers noticed a light coming from behind the bathroom door. He nudged the door with his foot, slowly swinging it open to reveal a man sitting on the toilet with his face buried in his hands.

"What's going on here?" asked one of the officers. "What happened?"

"I woke up when I heard a sound," Lashbrook said. "I'm not sure what happened."

"You didn't see the guy go out the window?"

"No. I just heard a noise and then I woke up."

The officer didn't know what to make of Lashbrook or his story. "Is there a reason you stayed in the room?"

Lashbrook shrugged. "What could I do?"

"You didn't think of going down to check on Mr. Olson?"

"I looked out the window. I saw him lying there. There were people running from the station. What could I have done? I could see that he had help. I thought it best to wait here."

While the officers questioned Lashbrook, Pastore went back down to the ground floor to ask the hotel's operator if any calls had been made from room 1018A that night. The operator said that there had been one. During the call, a man had said, "It's all over." The voice on the other end replied, "That's too bad." That was the extent of the conversation.

Five hours later, at 7:50 A.M., CIA officer James McCord, Jr. (later an accomplice in the Watergate scandal), met with Lashbrook in room 488 of the Statler Hotel to interview him about what had happened. Lashbrook started by saying that Olson had been suffering from "persecution delusions and guilt feelings." He then gave McCord a brief overview of the previous week, never once mentioning that he had put LSD in Olson's drink at Deep Creek.

McCord shadowed Lashbrook for most of the day. At 9:00 A.M., they went to the police station for more questioning. Two detectives searched Lashbrook's pockets and found a postcard, a travel ticket, a receipt for $115 signed by magician John Mulholland, a piece of paper with the address of the Chestnut Lodge sanitarium written on it, and another piece of paper with the contact information for a "G.W." Lashbrook refused to disclose the identity of this person—George White—for "security reasons." The detectives noted that it was "like pulling teeth to get anything out of him." Before Lashbrook left, he mentioned, falsely, that he was an employee of the Department of Defense, not the CIA.

Lashbrook next went to the morgue, alone, to identify Olson's body. At noon, he and McCord met back at the Statler Hotel, where Lashbrook made a series of phone calls. Other than "exhibiting fatigue," he appeared "completely composed."

At 5:00 P.M., an unknown agent identified only as "Walter" relieved McCord. He and Lashbrook went to a showing of the Korean War movie *Cease Fire!*, ate dinner at McGinnis's Restaurant, and at 9:15 visited Dr. Harold Abramson at his office. Lashbrook wanted to talk to Abramson privately about what had happened. He asked Walter to wait in the reception area while he and Abramson went into an adjacent room. Walter, however, did his best to eavesdrop on their conversation.

As far as Walter could tell, Lashbrook and Abramson listened to a recording of one of Olson's appointments. Walter then heard them move to yet another room, presumably to better insulate their voices, and share a drink together. Abramson mentioned that he was "worried as to whether or not the deal was in jeopardy" and that "the operation was dangerous." The precise meaning of these statements is unclear, but Abramson may have been referring to MKULTRA in general.

At 10:30, Lashbrook rejoined Walter in the reception area. They bid Abramson goodbye, took a taxi to Pennsylvania Station, and caught the midnight train back to Washington, D.C.

Vincent Ruwet had been the one to tell Alice Olson that her husband wasn't coming home for Thanksgiving. Now it was his responsibility to tell her that her husband was dead. As a light snow fell outside, he pulled his car into her driveway with a heavy heart.

On hearing the news, Alice sank to the floor. Ruwet helped her into a chair.

"There was some sort of accident," he said.

"What kind of accident?"

"I'm not sure. I think he fell . . . or jumped, out of a window."

"Jumped?"

"Or fell. Yes."

"But how? What happened?"

"I'm not sure. I'll try to find out."

Alice's sobs woke up her nine-year-old son, Eric, who walked into the living room. Ruwet spoke to him calmly: "Your father had an accident. He fell or jumped out a window." Eric later said, "There's a big difference between a fall and a jump, and I couldn't understand how either of them could've occurred."

A few days after Alice buried her husband, Sidney Gottlieb and Robert Lashbrook paid her a courtesy call to express their condolences. She didn't know who they were, aside from the fact that they had worked with her husband, but she treated them as cordially as possible given the circumstances, even making them a pot of coffee. Between sips of his cup, Lashbrook told her that he would be happy to talk about what had happened whenever she wanted. Gottlieb said something to the same effect. To Alice, they seemed "very sympathetic."

Following the Frank Olson incident, Willis Gibbons, Gottlieb's immediate supervisor in the TSS, temporarily impounded all of the CIA's LSD. Only three caches of the drug escaped his dragnet. Two were overseas, in Japan and the Philippines. The third was in the possession of a field agent named George White.

On November 30, 1953, Director of Central Intelligence Allen Dulles summoned CIA inspector general Lyman Kirkpatrick to his office. As inspector general, it was Kirkpatrick's job to scrutinize the actions of CIA personnel to ensure that they complied with the law and other internal policies. He was the conscience of the CIA, the internal watchdog, the one person with both the clearance and the responsibility to provide oversight and maintain accountability. For obvious reasons, Kirkpatrick wasn't always a welcome figure around the office. "You can't have a nice IG," he once said. "You have to be a son of a bitch." Dulles, talking through the smoke of an ever-present briar pipe, asked Kirkpatrick to launch an investigation into the death of Frank Olson.

Kirkpatrick had worked for the CIA since its inception, and for the OSS before that. Tall and bulky, he had been the picture of health until, on a trip to Asia in 1952, he contracted polio and lost the use of his legs. Over the next year, his skin turned pale, his body shed an unhealthy amount of weight, and his right arm became so weak that he had to lift it with his left arm to shake hands. He nevertheless felt compelled to work harder than ever.

Kirkpatrick's diary indicates that as part of his investigation, he interviewed Gottlieb on December 3, 1953. The interview wasn't recorded, but the diary contains a number of other clues about the investigation. The entry for December 18 reads, "[Sheffield] Edwards and [Harris] Chadwell: advised me that Stanley Lovell had considerable information about the Olsen [sic] case." After World War II, Lovell, the former head of the OSS R&D Branch, occasionally consulted for the CIA. Whatever he knew about Olson remains vague, though a small hint is contained in the summary of a cryptic conversation between two CIA officers. One month after Olson died, Lovell apparently told them that someone was "about to kill the Schwab activity at Detrick as 'un-American.' Is it necessary to take action at a high place?" The summary continues, "Lovell knew about Frank R. Olson. No inhibitions. Baring of inner man. Suicidal tendencies. Offensive usefulness?"

Perhaps Lovell knew about the LSD experiment at Deep Creek, knew that the drug removed "inhibitions," knew that it led Olson to bare his "inner man," and knew that it provoked "suicidal tendencies." If so, then Lovell may have realized that LSD had "offensive usefulness." In other words, he may have realized that the Olson incident proved that LSD could be used to control someone's behavior: to make them tell the truth during an interrogation, to make them appear foolish in front of others, or even to make them commit suicide.

The "Schwab activity" mentioned in the summary of the conversation apparently refers to a series of experiments conducted by Camp Detrick's director, John Schwab. In 1949, Schwab received permission to assess government buildings for their vulnerability to a biological attack. On a warm day in August, a team of his men disguised themselves as air quality testers and snuck spray disseminators containing an innocuous strain of bacteria into the Pentagon. When they turned on the spray disseminators, the Pentagon's air conditioning system spread billions of the harmless microbes throughout the building, demonstrating its vulnerability.

Schwab himself blamed Gottlieb for Olson's death. "As long as I am head of . . . Detrick," he said, "Sid Gottlieb will never be allowed inside the gates."

At the conclusion of Lyman Kirkpatrick's investigation into the Olson incident, he wrote a report detailing his findings. Among them: Olson had received a typical dose of LSD; the CIA's mechanism for approving human experiments was inadequate; such experiments "could seriously affect the record and reputation of the Agency"; and, most importantly, "there is a strong possibility that the drug was a trigger mechanism precipitating Olson's suicide." Lawrence Houston, the CIA's general counsel, was even more emphatic, flatly stating in a memo, "It is my conclusion that the death of Dr. Olson is the result of circumstances arising out of an experiment undertaken in the course of his official duties for the U.S. government and that there is, therefore, a direct causal connection between that experiment and his death." Houston went on to say, "I have been authorized by the Deputy Director of Central Intelligence to state that this is the official position of the Central Intelligence Agency."

Kirkpatrick and Houston had laid the blame for Olson's death on LSD, and therefore on Gottlieb and Lashbrook for surreptitiously giving it to him. In light of the situation, Gottlieb worried about his future at the CIA. Already an outcast, he might now be seen as a liability. "I brought out his stutter," Kirkpatrick said.

The CIA struggled with what to do next. Should it punish Gottlieb and Lashbrook for their reckless behavior? Luis de Florez, the CIA's chairman of research, didn't think so. In a letter to Allen Dulles, he argued that a formal reprimand would be "an injustice, since reprimands are applicable to those guilty of negligence, disloyalty, willful acts detrimental to an organization, rather than those involved in difficult circumstances caused by mischance or factors beyond our control." De Florez believed that Gottlieb and Lashbrook had "acted in good faith" when they served Olson a drink spiked with LSD.

Gottlieb later claimed that he was reprimanded for his actions. Indeed,

Dulles sent him a letter saying, "It is my opinion that you exercised poor judgment in this case." But the letter constituted an informal reprimand only. No other disciplinary action was taken.

As for Lashbrook, he didn't receive any reprimand whatsoever. Instead, the CIA "backstopped" him, meaning it gave him an alias and fake credentials to make it seem as if he worked for the Army, not the CIA. Rumors were circulating that Alice Olson wanted to file a double indemnity insurance claim, and the CIA was worried that the insurance company would discover that Lashbrook was on its payroll. Such a discovery would open the floodgates to negative publicity, so the CIA covered up its connection to Lashbrook.

Attorney Thomas Maddox asked Gottlieb, "Did [Olson's death] cause you and other members of the agency to take a closer look at the [MKULTRA] program?"

"It certainly did."

"You decided, notwithstanding that, to go forward with the research?"

"Yes," Gottlieb said bluntly, then he sat there for a second in silence. Court reporter Rosanna Del Guidice's hands hovered above her stenograph machine, ready to transcribe the thought that was percolating in his head. "You know," he finally spoke, "let me say—and I have said it before—that was a very traumatic incident. It caused me personally, and a lot of other people, a lot of anguish. I resent any implication . . . that we just sailed along and hardly noticed the fact that this man had died in circumstances that could have been related to LSD. But I want to very carefully say that the relationship between Dr. Olson's death and LSD specifically has never been made, as far as I am concerned."

This was an odd statement for Gottlieb to make, especially given the conclusion of Kirkpatrick's report, the official position of the CIA, and the fact that during a meeting ten months *before* Olson died, Gottlieb had said, "LSD is quite capable of producing very strong mental derangement when used in amounts so small as to be unseeable and incapable of being tasted or smelled." Furthermore, Gottlieb's own stated reason for sending Olson to Abramson was because Abramson was an expert on LSD. Gottlieb had obviously seen a connection between LSD and Olson's mental state back in 1953. During his depositions, however, he was reluctant to say as much.

At one point, Gottlieb told attorney Joseph Rauh, "I was very upset that a human being had been killed. I didn't mean for that to happen. It was a total accident."

Rauh pressed him, "What do you mean it was an accident? It is the official position of the CIA that you caused—"

"I don't care," Gottlieb interrupted. "I am giving you my position."

When Gottlieb regained his composure, Rauh asked, "The Olson death didn't in any way inhibit you from going forward with the safe houses?"

Gottlieb took a deep breath. "The answer to that is, no, it did not."

7

Operation Midnight Climax

Sidney Gottlieb decided that it was time to test LSD in an operational setting. He had already taken the drug himself and given it to his colleagues, but those circumstances were a poor approximation for how the CIA would use it in the field. If Gottlieb and the handful of TSS scientists working on MKULTRA were going to make a breakthrough in mind control, they would have to expand their research to include experiments on unwitting test subjects.

Gottlieb initially considered targeting foreigners, but he feared that if he did, the Soviets would somehow find out. Instead, he decided to target Americans. But not just any Americans would do. Gottlieb needed test subjects who would keep quiet even if they suspected that they had been drugged. After careful consideration, he realized that criminals fit the bill perfectly. They certainly wouldn't be eager to call the police.

Gottlieb knew just who to contact to help him navigate the criminal underworld. Earlier when perusing the old OSS files for guidance, he had come across the work of George White, a short and squat, bald-headed Bureau of Narcotics agent who had helped Stanley Lovell test different truth drugs during World War II. As part of those tests, White would surreptitiously dose his criminal contacts, monitor their reactions, and report the results back to Lovell. He once gave a cigarette laced with THC (the main psychoactive ingredient in marijuana) to New York gangster August Del Gracio and got him to name multiple public officials who were either being extorted or had taken bribes. White wrote in a subsequent report, "There is no question but that the administration of the drug was responsible for loosening the subject's tongue." For Gottlieb, those OSS files served as White's résumé.

Attorney James Turner asked Gottlieb, "You knew a George White while you were at the CIA, didn't you?"

"Yes, I did."

"Is that an alias? He had an alias, did he not?"

"Yes."

"What was it?"

"Morgan Hall."

"What were his functions?"

Gottlieb stuttered, "We had an arrangement with him where he administered LSD . . . and would report to us on what the results of those [tests] were."

"When did he become a consultant to the Agency?"

"Approximately in 1952, 1953."

"When did he begin to conduct the LSD tests that he reported on to the Agency?"

"Approximately 1954 or thereabouts, I don't remember the exact dates."

"Those tests were funded by MKULTRA, weren't they?"

"When you say funded, we never—we supported the facilities and provided the LSD."

"And that was through MKULTRA, was it not?"

"I think so."

"How long did that relationship with Mr. White continue?"

"I am not sure, but it continued for three or four years. I am not sure what the precise length of that term was."

"Who supervised Mr. White on behalf of the CIA?"

"There is some confusion in my mind about that. My remembrance is that Dr. Lashbrook was the regular link advisor to White, but I saw him from time to time also."

"When did you first become involved with Mr. White?"

"I said 1952."

"You personally?"

"1952. I think that was the question you asked earlier. I was the one who made the original contact, had the original conversation with him."

"At CIA? You were the original person from CIA who made contact with White?"

"That is correct."

After reading about White's work for the OSS, Gottlieb recruited him to do essentially the same thing for MKULTRA: dose people with drugs, monitor their reactions, and report the results back to Gottlieb. Except that White's reputation preceded him, and others within the CIA had their reservations. In a personal diary, White wrote, "A couple of crew-cut, pipe-smoking punks had either known me or heard of me during the O.S.S. days and had decided I was 'too rough' for their league and promptly blackballed me. It was only when my sponsors discovered the root of the trouble they were able to bypass the blockade. After all, fellas, I didn't go to Princeton."

White certainly ran in different circles from the "crew-cut, pipe-smoking punks" at the CIA. He was as comfortable around pimps and heroin dealers as he was his own friends and family. In fact, the two groups were often one and the same.

Gottlieb quickly grew fond of White, whom he described as being "always armed to the teeth with all sorts of weapons; he could be gruff and loutish, vulgar even, but then turn urbane to a point of eloquence." The two men were opposites in many ways. Gottlieb was calculated and unassuming while White was impulsive and domineering. They nevertheless formed a mutually beneficial bond. Through White, Gottlieb got research data and a chance to live vicariously. Through Gottlieb, White got funding and immunity from the consequences of his actions.

True to form, White dubbed his MKULTRA subproject "Operation Midnight Climax." Beginning in June 1953, he established a safe house in Greenwich Village, New York City, where he dosed his guests with drugs. It was "a small three-room apartment," Gottlieb said, "and it was equipped with [a] one way mirror so that things going on in the one side of the mirror could be viewed from the other side." Back in the OSS days, White had injected THC into cigarettes; now he injected LSD through the cork of a wine bottle.

One of his first targets was gangster Eugene Giannini. Journalist Ed Reid, a close friend of White's, witnessed the drugging and described what happened: "Giannini, glass in his hand, looked around and smiled. He leaned back and talked and talked and talked. He talked about the syndicate in Manhattan, about its friends in high places, in political clubs, in the halls of Justice, in the United States Attorney's office in the Federal Building on Foley Square. He gave names, dates, places. . . . He talked." Five months later, Giannini's body was found sprawled in a gutter with two bullets in his head.

George White was obsessed with sex. His friend Gilbert Fox said that White had a high-heel fetish stemming from a childhood infatuation with an aunt who wore high heels. Fox often told a story about a time when he and his wife accompanied White to see a prostitute at a hotel. The prostitute "tied him up and strapped him to the bed and whipped his ass. She had on high heels."

Using magician John Mulholland's sleight-of-hand tricks, White occasionally slipped LSD to his unsuspecting friends and tried to seduce them into orgies. "I was angry at George for that," Fox said. "It turned out to be a bad thing to do to people, but we didn't realize it at the time."

White once tried to tempt Eliot and Barbara Smithe, a married couple, into an orgy. Eliot recalled, "It was obvious that [he was] trying to get us into a sex scene. But because White was so gross I moved away and there never was one." At least not for Eliot.

On a separate occasion when Eliot was away, White drugged nineteen-year-old Barbara and her friend Clarice Stein with LSD, even though Barbara had brought along her baby daughter. White wrote in his diary that the women contracted the "Horrors" that night. Afterward, Barbara left Eliot and moved back in with her parents. When Eliot visited her, "She was cowering in a corner," he said. "She thought the Mafia was out to get her. Her parents were unable to cope with the problem, so on our psychiatrist's advice I admitted her to Stony Lodge Hospital in December 1958. Not long after that we got divorced, and Valerie," their daughter, "went to live with my parents." At the hospital, Barbara exhibited a paranoia eerily reminiscent of Frank Olson's and insisted that her telephone was being tapped by an unidentified "they."

White was known to treat his pet parrot better than the women that he objectified. When it died, he wrote in his diary, "Poor little bastard just couldn't make it. Tried hard. I don't know if I'll ever get another bird or pet. It's tough on everyone when they die."

* * *

PROJECT MIND CONTROL

Attorney James Turner asked Gottlieb, "What do you know of any activity vis-à-vis LSD or other drugs conducted by Mr. White prior to his departure from New York City?"

Gottlieb replied, "I have a memory that he might have administered LSD to his own contacts and informants several times, by that I mean four or five times before he left New York City."

"Did he report to you . . . or someone at [the] CIA on those incidents?"

"In an informal way, yes."

"What do you mean by 'informal'?"

"He verbally passed them on to somebody . . . He might have told me about one or two directly but that is what my remembrance is."

"It was not committed to writing?"

"No, as far as I remember."

"What did he tell you about those five or six incidents?"

"I couldn't remember whether he told me directly but by and large they involve sort of one-time administration of LSD and talking about persons getting disoriented and most of them involve kind of a high experience."

"Was a doctor present?"

"The circumstances of all of Mr. White's work on LSD precluded the attendance of a doctor."

"So as to those five or six incidents, the answer is no?"

"No, as far as I know."

Turner then asked, "Did Mr. White tell the individuals receiving LSD that they were going to receive a drug?"

"Certainly not."

"Those individuals were unwitting participants for the administration of the LSD?"

"That is correct."

According to Gottlieb, some CIA personnel were concerned about what White was doing in New York, mainly because he could get caught and embarrass the CIA. Richard Helms, the CIA's new deputy director of plans, wanted White transferred to a "looser environment." In 1955, the Bureau of Narcotics agreed to transfer him to San Francisco, where he could escalate his seedy activities without fear of exposure. His new safe house, nicknamed "the pad," was a picturesque apartment on Telegraph Hill overlooking the Golden Gate Bridge.

Ira "Ike" Feldman, another short and squat Bureau of Narcotics agent, assisted White in San Francisco. One evening toward the beginning of their partnership, White called Feldman into his office and revealed that their assignment was to dose people with "mind-bending drugs" and monitor the reactions.

Feldman asked, "Why the hell do you want to test mind-bending drugs?"

White told him that it was because the CIA thought that the Communists might possess methods of mind control. MKULTRA was trying to determine whether such a thing was possible. Could drugs make someone talk during an interrogation? Could they make someone obey commands? "If we can find out just how good this stuff works, you'll be doing a great deal for your country."

As Bureau of Narcotics agents, White and Feldman knew "the whores, the pimps, the people who brought in the drugs," said one acquaintance. In San Francisco, they relied on these contacts to help them conduct Operation Midnight Climax. Most notably, they hired prostitutes to surreptitiously dose johns with LSD. In exchange for their services, White paid the prostitutes one hundred dollars a night or gave them a veritable get-out-of-jail-free card with his personal phone number on it.

To recruit the prostitutes, Feldman would walk around San Francisco wearing a fedora and pinstriped zoot suit, chewing on an unlit cigar, pretending to be a pimp and heroin dealer. His heavy Brooklyn accent and penchant for profanity gave his disguise some added authenticity. "I always wanted to be a criminal," he later said, "so I was good at it. Before long, I had half a dozen girls working for me. . . . These cunts all thought I was a racketeer."

A declassified inventory of the San Francisco safe house paints a picture of the scene that White created for the prostitutes and their clients. It lists everything that you would find in a typical home, from rugs and lamps to throw pillows and a typewriter. An informant keeping tabs on White for the FBI couldn't help but mention to his director, J. Edgar Hoover, that "the bedroom has been decorated in a style attractive to the feminine sex."

The safe house also had bookcases containing what one agent called a "comprehensive library" of porn, "the most pornographic library I ever saw: dirty movies, pictures, everything." Unsurprisingly, White gave the CIA audit staff, which wisely questioned many of his purchases, a constant headache.

The declassified inventory contains a few other items that reveal the uncomfortable truth about what White was doing in the safe house. These include a tripod, microphones, audio and visual recording equipment, and a "handi-dandi portable toilet." A CIA memo further clarifies, "A 'doorway' was constructed in the wall between the operational and monitoring apartments to allow visual surveillance and the testing of experimental photographic surveillance equipment, and a 'window' was constructed in a bedroom wall to permit visual surveillance techniques." One agent joked that the safe house was so wired for spying on its occupants "that if you spilled a glass of water you'd probably electrocute yourself." A spilled glass, though not containing water, wouldn't be out of place. White often guzzled booze in an apparent attempt to exceed his legendary constitution. He always kept a martini pitcher stashed in the refrigerator.

Inside the San Francisco safe house, from the perch of his $25 portable toilet, peering through a one-way mirror, drunk off the liquor that he bought with CIA funds, White secretly recorded his hired prostitutes drugging and bedding their clients.

Ike Feldman sometimes joined White on these indoor stakeouts. The sex, drugs, and surveillance were at least less violent than some of the other methods that he had used in the past. "Sometimes," he said, speaking of his early career in the Bureau of Narcotics, "when people had information, there was only one way you could get it. If it was a girl, you put her tits in a drawer and slammed the drawer. If it was a guy, you took his cock and hit it with a hammer. And they would talk to you. Now, with these drugs, you could get information without having to abuse people."

Jean Pierre Lafitte, another of White's accomplices, wrote a descriptive account of the unsettling events that regularly occurred inside the safe house:

> Two men sit side by side in straight-backed chairs watching the couple in the opposite bedroom through a large [one-way] mirror. On the floor beside them rests an RCA reel-to-reel tape recorder, its twin spools slowly, silently revolving. A few feet away from the recorder . . . is a Kodak movie camera mounted on a tripod. . . .
>
> In the opposite room, a slim, light haired man dressed in a sleeveless white undershirt and dark dress slacks lies half reclined on an unmade bed watching a shapely brunette wearing only a lacy brassiere,

matching panties, and a garter belt fastened to sheer stockings. She is standing before the mirror's other side, pouring two small glasses, which rest atop a dresser, half full of scotch. As the woman turns and approaches the bed holding the drinks, the reclining man says, "I don't know if I need that."

"One more won't hurt," says the woman. . . .

[She] hands him one of the drinks and sits on the edge of the bed, running her free hand gently up and down the man's back. Upright now, the man takes a sip from the glass. He leans forward, sets the glass on a nightstand, and lies back heavily on the bed. He stares up at the ceiling for a moment, an astonished look on his face.

"See," the woman says, smiling seductively. "Just what the doctor ordered, wasn't it."

"Jesus," the man says, a dazed look now on his face. He moans and begins absently rubbing his forehead.

"What's the matter, sweetheart?"

"I'm not sure. I feel really strange."

The woman leans over the man and places her mouth close to his ear. Her lips purse and lightly touch his lobe. She says, "You're not going to go to sleep on me now, are you?" But the man does not hear her. His eyes are now closed and he is oblivious to his surroundings.

During his depositions, Sidney Gottlieb became uncomfortable when confronted about White's surveillance methods. He claimed not to remember the details, which is unlikely, especially considering the fact that he visited the San Francisco safe house multiple times. Ike Feldman described one of the more intriguing stunts that Gottlieb performed there:

White used to send me to the airport to pick up Sidney and this other wacko, John Gittinger, the psychologist. Sidney was a nice guy. He was a fuckin' nut. They were all nuts. I says, "You're a good Jewish boy from Brooklyn, like me. What are you doing with these crazy cocksuckers?" He had this black bag with him. He says, "This is my bag of dirty tricks." He had all kinds of crap in that bag. We took a drive over to Muir Woods out by Stinson Beach. Sidney says, "Stop the car." He pulls out a dart gun and shoots this big eucalyptus tree with a dart. Then he tells me, "Come back in two days and check this tree." So we go back in two days, the tree was completely dead. Not a leaf left on it.

Feldman remembered Gottlieb being "cock crazy" at the safe house. "All he wants me to do is get him laid!" In a deposition of his own, Feldman said, "Anytime that fuck [Gottlieb] came to San Francisco—'Get me a girl.' He always needed a girl." Apparently Gottlieb even had an affair with White's wife. In the evenings, whenever White inevitably passed out from taking too many drugs and drinking too much liquor, "Sidney was on the couch with the old lady, humping her brains out." According to Feldman, "George knew, but he—I think he loved her very much."

In addition to LSD, White experimented with marijuana, drugs to induce diarrhea, and "hush puppy" pills to temporarily subdue guard dogs. The latter he wrapped in hamburger meat and fed to random dogs in neighborhood yards. A glutton for adventure—and pretty much everything else—White tested the rest of the drugs on himself as well as his unwitting victims. "He always said he never felt a goddamn thing," Feldman recalled. "He thought it was all bullshit. White drank so much booze, he couldn't feel his fucking cock."

Luckily for White, one of the drugs was supposed to increase sexual performance. He happened to receive a supply of it at the same time that a group of Russian sailors arrived in the harbor. Feldman said that White "wanted to know all kinds of crap" from the Russians, "but they weren't talking. So we had the girls slip 'em this sex drug. It gets your dick up like a rat. Stays up for two hours. These guys went crazy. They fucked these poor girls until they couldn't walk straight. The girls were complaining they couldn't take any more screwing. But White found out what he wanted to know."

In total, Gottlieb estimated that White conducted thirty to forty unwitting drug tests in San Francisco, though the hundreds of checks issued to White suggest that there were many more, as does the testimony of the safe house's next-door neighbor, John Erskine, who said that for years "I had a feeling that things were going on in there that were none of my business. It wasn't [c]overt. People were screaming out the windows." All the while, George White, still an agent of the Bureau of Narcotics, patrolled the streets of San Francisco by day, arresting junkies for illegal possession.

When White and Feldman weren't doling out drugs (or confiscating them), they tested secret devices for the CIA, such as stink bombs, swizzle sticks, itching and sneezing powder, and an experimental fountain pen that shot out tear gas.

"C'mon, Ike," White had said upon receiving the fountain pen. "I'll shoot you with it, then you shoot me."

"Fuck that," Feldman told him. "You ain't gonna shoot me with that crap."

White went outside and sprayed himself in the face. Feldman remembered, "He coughed, his face turned red, his eyes started watering. He was choking. Turned out, that stuff was the prototype for Mace."

White also received a pen that shot out deadly nerve gas, but he was at least smart enough not to spray himself with it.

Besides the safe houses in New York and San Francisco, the CIA sponsored a third safe house in Mill Valley, California. Gottlieb didn't remember much about it during his depositions—"I was overseas when it took place"—but he thought that the personnel there had worked on the aerosol delivery of LSD.

Indeed, in 1959, CIA officers Walter Pasternak and David Rhodes visited the Mill Valley safe house to test a new device that sprayed a fine mist of LSD into the air. Pasternack later said that when they knocked on the door, White "showed up with a snub pistol on his hip, belted down three or four martinis in about 45 minutes or so, and mostly just strutted about." That evening, Pasternak and Rhodes prowled the local bars looking for random strangers to invite to a party at which they planned to secretly spray the LSD mist.

Things didn't go as planned. It was a hot day, and the only way to keep the safe house cool was to open the windows and let the breeze blow through. This would have disrupted the experiment, so the party was canceled.

CIA psychologist John Gittinger soon joined his colleagues at the Mill Valley safe house. Frustrated that they hadn't yet tested the aerosol device, he took it to a back room, closed the door, sprayed the mist, and, he said, "got no effect from it. And that was the end of that. That whole thing was benched."

Attorney James Turner asked Gottlieb, "How does administering LSD to someone assist in getting information from them?"

"That is what [White] was trying to find out," Gottlieb said. "I think our final conclusion [was] that it was a very variable thing and very situation dependent and was in fact not a reliable way to get information."

In other words, Operation Midnight Climax had been a failure. There was no breakthrough. There was no revelation about mind control. LSD wasn't an effective truth drug.

However, White did inadvertently discover a way to make men spill their secrets. They would do so not because of the drugs but because of the sex. One anonymous CIA agent revealed that during the awkward postcoital situation when a man expects the prostitute to take her money and leave, if she stays instead, "it has a tremendous effect on the guy. It's a boost to his ego if she's telling him he was really neat, and she wants to stay for a few more hours. . . . Most of the time, he gets pretty vulnerable. What the hell's he going to talk about? Not the sex, so he starts talking about his business. It's at this time she can lead him gently. But you have to train prostitutes to do that. Their natural inclination is to do exactly the opposite."

The idea that sex can help elicit information wasn't new. Prostitution is often considered to be the world's oldest profession, espionage the second-oldest. Perhaps the order isn't coincidental. For all of his time, effort, and abusive actions, George White had simply reinvented the wheel.

Operation Midnight Climax ended a decade after it began. Despite its moral repugnancy, Ike Feldman defended it for the rest of his life. He insisted that it had been "good for the country." When pressed on how it had been good, he yanked the cigar from his mouth and said, "Well, look, we're goddamn free, aren't we?"

Years after White stopped working for the CIA, he wrote a letter to Sidney Gottlieb reminiscing about Operation Midnight Climax. During Gottlieb's depositions, attorney James Turner asked him if he still had the letter.

"No," Gottlieb said, "I certainly don't." He added that White was an "unpredictable character" with a "flair for writing." The letter couldn't be taken seriously. It was nothing more than "a flight of poetic license."

What did the letter say? What was Gottlieb so eager to dismiss? White had written, "I was a very minor missionary, actually a heretic, but I toiled wholeheartedly in the vineyards because it was fun, fun, fun. Where else could a red-blooded American boy lie, cheat, steal, rape and pillage with the sanction and blessing of the All-Highest?"

8

Overseas Operations

George White had dosed unwitting Americans—and a few others—with various drugs, including LSD. Having established this fact during the depositions, fiery veteran attorney Joseph Rauh asked Sidney Gottlieb whether the CIA had ever administered those same drugs overseas as part of an interrogation.

CIA attorney Lee Strickland, who was to become the persistent thorn in Rauh's side, objected to the question because "it is a fact not in evidence" and would require Gottlieb to disclose classified information.

Rauh was annoyed, but he didn't back down. He cleverly rephrased the question to bypass Strickland's objection. Instead of asking whether the CIA had ever administered the drugs overseas, he asked whether it was CIA policy to keep any such administrations a secret. If Gottlieb answered in the affirmative, it would indicate that the CIA was at least interested in doing such a thing.

Gottlieb was too smart to fall for the trap. "I don't know whether that is the CIA's position."

Rauh tried again, this time asking whether the administration of drugs overseas was the kind of thing that the CIA would *want* to keep secret.

"That is why I consulted with Mr. Strickland," Gottlieb said, "and he said I am not allowed to talk about overseas operations."

"You are not allowed to talk about any overseas operations?"

"That is right."

Strickland had grown frustrated by Rauh's antics. He confronted him, "You are not supposed to ask questions which presuppose a whole set of facts which have not been established. That is our chief problem. And I

69

have explained time and time again, it is unfair." He further accused Rauh of harboring a political vendetta against the CIA, and while it was "absolutely your prerogative to do so as it is the prerogative of every American," Strickland didn't think that Rauh should let personal politics influence his questions.

Rauh was offended. "I have not asked one question based on political—"

"You have not asked one question that has your client's interest."

Rauh sneered, "Time alone will answer that, Mr. Strickland."

In 1953, Morse Allen, the head of Project Bluebird, drafted a memo connecting Gottlieb to the administration of drugs overseas. "Sometime during the fall of 1953," it says, "Mr. Sidney Gottlieb made a tour of the Far East for reasons unknown, but undoubtedly in connection with official business of TSS. According to [redacted] and according to other sources [redacted], Gottlieb gave out samples of psychogenic drugs and ran some tests on various people out there using this drug." Allen suspected that the drug was LSD.

The next year, Willis Gibbons, head of the TSS, received unofficial reports that Gottlieb and other members of his staff had conducted "operations-type tests using chemicals on various subjects in both the Far Eastern and European areas." With the death of Frank Olson still fresh in his mind, Gibbons warned them that the uncontrolled use of LSD "may very seriously embarrass the Agency and possibly the Government."

Where had these "operations-type tests" occurred? Who were the targets? Another memo by Morse Allen provides a vague answer: "Gottlieb also is reported to have given some of the chemical to one of our staff officers in the [redacted] with the idea that the staff officer would place the chemical in the drinking water to be used by a speaker at a political rally in the [redacted]." Circumstantial evidence places the operation in the Philippines, one of only two overseas locations where Gibbons had allowed the local CIA station to keep its cache of LSD following the Olson incident. The target was President Elpidio Quirino, whom the CIA wanted to replace with someone more pro-American. An unidentified agent tried to slip Quirino ninety micrograms of LSD to make him appear insane, thereby ruining his chances in the upcoming election.

Attorney Joseph Rauh confronted Gottlieb about the operation. He read aloud Allen's memo and asked, "Is that correct?"

"I am not going to comment on that. The inference is that it is an operational activity and I don't feel free to discuss those with you."

"You don't feel free to discuss it even though this document was publicly released?"

Gottlieb, normally composed, became combative. "I have no idea what the validity of this [document] is."

Rauh knew that he had struck a nerve. He pressed harder, "You are asking Mr. Strickland everything. Ask him if this document wasn't released to us."

"Why don't you ask him?" Gottlieb snapped.

"This document is now a matter of public release. I don't see how you can say it is a matter of security not to answer my question."

Gottlieb stuck to his story. "This could be a lot of nonsense."

"Coming out of the CIA files?"

"I don't know. Every memo that a person writes isn't necessarily accurate."

Precious little information exists concerning the CIA's efforts to administer drugs overseas. Only a few other pertinent facts have emerged. First, the overseas operational side of MKULTRA was called MKDELTA. Second, by 1957, the CIA had administered six different drugs in six different overseas operations to a total of thirty-three different subjects. Third, in testimony before the Senate, medical officer Edward Gunn said that he had once walked into a meeting where CIA personnel were discussing "an individual in conjunction with a foreign government" who had been given drugs and, "shall we say, had a fatal outcome."

Perhaps more information can be gleaned from a letter that Gottlieb's wife, Margaret, wrote to her mother. In it, she talks about a trip to the Philippines that Gottlieb took in 1953:

> The novelty of having him home has not worn off yet. His trip was very successful and, to him, very exciting. He enjoys all of life's experiences to the full, and this one was so new to him and he had so much to see and absorb that he came back just about ready to burst. He spent almost all of his free time learning some native Phillipino [*sic*] dances and getting the right costumes to do them in.

Margaret then confided that Gottlieb had returned from the trip wanting to quit his job:

Sid is considering a new idea these days. He thinks he would like to stop his career for a while and get an MD with the emphasis on psychiatry, and then do research in that field with maybe some private practice to keep us in bread and butter. This, of course, would take five or six years, and whether or not we could swing it is doubtful. . . . This is a big step to take at this late date and it will take nerve to do it, but I would really like for him to at least try to do it.

Why did Gottlieb want to quit his job? He would later say that it was because of the Olson incident. But was that the truth, or was he just trying to elicit sympathy? Was he morally conflicted about his work, or was he just tired of it? Whatever had caused him to question his career, it was fleeting.

9

The Cutouts

Sidney Gottlieb was ready for MKULTRA to explore other methods of mind control beyond drugs. In particular, he was hopeful that new innovations in the fields of psychology and psychiatry would illuminate a path forward. But there was one major problem. Gottlieb didn't have the personnel necessary to conduct psychological and psychiatric experiments. Nor did he have the test subjects. He therefore decided to recruit non-CIA researchers at prisons, hospitals, and universities to conduct the experiments for him.

During Gottlieb's depositions, attorney Thomas Maddox asked him whether it had been difficult to recruit researchers from an academic community where the scientific spirit of open collaboration clashed with the secrecy demanded by the intelligence community.

"We had no trouble whatsoever recruiting," Gottlieb said. "I don't remember anybody ever saying, 'I would rather not work on this.' I mean, here was an official representative of the U.S. government saying this is a government problem. There was no pressure put on them. If they wanted to refuse—but I don't remember that being any kind of problem whatsoever."

Maddox was surprised. "Most of the researchers didn't reject the use of the Agency money for Agency purposes?"

"No. My remembrance was they felt they were doing a patriotic and valuable thing."

Gottlieb understood that once he began funding researchers to conduct experiments, the researchers' colleagues would inevitably ask where the money had come from. Word might leak that the CIA was involved, which could prompt other countries to conduct similar experiments of their own. Gottlieb had to prevent this from happening so that the United States could gain a lead in the mind control arms race. He had to somehow hide the CIA's hand.

At first, he simply gave the researchers cashier's checks from an innocuous bank account, but the process became unmanageable as MKULTRA grew. He eventually settled on funding the researchers through cutout organizations, independent institutions that agreed to launder the money for a "handling fee" of 4 percent. In essence, the money would go from the CIA to the cutout organizations, and from there to the researchers. Many of the researchers who were funded through the cutout mechanism didn't even know that the CIA was their true patron.

What's more, the cutout mechanism gave the CIA a degree of plausible deniability. If one of the researchers did something illegal or unethical, the cutout organization would take the blame while the CIA watched safely from the shadows.

The Geschickter Fund, a private research foundation at Georgetown University, served as one of the first cutout organizations. In total, it funneled over $2 million to various researchers and received another $1 million for its own programs. "We struck oil," said Charles Geschickter, the pathologist who had founded the fund. "That is the one thing that came out of it."

With the money that he received from the CIA, Geschickter paid for the construction of a new research building at the Georgetown Medical Center. The federal government, thinking that the money had come from the Geschickter Fund and not the CIA, matched the "donation," thereby paying twice. In exchange, the CIA received one-sixth of the building's laboratory space, professional cover for three employees, and Geschickter's cooperation in using his patients for experiments.

Attorney James Turner asked Gottlieb to describe the nature of Geschickter's research.

Gottlieb replied, "Dr. Geschickter was primarily interested in cancer chemotherapy. He was designing ... organic chemical compounds that might be effective. He ran both animal and, I am a little vague on this but I believe he ran some human experiments."

Turner followed up with a barrage of questions: Did the CIA supply

Geschickter with the compounds? Could the compounds render someone unconscious? Could they be used to increase stress levels?

Gottlieb wasn't sure about the first two questions, but the third jogged his memory. "[Geschickter] might have done that," he said. "I have a vague memory that he had a stress test that he used that was very unusual at the time and it makes me think he did some of that research."

Geschickter's MKULTRA subproject files contain a list of the compounds that Gottlieb wanted him to investigate. Among them were substances to produce amnesia, euphoria, paralysis, impulsiveness, mental confusion, lowered ambition, illogical thinking, resistance to torture, altered personalities, heightened suggestibility, and signs and symptoms of disease. Geschickter tested them on animals and, according to some reports, terminally ill cancer patients. His files also indicate that he withdrew the spinal fluid of comatose patients in an attempt to identify the compounds that cause "maximum levels of physical and emotional stress in human beings." When asked during a 1977 Senate investigation why the CIA was interested in such a grim topic, Geschickter said, "I can only give you the report that came to me from Allen Dulles, and I will quote it: 'Thank God there is something decent coming out of our bag of dirty tricks. We are delighted.'"

Gottlieb also used the Josiah Macy, Jr., Foundation and the National Institutes of Mental Health as cutouts. The primary cutout, however, was an organization of the CIA's own making, known as the Society for the Investigation of Human Ecology (SIHE). On its surface, the SIHE looked like any other organization, but in reality, it was nothing more than a false front for the CIA. By funding researchers through the SIHE, Gottlieb could save the handling fee that he would otherwise have to pay an independent cutout. And just so that nobody became too suspicious, the SIHE funded a few studies unrelated to mind control as a smoke screen to cover its true purpose.

Neurologist Harold Wolff and cardiologist Lawrence Hinkle, research partners at the Cornell Medical School, headed the SIHE. A series of serendipitous events had led them to work for the CIA. For one, Dulles's namesake son suffered a traumatic brain injury. On November 15, 1952, Allen Dulles, Jr., of the First Marine Division went on patrol near Outpost Bunker Hill in Korea. As he was repairing a barbed wire fence, a mortar exploded nearby, knocking him unconscious. Commander Robert Abboud remembered seeing "a lot of his head in the helmet. . . . I didn't think he'd live." Dulles Jr. remained unconscious for a month and lost the ability to form new memories. Harold Wolff treated him throughout the ordeal, endearing Wolff to the elder Dulles.

Furthermore, CIA psychologist John Gittinger had a bad back. One day while mowing his lawn, the pain became so severe that he went to the hospital for treatment. The doctor attending to him accidentally grabbed the X-rays of the man in the next room over and told Gittinger that he needed surgery. As a result, the CIA temporarily transferred Gittinger to Cornell University, where the surgery was scheduled to take place.

At Cornell, Gittinger met doctors Wolff and Hinkle. The three men, it turned out, shared many of the same interests and became fast friends. When Gittinger learned that Gottlieb and Dulles were creating the SIHE, he suggested that they recruit Wolff and Hinkle as figureheads to give it an air of legitimacy.

Besides nominally heading the SIHE, Wolff and Hinkle also wrote a report for the CIA detailing Communist methods of mind control. They obtained most of their information from Soviet prisoners and former members of the KGB. Issued in 1956, the report ominously begins by acknowledging that the Communists can make prisoners "do their bidding," confess to imaginary crimes, and wholeheartedly believe in those false confessions. The conclusion, however, is less revelatory. The Communists weren't controlling people through drugs, hypnotism, or "occult methods." Instead, they were using the same methods that had been employed for centuries: hunger, beatings, isolation, stress positions, and sleep deprivation.

Robert Vogeler, an American businessman imprisoned in Hungary on false charges of espionage, confessed to the crimes not because of any drugs but because, he said, "the toxins of fatigue are enough in themselves." He recalled how, during sleeping hours, "they made me lie on a day-bed with my face exposed to the light. I was never allowed to sleep for more than three hours at a time." Vogeler's interrogator had previously extracted Cardinal Jósef Mindszenty's false confession and made it clear that resistance was futile, saying, "Even if Jesus Christ were sitting in your chair, He'd tell me everything I wanted Him to." The interrogator warned Vogeler that refusing to answer a question "in the proper spirit" would result in a "treatment" that would cripple him for life. "We have better methods than drugs to obtain the truth."

PROJECT MIND CONTROL

In their report, Wolff and Hinkle marvel at the dramatic effects that mere isolation can have on a person's psyche:

> The profound boredom and complete loneliness of his situation gradually overwhelm the prisoner. There is literally nothing for him to do except ruminate and because he has so much to worry about, his ruminations are seldom pleasant. Frequently, they take the form of going over and over all the possible causes of his arrest. His mood becomes one of dejection. His sleep is disturbed by nightmares. . . . Some prisoners may become delirious and have hallucinations. God may appear to such a prisoner and tell him to cooperate with his interrogator. He may see his wife standing beside him, or a servant bringing him a large meal. In nearly all cases the prisoner's need for human companionship and his desire to talk to anyone about anything becomes a gnawing appetite. If he is given an opportunity to talk, he may say anything which seems to be appropriate, or to be desired by the listener. . . . He may be unable to tell what is "actually true" from what "might be" or "should be" true. He may be highly suggestible.

The similarities between the effects of isolation and LSD, down to the hallucinations, are striking. Although the Communists didn't use LSD in their interrogations, it's little wonder why the CIA thought that they might have. Ironically, Wolff and Hinkle headed the cutout organization—the SIHE—that would allow MKULTRA to flourish, even though they also wrote the report that debunked the claims that had led to the creation of MKULTRA in the first place.

John Gittinger's bad back had brought him to Wolff and Hinkle. Now fate brushed him again. While flipping through academic journals, he came across an article in the January 1956 edition of the *American Journal of Psychiatry* on something called "psychic driving." The name of the author, Dr. Ewen Cameron, didn't ring any bells, but the content of the article gave Gittinger a rush of excitement. This, he thought, was the future of MKULTRA. He ran—gingerly—to show Gottlieb.

10

Psychic Driving

"Dr. Gottlieb . . . when did you personally become aware of Dr. Cameron's research?"

"I can't remember."

"Why was the CIA interested in the research Dr. Cameron was performing?"

"The CIA . . . was interested in anything which bore upon the question of the major changes in human behavior."

"What were your responsibilities in relation to the grant made by the Society for the Investigation of Human Ecology to Dr. Cameron?"

"My responsibilities, as I remember them now, were to ensure that the work was relevant to the goals of Project MKULTRA and to satisfy myself that the investigator was a serious and reputable one."

"You stated that MKULTRA and the Society were interested in funding research on things which bore on the question of major changes in human behavior. Would you please explain how Dr. Cameron's research was funded by the Society within that broad category?"

"Well, as I remember it . . . he was interested in the effects of sensory deprivation, in electric shock. I am not sure of this, but I believe in the use of psychotropic drugs or psychochemical. Each of these things brings about major behavioral changes."

Ewen Cameron was a giant in the field of psychiatry. At the end of World War II, he had been on the psychiatric team that evaluated Nazi leader Rudolf Hess for signs of insanity and deemed him fit to stand trial at Nuremberg. Those same Nuremberg Trials spawned the Nuremberg Code, a set of ethical principles designed to guide researchers in their experiments on humans. Its authors hoped to prevent the kinds of horrifying medical experiments that had occurred inside the Nazi concentration camps from ever happening again.

The Nuremberg Code consists of ten points, the first of which reads, "The voluntary consent of the human subject is absolutely essential." The fourth point declares that any experiment involving humans "should be so conducted as to avoid all unnecessary physical and mental suffering and injury." If anyone had reason to adhere to the Nuremberg Code, it was Ewen Cameron.

A tall Scotsman with a thick accent, Cameron's kind face betrayed a personality that was as cold as the mountains that he loved to climb. After World War II, he became president of the American Psychiatric Association, the Canadian Psychiatric Association, and the World Psychiatric Association. His staff and patients alike viewed him with both reverence and fear. "He was a dictator in many respects," said one colleague. Another put it differently: "He was God."

Cameron directed the Allan Memorial Institute in Montreal. Perched on a hill overlooking the city, the Allan was an intimidating stone mansion turned psychiatric hospital. The mere sight of its weathered walls was enough to frighten former patients, one of whom called it "a spooky old place."

In 1951, Cameron became interested in mind control after reading an article by British psychiatrist William Sargant on Communist brainwashing techniques. Sargant argued that the Communists were subjecting people to extreme stress, which was somehow wiping their minds clean and making them susceptible to propaganda. The theory sprang from Sargant's knowledge of religious conversions. In particular, he recounted how certain Christian preachers would begin their sermons by describing the eternal torments of Hell. Such fire-and-brimstone fearmongering distressed the listeners and made them susceptible to indoctrination. In Sargant's words, "An overwhelming emotional stimulus carries the subject to the point of emotional collapse and increased suggestibility." Maybe the Communists were doing something similar.

Sargant was a behaviorist. According to this view, people are born as blank slates and are conditioned by their environments to behave in certain ways. A positive stimulus will cause a person to adopt a behavior, whereas a negative stimulus will cause them to avoid it. Nurture, not nature, reigns supreme. Behaviorism was best summarized in a famous phrase attributed to American psychologist B. F. Skinner: "Give me a child and I'll shape him into anything."

Ewen Cameron adopted Sargant's views and applied them to psychiatry. He reasoned that mental illness must be the result of a bad environment reinforcing bad behaviors. In that case, would it be possible to reduce a person back to a blank slate via stress, and upon that blank slate write better behaviors? Cameron thought so. If he could find a way to induce enough stress in his patients so that they forgot their bad behaviors, then he could build them back up in his image and cure all mental illness.

Cameron had long pioneered unorthodox treatments for mental illness. Whenever he learned of a potential treatment that showed any sign of promise, he pursued it with reckless abandon. Once, a schizophrenic boy and former patient at the Allan tried to commit suicide by sealing himself inside a garage and breathing in the noxious fumes of a running car. He survived, barely, and was sent back to the Allan for help, whereupon Cameron noticed that his symptoms of schizophrenia had diminished. Perhaps the carbon monoxide had somehow cured the boy. Overcome with excitement, Cameron sent a reluctant colleague to go buy a cylinder of carbon monoxide for experiments. The cylinder was $500, but the colleague, thinking the idea mad, lied to Cameron and said that it was $2,500, too expensive for him to buy.

In 1953, Cameron accidentally discovered what would become his favorite treatment for schizophrenia. He was recording the therapy session of a female patient—"a blonde and sultry girl from Bermuda whom I roundly suspected of incestuous . . . feelings for her father"—and noticed that whenever he played back the audio for her to listen to, she became visibly upset. Fascinated, he replayed the audio over and over, each time provoking a stronger reaction. "You're a damn fool," she finally yelled before storming out of the room.

Soon afterward, another patient told Cameron that her mother used to threaten her by saying, "If you don't keep quiet, I'm going to leave you behind." Cameron played these words back to her and asked, "Do you feel anything, lassie?"

His notes of the session capture her dramatic response:

> 19 repetitions: "Does it go on all the time? I hate to hear that—it upsets me; look at me shaking."

> 21 repetitions: "It upsets me enough. It is the future that I think of—I know now that I can't count on my husband and my mother." (At this point the patient became red, restless, and began to breathe rapidly.)

> 30 repetitions: "I hate everything; it makes me so resentful—I am so alone, I might as well go and do something silly; I am so different—I want to be like others; I want to hear nice words—my mother and husband never did—but I can't go out for necking—I want to be protected—I never got it."

> 35 repetitions: "I hate. I hate."

> 36 repetitions: "Oh stop it. I don't want—"

> 39 repetitions: "Stop it! Stop it!" (The patient began to threaten with her hands).

Cameron realized that by subjecting mental patients to repeated auditory messages—what he called "psychic driving"—he might be able to induce enough stress in them to reprogram their behavior. The idea at first filled him with unease. "I even noticed in myself a reluctance to do this," he said. "I felt that I was being unkind, insensitive, imperceptive.... One simply didn't do this sort of thing to people." Yet *because* of his feelings of unease, Cameron reasoned that he must be on the right track. In his view, only those who dared to go where nobody had gone before would discover anything new. It was a view shared by Sidney Gottlieb, on whose desk sat a carving of a turtle bearing the inscription, "Behold the Turtle—it never advances unless it sticks its neck out."

Cameron thought that psychic driving was the key to curing mental illness. In 1956, he published his findings in the *American Journal of Psychiatry*, a copy of which happened to land in the hands of John Gittinger.

Attorney Joseph Rauh wanted to get Gittinger's story straight. "Well, now, let's go back. You read the article by Cameron?"

"Yes, sir."

"And then someone suggested to Cameron he file an application. And who was that, [James] Monroe?"

"I would assume so, yes."

"You suggested it to Monroe?"

"Yes."

"And Monroe suggested it to Cameron. Now, it comes back from Cameron as an application. Monroe approves it and he sends it to Washington?"

"That's right."

"What happens in Washington?"

"I just explained, sir, that it went to the fiscal group for the allocation of funds."

"And then?"

"The funds were given to the Society for the Investigation of Human Ecology for dispersal and for whatever accounting they required."

"But wasn't it approved by you and Mr. Gottlieb?"

"Oh, yes. We certainly would indicate that we were interested in having this done, sir."

In Cameron's application for funding from the SIHE, solicited by the CIA, he proposed to investigate psychic driving, the administration of LSD, and other techniques "as a means of breaking down the ongoing pattern of behavior" in his patients. Given the fact that Frank Olson had died as a result of an LSD experiment, Rauh was surprised to learn that Gittinger and Gottlieb had approved an application that called for the administration of LSD.

"Did you do anything to have the [SIHE] tell him that he shouldn't use LSD?"

"Absolutely not," Gittinger said.

"You can't remember a sentence about LSD after a man died from having the agency give him LSD?"

"Well, I didn't know that."

"In 1957 you didn't know that Olson had died from LSD?"

"I did not."

Rauh didn't believe Gittinger for a second. He raised his voice: "Look, friend, you and I are both pretty close to our maker and let me tell you that I think you have done something terrible, but lying about it today you ought to think about." Rauh then requested a five-minute break to calm down.

Ewen Cameron had always believed that he was destined for glory, the next Sigmund Freud, the future recipient of the Nobel Prize in Medicine. He didn't know how he would achieve his fantasy—until he discovered psychic driving. This was his ticket to the awards and accolades that he so desperately craved. First, though, he needed to prove that psychic driving actually worked, and he could only do that through experiments.

Having secured funding from the SIHE, Cameron began subjecting his patients to psychic driving for up to twenty hours a day. The patients had sought his care thinking that they would receive tried-and-true treatments, but instead they became his unwitting guinea pigs. The CIA itself later admitted, "It is doubtful that any meaningful form of consent is involved in this case."

Each patient had his or her own psychic driving message specifically tailored to them. The message for one female patient was, "Do you realize that you are a very hostile person? Do you know that you are hostile to the nurses? Do you know that you are hostile with the patients? Why do you think you are so hostile? Did you hate your mother? Did you hate your father?" It looped over and over, tens of thousands of times through a set of headphones that she was forced to wear. Whenever she became so desperate to escape the nonstop negativity that she ripped off the headphones, Cameron's assistant put them inside of a leather helmet and strapped it to her head.

Oftentimes, Cameron would ask a patient's husband, wife, or other close relative to record the psychic driving message for added impact. On the rare occasions when Cameron switched a patient from a negative to a positive message, he would record the positive message himself.

Jeannine Huard, a thirty-year-old mother of three suffering from depression, later recalled her first experience with psychic driving: "They had this machine on top of the bed and I said, 'What is that?' The nurse said, 'You have to listen to that.' I said, 'No, no, no! I'm not in Russia! I'm not going to listen to anything!'" Cameron nevertheless forced her to listen to the haunting message, which went, "Jeannine, you are running away from responsibility! Why? You don't want to take care of your husband! Why? You don't want to take care of your children! Why? Why, Jeannine? Why?"

She somehow managed to turn off the device, but afterward she was given nitrous oxide and forty pills a day to subdue her. "I tried not to listen," she said, "but it was so hard. . . . How can you be strong enough?" Once, she escaped her room and ran down the hall to the cafeteria. Cameron spotted her and barked, "Jeannine! Go back there! Go back and listen!" On catching up to her, he put his arm around her shoulders and sighed, "Don't you *want* to get well?" As far as he was concerned, any attempt to avoid psychic driving was undeniable proof that a patient required more of it.

Jeannine began to question whether Cameron had her best interest at heart:

> In my mind, they wanted to drive me crazy. Why would they do such a thing to me? So, on the tape, I remember it was saying if you see a paper on the floor, pick it up. So, I'm all alone in a little room, with a bed and a tape machine. There is nothing but a little waste basket. And I hear, you pick it up, you pick it up, if you see a paper. So, I look all around, because it gets in my mind and I don't see any paper. . . . They were driving me crazy, and they were watching me, telling me all these crazy things. Why in the world would they tell me to pick up a paper on the floor, when there is no paper?

Another psychic driving patient referred to as "Lauren G." became so disillusioned that she tried to run away. One day, while still groggy from the treatment, she stumbled out of the front door of the Allan Memorial Institute, her long hospital gown trailing behind her. When she reached the base of Mount Royal, she started climbing as fast as she could. But she didn't get very far. Staff members soon found her and pumped her full of sedatives.

Cameron sent his most unruly patients to an isolated dormitory called the "Sleep Room." Here they were put in chemically induced comas and forced to listen to endlessly repeating psychic driving messages played through speakers placed next to their pillows. The patients woke up three times per day to eat and to use the bathroom. Otherwise, they remained unconscious for up to two months straight.

The concept for Cameron's "sleep therapy" wasn't entirely new. In Aldous Huxley's 1932 novel *Brave New World,* the World State indoctrinates its citizens by making them listen to recorded slogans while sleeping. Within a decade of the novel's publication, American businessman Max Sherover created a real-life version of the technology—the "Cerebrophone"—that could supposedly teach people new languages overnight. Cameron, inspired by an advertisement for the Cerebrophone, decided to replace the foreign language tapes with psychic driving messages. Science fiction had become science fact.

Peggy Mielke, a nurse in the Sleep Room, recorded the patients' behaviors during their brief moments awake. Her notes include phrases like "only babbles," "infantile responses," and "unable to say her own name." The overall scene, not to mention the room's pungent smell of body odor, was "highly unpalatable," she wrote. Cameron sensed her unease and tried to reassure her, "This treatment is helping. Never you forget that. When you take away everything that is bad, you have room to put back the good."

A rebellious Jeannine Huard was sent to the Sleep Room—while pregnant. Whenever she refused to take her cocktail of drugs, the nurses would tell her, "You are no good to your family" and threaten to call the police. Cameron eventually let her leave the Allan, but only because she almost had a miscarriage.

Jeannine soon gave birth to a baby girl who developed severe gastric trouble and teetered on the edge of death. "I think that it's on account of all the drugs that I took," she later said. Worried sick about her daughter, her mental state collapsed. Two months after giving birth, she found herself back at the Allan under the watchful eye of Ewen Cameron. This time around, "I had no more fighting power. And I am a very fighting person. . . . I had no more resistance whatsoever. So, I did not discuss, I did not argue. I did—" She hesitated. "I became the way that Dr. Cameron wanted me to be."

To further break down his patients, Cameron placed them in sensory deprivation chambers for up to thirty-five days at a time. The chambers were essentially dark rooms in which the patients lay with plugs in their ears, masks on their faces, and mitts over their hands.

Cameron had first become interested in sensory deprivation through the work of psychologist Donald Hebb, another researcher in Montreal. In the early 1950s, Hebb had paid seventy student volunteers twenty dollars a day to plug their ears with cotton, cover their eyes with a translucent visor, wrap their arms in cardboard tubes, and lay in bed for as long as possible. They could only move to eat and to use the bathroom. Some of the students tried to pass the time by counting in their heads. Others imagined the plots of their favorite movies. Most, however, found it difficult to concentrate on anything for any appreciable amount of time.

Over the course of the experiment, the students became "markedly irritable," said Woodburn Heron, a member of Hebb's team. Several of them experienced hallucinations, ranging from squirrels running through a field to eyeglasses marching down a street. Given the insufferable boredom of just lying there, the hallucinations were often a welcome distraction. "But after a while," Heron said, "the pictures became disturbing, and so vivid that they interfered with sleep."

Half of the students quit within a day. The longest lasted almost six days, still only a fraction of what Cameron would make his patients endure. (Hebb later called Cameron "criminally stupid.") Four of the students insisted that sensory deprivation was undoubtedly a form of torture. The results startled Hebb, who said, "It is one thing to hear that the Chinese are brainwashing their prisoners on the other side of the world; it is another to find, in your own laboratory, that merely taking away the usual sights, sounds, and bodily contacts from a healthy university student for a few days can shake him, right down to the base."

After Hebb published the results of his experiment, the CIA began funding his work through a cutout organization. It also funded the related work of Hebb's former student Maitland Baldwin. A sinister-looking brain surgeon, Baldwin took sensory deprivation to a new and unsettling level. One of his experiments involved confining an Army volunteer in a small padded box for forty hours, at which point the volunteer began "sobbing in a most heartrending fashion," Baldwin reported. The panicked volunteer then proceeded to kick his way out of the box.

Baldwin next wanted to conduct "terminal type" sensory deprivation experiments, but a CIA medical officer rejected the idea for being "immoral and inhuman." In a scathing note to his colleagues, the medical officer suggested that "all who are in favor of the above-mentioned operation volunteer their heads for use in Dr. Baldwin's 'noble' project." Baldwin never did conduct "terminal type" experiments, at least not on humans. Monkeys were another matter. His experiments on them included lobotomies, beaming microwaves into their brains, and attempting to transplant the head of one monkey onto the decapitated body of another monkey.

Charles Geschickter, the pathologist whose foundation the CIA used as a cutout to fund Baldwin, elaborated on the monkey experiments during his 1977 testimony before the Senate. He said that Baldwin once "rocked the heads of animals back and forth to try to cause them amnesia by concussion of the brain. And that was for $110,000." As for the microwave experiments, the goal was "to put monkeys to sleep, to see if they could be, should I say, instead of Mickey Finn, they could put them under with radar directed toward the monkey brain."

"Could they?" asked Senator Richard Schweiker.

"Yes, sir," Geschickter said. "But, Senator, it showed that if you got into too deep a sleep, you injured the heat center of the brain the way you cook meat, and there was a borderline there that made it dangerous."

Meanwhile, at the Allan Memorial Institute, Ewen Cameron was doing something similar to his own patients. Except instead of blasting their brains with microwaves, he was frying them with electricity.

11

Depatterning

Ever since the birth of her daughter in 1949, Velma Orlikow had suffered from bouts of depression. She had tried getting help from her general practitioner, but, she said, "he just laughed at me."

In 1955, Velma's depression spiraled out of control. She was pregnant again and "didn't know what another person entering our lives would do." Feeling overwhelmed, she and her husband decided to have an abortion. When she arrived at the hospital for the procedure, a young intern asked her to consent to a tubal ligation.

"What's that?" she asked.

"They're going to see that you don't have any more children."

"Well, I've never discussed this with the doctors, nobody told me about that."

"I'm sorry, but that's the paper I have."

The Orlikows were flabbergasted. They sat in the hospital all evening contemplating what to do. In the end, "we signed the paper," Velma recalled. "Oh, God. And we lost our child and we never had another child."

A year later, Velma checked into the Allan Memorial Institute. Out of all of Cameron's "treatments"—drugs, psychic driving, sleep therapy, sensory deprivation—she came to dread the "depatterning" the most. It was a form of high-voltage electroshock therapy that Cameron believed could eliminate a person's destructive patterns of thought. An official Canadian government report on the Allan used a helpful analogy to describe the goal of depatterning: "Under Cameron's theory, one might compare the patient's brain to an old-fashioned telephone switchboard, in which all the wires were plugged into the wrong holes. In depatterning, all the wires were pulled out. In repatterning," which involved making the patient listen to a positive psychic driving message, "the aim was to plug all the wires back into the right holes."

The CIA was particularly interested in electroshock therapy because of its reported ability to induce amnesia. Although some of the CIA's unidentified consultants argued that "short of cutting a subject's throat, a true amnesia cannot be guaranteed," others held out hope. One declassified memo says that a standard electroshock machine could "guarantee amnesia for certain periods of time." The same memo, written *before* the CIA started funding Cameron, also says that people who had been subjected to electroshock therapy "complained that their whole head was on fire and it was much too painful a treatment for any medical practice." One anonymous CIA officer was of the opinion that "an individual could gradually be reduced through the use of electro-shock treatment to the vegetable level."

During a later deposition, Velma Orlikow became distraught when asked about depatterning. "Please don't talk about it."

"I'm sorry," said the attorney, "but I feel that I must."

"You're really upsetting me very much. Please do not do this."

Velma may have been reluctant to revisit that traumatic chapter of her life, but she made it clear that she had complained to the staff, nurses, doctors, and even to Cameron himself. "I don't want to do it," she would tell them, "It's killing me. It's killing me."

Jeannine Huard, the patient who nearly lost her baby daughter, was more open about her experience. She remembered being put on a stretcher and wheeled into a strange room full of male assistants who were there to restrain her convulsing body. (Some patients were given Anectine to cause temporary muscle paralysis and reduce the magnitude of their convulsions.) "It was like they were going to put me on the electric chair," she said. "That's what I had in my mind." The assistants placed a firm object between her teeth so that she wouldn't bite off her tongue, then they placed the electrodes on her temples. From the corner of the room, Cameron's voice called out, "This will help you, lassie. You won't feel anything." Six consecutive jolts of electric fire rattled her brain.

Gail Kastner, a young nursing student at McGill University, similarly received depatterning for her depression. After one of her thirty-six sessions, Cameron wrote in her medical file, "The shock treatment turned the then 19-year-old honours student into a woman who sucked her thumb, talked like a baby, demanded to be fed from a bottle and urinated on the floor."

By the time that Gail left the Allan, she had lost most of her memories as well as her ability to form new ones. She lived for a time with her identical twin sister, Zella, but the ever-present reminder of what could have been was too much for her to bear. Demoralized, she moved to an empty garage and scavenged food from garbage bins outside of a nearby grocery store. Years later, Zella told her, "You have no idea what I went through. You would urinate on the living room floor and suck your thumb and talk baby talk and you would demand the bottle of my baby. That's what I had to put up with!"

Few people were as equipped to judge the effects of depatterning as Mary Morrow. Ever since she was twelve, she had wanted to become a doctor like her father. Driven by ambition, she went to nursing school at St. Mary's Hospital in Montreal and spent two years in the Royal Canadian Army Medical Corps. Afterward, she enrolled in medical school with the goal of becoming the head of neurology at St. Mary's. "I wanted to be a doctor," she said in a deposition. "My mother wanted me to be a stenographer. We were fighting. I won."

Mary had an indomitable spirit—"Nothing deters me in this world, ever"—but her body was petite and frail. Too poor to afford proper food, and too busy studying to get a job, she survived medical school on a meager diet of bread and Cheez Whiz. Moreover, because of the academic pressure and constant fights with her mother, she developed anorexia. At ninety-five pounds, her dark brown hair framed a sunken face studded with hollow eyes. "I guess my life is kind of tragic," she said.

In late 1956, Mary became a resident-in-training at the Allan. For six months, she watched Cameron dole out his unorthodox treatments with "satanic vigor." The depatterning in particular turned her stomach. "You push the button once, and they'd go into a convulsion. And then in quick succession you do it six times, and they'd go from one shock into another with apnea. That means their breathing would stop. And it was the most terrifying thing I've ever seen in my life before or since." The only thing that eased her conscience was the fact that the patients had signed a consent form.

When Mary finished her residency at the Allan, she developed a severe sinus infection requiring hospitalization. The new head of neurology at St. Mary's, Preston Robb, took care of her. "He had been given the job that I had worked for for twenty years. . . . So you know, it was pretty tough." To make matters worse, Mary failed her certification exams in neurology, causing her to sink into a deep depression.

Not only had her pride taken a severe blow, but so had her income—what little there was—because she could no longer accept private patients. "They gave all my private patients to Robb who could give continuing care. And I was just in a bottomless pit. I was just in a hole. . . . I couldn't talk to anybody, look at anybody, not even my own family." She started self-medicating with uppers in the morning and downers in the evening. "The only way I could hold my head up was with amphetamines. I would weep copiously or be irritable and cranky with everybody. And I just went from bad to worse." Having hit rock bottom, she swallowed a handful of pills in an unsuccessful attempt to commit suicide.

Ashamed and embarrassed, Mary isolated herself from her friends, family, and colleagues. She got a job as a nurse in a convalescent hospital an hour's drive from her home. She then re-took her certification exams and failed them again. Out of desperation, she visited Cameron at the Allan to ask him if she could continue training under him. He tentatively agreed, but given her sickly, disheveled appearance, he wanted her to get a medical evaluation first. "I must have been an awful mess," she later said.

Mary quit her job and checked into the Royal Victoria Hospital for the medical evaluation. Cameron visited her there multiple times, apparently in an attempt to recruit her to come to the Allan not as a resident but as a patient. The doctors at the Royal Victoria warned her not to do it. "Go home and think about it," they would say. But in her mind, Cameron represented her last chance to become a doctor. At his request, "like a fool," she went.

Upon checking into the Allan, Mary was diagnosed with schizophrenia. She soon heard Cameron tell a resident just outside her door, "We'll give her shock treatments." Mary let out an involuntary yelp in horror. She knew firsthand the awful effects of depatterning. Her only solace was the fact that she hadn't signed a consent form. Unbeknownst to her, in the short time since her residency, Cameron had stopped using the consent form.

Mary remembered little else about her stay at the Allan, though her medical records indicate that she received eleven rounds of depatterning. On the days of her "treatment," she would call her mother to talk, each time making less and less sense. Her mother grew so concerned that she sent another daughter, Margaret, to go make sure that Mary was all right. Margaret arrived at the Allan late one evening and demanded to see her sister. The staff only obliged when she threatened to call the police.

Margaret found Mary sitting alone in the corner of a small room, her swollen eyes staring into nothingness.

"Mommy is going to have the treatments stopped," Margaret said.

"What treatments?" Mary replied.

The next morning, Mary struggled to perform even simple tasks like getting dressed and applying her makeup. She later said that she had felt as if she were "in a deep, dark, pitch-black hole with no sense of appendages, like a worm. But I had no—I didn't know that I should have appendages. There was no sense of solidity." It took her two days to recognize Margaret. During that time, their mother called every doctor in every ward of the Allan and told them not to put another finger on her daughter.

"Cameron never came near me after my mother demanded that everything be stopped," Mary said. "He never came near me to find out what I had gone through. He abandoned me." She at least considered herself more fortunate than the many patients whose families never rescued them. "What further tortures they went through before they got to be a legume I can't tell you." Contemplating their fates, she became irate. "How much longer is this torture going for these people? Do you understand what I'm trying to tell you? To hell with me. I'm able to tell you what I went through for two or three days. I'm not able to tell you what some of these victims have gone through for 26 or 30 years. It's just horrible. Just absolutely horrible."

Weeks after escaping from the Allan, Mary returned to confront Cameron in his office. "I went in uninvited. He never came near me. I said, 'I want to know, man to man, what you've done to me.' Man to man, my words. He laughed in my face, facetiously, like the Satan that he was, and said, 'I can't discuss it with you; you're a woman.' I left. I never saw him again."

Mary had always prioritized her career over everything else, thinking that one day when she was established she would start a family. Now, given the state of her mind, she lost hope that she ever would. "My biological clock . . . was ticking. And I desperately wanted to marry and have a child. And that, as much as my career, was over."

Mary sued Cameron for $1.5 million, but the judge ruled in his favor. She appealed the ruling, but another judge dismissed the case. Unable to find a job in Canada (Cameron sabotaged her attempts), she moved to Louisville,

Kentucky, and became a teaching consultant. In 1979, she again tried to commit suicide.

During Cameron's keynote speech at the 1963 meeting of the American Psychopathological Association, he admitted that his experiments had been futile: "We tried [psychic] driving under hypnosis, immediately after electroshock, we tried innumerable combinations of voices, of timing and many other conditions, but we were never able to stop the mechanisms [of mental illness]." He had been on a wild goose chase the whole time.

Cameron resigned from the Allan the following year. By then, a growing number of his colleagues had begun to question the therapeutic value of his unorthodox treatments. Three years later, he died of a heart attack while hiking in the Adirondack Mountains.

In all likelihood, even if Cameron hadn't received funding from the CIA, he still would have conducted the same experiments. Nobody at the CIA told him what to research. Instead, they funded him because of his research. Frederick Lowy, a fellow Canadian psychiatrist, made an analogous point:

> [Cameron] conducted these treatments in an open atmosphere where everybody knew what he was doing. He, if anything, sought publicity. He lost no occasion to report to the public in Montreal papers and to psychiatrists at meetings what he was doing. He was elected to high psychiatric office despite these treatments, so the fact of the matter is they were accepted, even though I myself would not have done them. . . . [In the 1950s], whether it was in surgery or in psychiatry, every physician pretty well was his own ethics committee, and if he felt he could benefit the patient by trying something new . . . he would go ahead and do it, and then let experience dictate whether to continue to do it.

The CIA didn't instigate every wicked act that occurred under the MKULTRA umbrella. It did, however, aid and abet the perpetrators.

12

The Wild West

In the early morning hours of July 4, 1954, a search party of two hundred volunteers combed through the woods near San Antonio, Texas. They were looking for a missing three-year-old girl named Chere Jo Horton. The night before, Horton's parents had left her outside to play in the parking lot of the Lazy A Bar while they went inside for a drink. When they returned a few minutes later, she was gone. They initially thought that she had wandered away and gotten lost, but as the hours passed, they began to fear something much worse.

Their fears were realized when a member of the search party discovered Horton's twisted body lying in a gravel pit. Her skull had been fractured. Her clothes had been ripped off. She had been raped.

Shortly after the discovery, highway patrolman Eugene Talbert spotted a blue 1941 Plymouth car parked a few hundred yards from the murder scene. A torn pair of girls' underwear hung from one of its door handles. Talbert then saw a shirtless man stumbling down a bluff overlooking the gravel pit. The man's arms and chest were covered in fresh scratches and his pants were speckled with blood.

His name was Jimmy Shaver. He was a twenty-nine-year-old airman at nearby Lackland Air Force Base. He had a wife, two children, no criminal record, and no history of violence. Talbert immediately arrested him and, out of concern that the search party would try to lynch Shaver if they saw the blood on his clothes, made him squat down on the floorboards of the patrol car while they sped to the police station for questioning.

Shaver insisted that he was innocent. The real culprit, he said, was a hitch-hiker whom he had picked up, a blond man with tattoos. The hitchhiker had hit him over the head and left him for dead in the mesquite brush. Over time, though, Shaver's story fell apart. He eventually admitted to abducting Horton and taking her to the gravel pit. "Then I blacked out," he claimed.

When the police learned that a lynch mob was forming in San Antonio, they transferred Shaver to a jail cell in Austin until the public furor died down. "I'd give my life if it hadn't happened," he told a journalist from the *Austin Statesman*. "I guess I'm guilty, but I just can't see me doing something like that."

Louis Jolyon West was the resident psychiatrist at Lackland Air Force Base. Nicknamed "Jolly" for his middle name as well as his uncanny resemblance to Santa Claus, he was renowned for having evaluated the American POWs who had given false confessions during the Korean War. Now it was his responsibility to evaluate Shaver to determine whether he had been sane at the time of the murder.

West's narcissistic tendencies rivaled those of Ewen Cameron. Being attached to the Shaver case would undoubtedly give him plenty of coverage in the newspapers, bringing him closer to the fame that he craved. On top of that, it would give him the opportunity to conduct a long-awaited experiment.

Back in early 1953, West had received an intriguing letter from Sherman C. Grifford of Chemrophyl Associates. "Sherman C. Grifford" was actually a pseudonym for Sidney Gottlieb. "Chemrophyl Associates" was a cover for the CIA. Even though West had argued that the American POWs in Korea hadn't been drugged or hypnotized into giving their false confessions, Gottlieb wanted his help in determining whether such a thing was possible.

In the first surviving letter of their correspondence, dated June 11, 1953, West described the experiments that he hoped to conduct for "S.G." These included "the degree to which information can be extracted from presumably unwilling subjects (through hypnosis alone or in combination with certain drugs), possibly with subsequent amnesia." He also wanted to explore "techniques for implanting false information into particular subjects . . . or for inducing in them specific mental disorders." Lastly, he sought to create hypnotic couriers who could carry secret messages in their subconscious minds. "Needless to say," he wrote, the experiments "must eventually be put to test in practical trials in the field."

West knew that if he conducted the experiments at Lackland Air Force

Base, his colleagues would condemn them as unethical. He therefore wanted to "cut down considerably the number of people who can call me to account." Perhaps, he suggested, Gottlieb could pull some strings and get Major Robert Williams transferred elsewhere. Williams was "an uncomfortably close scrutinizer of all my activities" and believed that hypnotism amounted to "tampering with the soul."

One year after West sent this letter, Jimmy Shaver murdered Chere Jo Horton. West spent the next two weeks running Shaver through a gauntlet of psychological exams. Others spent countless hours interrogating Shaver for information, but he maintained that he couldn't remember anything about the crime. Seeing as how the conventional methods of interrogation weren't working, West decided to try something unconventional. He decided to subject Shaver to the methods of mind control that he had been discussing with Sidney Gottlieb.

West hypnotized Shaver and injected him with sodium amytal. As the effects took hold, Shaver gradually lowered his defenses. He said that on the night of the murder, he had stopped by the Lazy A Bar for a drink.

"So what do you do now?" West probed gently.

"Well," Shaver said, "I walked around to the juke box and played a song, you know, stood looking over the place. Then I started outside, and here's this little girl. So the little girl wants to go for a ride, you know?"

"Sure."

"I figured no harm in that."

"That's right," West reassured him.

"She says, 'Please, sir, mister, will you take me for a ride in your car?' I says, 'Why sure honey.' I think you know I've got all kinds of kids at home. I love kids."

"Sure. Then what happens, Jimmy?"

"Well, we get in the car and drive down the road there. I always was an impulsive guy. I wonder doctor, if there's anything for that?"

"Well, we'll see, Jimmy. What happened next?"

"Well—I mean—I—you get times that are right. You know, at that moment—you know what I mean? And I can't understand it."

"Tell me, Jimmy."

"Well, when I get down there I turned the corner on Frio Road—you know that there?"

"Yes."

"And I went on up there and I didn't know nothing about that place up there but the girl did. . . . So we went in the place, you know and after I got her out there, I—don't know."

At this point, West wrote in his notes that Shaver "looks frightened, covers mouth." West prodded him to continue, "Yes, Jimmy. It's all coming back to you."

Shaver became agitated. "Hey, hey, let me out of here. Let me out, let me out of here. Please let me out."

"Don't worry," West said. "You remember what happens, Jimmy. Tell me. What were you thinking about? What did you do?"

"And I beat her until she was a pulp," Shaver howled as he sobbed into his hands.

Later in the interrogation, West asked Shaver to explain what had happened at the gravel pit.

"You see," Shaver said, "I didn't have no sexual desire for this little runt of a kid. She wasn't nothing to me. . . . I walked outside and that little girl was standing by my car. Just throwin' stones you know. Just throwin' stones at my windshield and at my body."

"Throwing stones at your windshield and at your body?"

"Yes."

"How did you feel?"

"I thought it probably wouldn't hurt it. But then she got to picking up bigger rocks and hittin' it in the body and knocking the paint off. I told the little girl to go home and leave. Well she could talk a little bit, but not too plain. She says, 'I ain't gonna do it.' Just like Beth used to say."

"Just like Beth used to say?"

"I don't know what got a hold of me at that time. I just don't realize how in the world I could do such a thing as I did."

Throughout the interrogation, Shaver referred to a girl named "Beth Rainboat," supposedly his cousin who had tormented him as a child. "She was always doing things . . . making me wash the dishes, taking food and cakes away from me. Hit me in the head with a rock. Almost had me drowned, knocked me out." He also claimed that she had sexually abused him, though her abuse was nothing compared to the abuse of his father.

"My father," he cried, "I'm telling you. He was the most rotten, the most deceiving man there was. I hated his guts. Absolutely hated his guts. Whip a horse to death with a chain cause it stepped on a little pig. Pig wasn't worth two cents. . . . He beat me with a lariat rope. A lariat rope!"

At the age of eighteen, Shaver had changed his birth name, Nebron Brown, to Jimmy Shaver because he refused to carry on his father's legacy.

West tried to bring the discussion back to the night of the murder, but Shaver kept dodging the questions. Eventually, West blurted out, "Tell me about when you took her clothes off, Jimmy."

Shaver then gave the most damning statement of his life. "Well, Doc, I don't know," he began:

> I thought of that kind of a little late I guess. I finally did take them off—well, I couldn't do no good with the little old girl. I couldn't get it in her. That kind of disappointed me, you know Doc, but then I said oh well. Maybe later on you know, you get somebody else. So I seen some lights and I run away real fast. No clothes on see Doc? I didn't have no clothes on. I [run], and all this brush were scratching me up, so I said oh well I better put on my shirt and pants, you know, Doc. Then so I did. Then I was running along there again and I stumbled over a fence. I didn't know which direction I was going.

The first part of the interrogation was now over. Inexplicably, West began the next part without turning on the tape recorder. Whatever was said during those thirty minutes remains lost.

West turned the tape recorder back on.

"Now you remember it all, don't you Jimmy?"

"Yes, sir."

"I want you to tell me again what happened . . . Tell me everything you can remember. Everything you felt. Everything that came into your mind."

"I went back to the Lazy A. There was this little girl. I put her in my car."

"Wait a minute. Don't go too fast, Jimmy, tell us everything that happened. You got back to the Lazy A and then what did you do?"

"Then I went inside. And the little boy and the little girl was in there. I came back outside and put the little girl in my car."

"Did you do anything before you put her in your car?"

"Yes, sir, I knocked her out."

"Why did you do that, Jimmy?"

"Because I hated her."

"Why did you hate her, Jimmy?"

"Because I thought she was someone else."

"Who did you think she was, Jimmy?"

"Beth Rainboat."

"What was the little girl doing to make you think such a thing?"

"Throwing rocks at my car."

"Why did that make you think of Beth Rainboat?"

"She hit me in the head once with a rock."

"So you got to the gravel pit. Then what happened?"

"Well then, I took her and I beat her and I beat her, and I beat her and I beat her, and beat her some more."

"How did you feel at the time, Jimmy?"

"Well, I didn't want to do it. I knew that it was God's will."

"You knew that it was God's will? How'd you know?"

"He sent an angel and told me."

"Was he there with you at the time?"

"Yes, sir."

"Did you see him?"

"Yes, sir."

"Describe him."

"Sir?"

"Describe him."

"He had a radiant white gown and he had a nice beard. Not rugged, but nice."

"Now let's come back to earth for a minute, Jimmy. You were back out there in the gravel pit. You beat and beat on this little girl. Did she bleed?"

"Yes, sir."

"Did you get blood all over yourself?"

"Yes, sir."

"Then what did you do?"

"I went down in the ditch there and washed off."

"Then what did you do?"

"Put on my clothes and started back after my car."

"Wait a minute, Jimmy. What else did you do to the little girl?"

"Oh, just beat her and beat her and beat her."

PROJECT MIND CONTROL

"What else did you do? Think. Try to remember Jimmy, what else you did."

"Nothing! That's all. I just beat her and beat her and beat her."

"After you took her clothes off what did you do?"

"I never did take her clothes off."

"Hmm?"

"I never did take her clothes off."

"Didn't you do something with your finger?"

"Then I run my finger up in her real far because I wanted to hurt her. For the way she hurt me so many times."

"Who was she, then?"

"She was Beth Rainboat."

West ended the interrogation by asking Shaver about the future. "Jimmy, look up here a minute, boy. What do you think is going to happen now?"

"I'll go to the electric chair, I guess."

"Are you afraid to go to the electric chair?"

"I don't know. I've never been there."

"Do you think you deserve to go to the electric chair?"

"Yes sir. I guess I do."

"Why?"

"You just said I killed the wrong girl."

"Would it be because you killed the wrong one? Let me ask you this, Jimmy. If you had killed the right one," Beth Rainboat, "then would you have had to go to the electric chair?"

"Oh, no, she was evil. She was evil. Nobody would send me to the electric chair for her."

The interrogation raises a number of questions. Why did Shaver emphasize the beating? Why did he keep mentioning Beth Rainboat? Why did he suddenly invoke "God's will"? If he had already confessed to trying to rape Horton, why did West ask the leading question about the finger?

West provided some answers in a preface to the transcript of the interrogation. He wrote, "In the last one third [of the interrogation], some leading questions were put in order to bring out in the tape recording those revelations which had occurred when no recording was made." Maybe he was telling the truth, but there's reason to think otherwise.

West vehemently opposed the death penalty, calling it "outdated, immoral,

wasteful, cruel, brutalizing, unfair, irrevocable, useless, dangerous, and ob-
structive of justice." If Shaver were deemed insane at the time of the murder, he could avoid getting the death penalty. During those thirty minutes
of unrecorded interrogation, perhaps West influenced Shaver to give answers that would prove his insanity, such as the emphasis on the beating,
the references to Beth Rainboat, and the invocation of "God's will." Perhaps West also influenced Shaver to downplay the rape, which might help
Shaver avoid getting the death penalty even if he were deemed sane. Perhaps
the hypnotism and sodium amytal weren't for eliciting the truth but rather
for "implanting false information into particular subjects . . . or for inducing in them specific mental disorders," as West had written to Gottlieb.

Of course, there are other possibilities. Perhaps Shaver altered his story
on his own accord. Or perhaps he really was insane.

At Shaver's sanity hearing, West testified that at the time of the murder,
Shaver had experienced temporary insanity. Sheriff Owen Kilday dismissed
the diagnosis, saying that he had seen thousands of insane people over his
fourteen years in law enforcement, and Shaver wasn't one of them. During
cross-examination, when Kilday was asked whether he was a doctor, he
scowled, "Better than some I've heard testify."

Despite West's credentials and "flowing, hypnotic voice," as one journalist put it, the jury sided with Kilday. They determined that Shaver had been
sane at the time of the murder and was eligible for the death penalty. The
case could now go to trial.

One of the first witnesses called to testify at the trial was Adela Sanchez, a
waitress at the Lazy A Bar. On the night of the murder, she had seen Shaver
at the bar, apparently sober, not drunk as the defense claimed. In a callous
attempt to tarnish her testimony, Shaver's defense attorney, Sam McCollum,
asked her, "Your profession is a common prostitute, is it not?" Sanchez
calmly denied it.

Next, Charles Theall testified that he had taken a nap in the gravel pit on
the morning of the murder and saw Shaver walking out of the pit with blood
on his clothes. "He had been drinking but he wasn't drunk," Theall said.
"He was talking straight, just telling one lie after another." McCollum demanded that the judge declare a mistrial for these "inflammatory remarks,"
but the judge ignored him.

The drama wasn't confined to the courtroom. The next day, Shaver's wife received an anonymous note under the door of her hotel room that read, "Why don't you leave town before you get hurt. Jimmy's going to burn anyway."

In a last-ditch effort to spare Shaver the death penalty, McCollum claimed that Chere Jo Horton had been alive but unconscious when she was found. The man who discovered her—the owner of the Lazy A Bar—took her pulse and didn't detect anything, but he wasn't a doctor. As such, Horton should have been taken to the hospital, not to the morgue. McCollum then claimed that the embalmer at the morgue had made an incision in Horton's body and saw blood flow out, an indication that her heart was still beating. The embalmer had killed the girl, not Shaver, and therefore Shaver shouldn't be found guilty of murder. Or so went McCollum's baseless theory.

Amid all of these courtroom theatrics, Shaver sat stoic and unmoving. He was "like a man in a trance," observed one journalist. Even during breaks he refused to stand and stretch. Nor did he flinch when the verdict was read: guilty of murder, with a sentence of death.

On June 22, 1955, an appeals court reversed the verdict because one of the jurors had apparently said prior to being selected, "I will burn the bum or hang the jury till doomsday." Shaver was granted a retrial.

Shaver's new defense attorney, Jarrard Secrest, had more scruples than McCollum. He told the jury, "I am convinced [Shaver] did it," and said that the only issue was whether Shaver should get the death penalty or life in prison. The jury deliberated for only one hour. They again found Shaver guilty of murder and sentenced him to death. Afterward, Chere Jo Horton's parents shook the hands of each of the jurors as they walked out of the courtroom.

On the evening of February 4, 1958, Shaver's mother stood beside a death vigil in her home, waiting to receive word that her son had been executed. At that same moment, Shaver stood in cell number 1 of the Texas State Penitentiary in Huntsville, waiting to be led into the execution chamber. He was wearing a cheap blue burial suit. His head had been shaved to allow for a better connection in the electric chair. His death warrant had already been read to him.

But then, quite literally at the eleventh hour, Shaver's cellmate, Donald Summers, made a startling confession. He said that he had been the one to kill Horton, not Shaver. On the night of the murder, he had gotten drunk and abducted her from the parking lot of the Lazy A Bar. From there, he took her to the gravel pit, raped her, smashed her skull, covered her with brush, and walked back to the parking lot where he stole a blue 1941 Plymouth car to make his getaway. While driving along Frio Road, a man (Shaver) who had been sleeping in the back seat rose up. Summers knocked him unconscious, turned in to the gravel pit, and dumped him out beside Horton. Summers then started to drive away, but the car stalled in the gravel, so he abandoned it there, too.

Summers, who was in prison for stabbing a San Antonio deputy sheriff, said that he hadn't confessed earlier because he thought that Shaver's death sentence would be commuted. When that didn't happen, he couldn't bear the guilt of watching an innocent man die for him. Based on his confession, Governor Price Daniel granted Shaver a stay of execution.

Sheriff Owen Kilday was skeptical of the confession. He suspected that Summers was just trying to keep his friend alive for as long as possible. "The best you can do," Kilday told him, "is get Shaver 15 or 20 days' stay. All you're doing is making it rough on that boy."

Indeed, Summers's confession quickly fell apart. Not only did he fail a lie detector test, but several pieces of his story contradicted the evidence. For example, how did the underwear get on the door handle if Summers had stolen Shaver's car after he had killed Horton? Summers didn't have an answer. What's more, an unidentified prisoner reported that he had heard Summers tell Shaver, "I'll see that you don't go to the chair. We'll wait, and if your sentence isn't commuted, I'll take the rap for you." Yet another prisoner reported that Shaver had bribed Summers to lie about the murder.

Shaver's execution was rescheduled for July 25, 1958, his thirty-third birthday. Just before midnight on the twenty-fourth, Chere Jo Horton's father called the prison to make sure that the execution would proceed without delay. He was assured that it would.

At 12:01 A.M., Shaver entered the execution chamber. He smiled as the prison guards strapped him into the electric chair. "May God bless every one of you," he said with a final breath.

Jolly West often treated the airmen at Lackland Air Force Base for their mental disorders. In one of his letters to Sidney Gottlieb, he suggested using the airmen, along with "prisoners in the local stockade," as guinea pigs for MKULTRA experiments.

Jimmy Shaver was known to have suffered from debilitating migraines. During West's interrogation of him, Shaver had said, "I was already sick, Doc. I have headaches. Seven-eight hours at a time, Doc, you know? And they drive you to do anything to get away from them. I've ducked 'em in almost solid ice, and drank, and done everything." At Shaver's trial, his wife testified that he had often complained of headaches.

Did West ever "treat" Shaver for his headaches prior to the murder of Chere Jo Horton? Was Shaver a guinea pig in an MKULTRA experiment? Curiously, all of West's patient records from 1954, the year of the murder, survive except for a single file: last names "Sa" through "St."

West soon left Lackland to join the University of Oklahoma medical school, though he frequently returned to the base to conduct experiments. In a 1956 research proposal submitted to the Geschickter Fund, he wrote that his experiments involving sensory deprivation "have yielded promising leads in terms of suggestibility and the production of trance-like states." Regarding hypnotism, he said, "Current experiments have definitely established a number of ways in which hypnotic suggestions can bring about states of marked psychological stress in suitable subjects." In another report, West claimed to have replaced "true memories" with "false ones" in his psychiatric patients.

Aside from a handful of letters and documents, West left behind little evidence of his association with MKULTRA. But there was one experiment that he couldn't keep hidden. In August 1962, standing before a crowd of onlookers at the Lincoln Park Zoo in Oklahoma City, he dosed a bull elephant named Tusko with 297 milligrams of LSD. West was attempting to artificially induce musth, a state of heightened aggression and strong sexual urges in bull elephants. Instead, Tusko ambled around as if in a drunken stupor. His mate, Judy, tried to support him with her body, but his hindquarters buckled. "Five minutes after the injection," West wrote in a postmortem, Tusko "trumpeted, collapsed, fell heavily onto his right side, defecated, and went into *status epilepticus*. . . . Despite a last-minute effort to save the animal with an intravenous injection of pentobarbital sodium, he died 1 hour and 40 minutes after the LSD had been injected." West concluded dryly, "It appears that the elephant is highly sensitive to LSD."

West's successor at the University of Oklahoma said that when Tusko died, everyone in the department wondered, "How in the world are we going to pay for that?" West told them not to worry. "All Jolly would say to anybody was that he would find a way to pay for it. I learned then, when I became chair, that the source was payment from the CIA."

For the rest of his career, West constantly chased the spotlight by attaching himself to sensational legal cases. In 1976, he examined Patty Hearst, the high-profile kidnapping victim who participated in a crime spree with her kidnappers. West argued that Hearst had been brainwashed into committing the crimes and lobbied for her release from prison.

West also examined Jack Ruby, the nightclub owner who killed Lee Harvey Oswald, President John F. Kennedy's assassin. According to West's notes, Ruby told him that "all the Jews in America were being slaughtered" because he had killed Oswald. West tried to persuade him otherwise.

"Don't tell me you don't know about it," Ruby screamed. "Everybody must know about it!"

West determined that Ruby had experienced a "psychotic break" and was now "positively insane," a diagnosis that could potentially delay Ruby's execution. Judge Joe Brown was skeptical of the diagnosis, saying, "I would like some real disinterested doctors to examine Ruby for my own benefit. I want to get the truth out of it." Brown asked Dr. William Beavers for a second opinion.

After examining Ruby, Beavers reached the same conclusion as West. Ruby had either snapped or, Beavers suggested, it was also possible that he had been drugged, making him appear insane. However, Beavers considered this second possibility highly unlikely because Ruby would have to have been drugged while isolated in jail. Almost nobody had access to him—except Jolly West.

Perhaps West drugged Ruby to spare him the death penalty. Or perhaps Ruby faked his insanity. Or perhaps Ruby really was insane. Regardless, Ruby died soon afterward of a pulmonary embolism.

West would go on to study how cults manipulate their members. He once singled out the Church of Scientology as a "science-fiction psychotherapy cult concocted by one of our century's most extravagant liars," L. Ron Hubbard, who was "a cross between Baron Munchausen and Rev. Jim Jones." West criticized Scientology's "deceptive, manipulative, exploititive [sic], dangerous, and even brutal practices, which have diminished the freedom and individuality of untold thousands of people."

In response, the Church of Scientology sued West for using taxpayer money to fund "anti-religious activities," including organizing the Cult Awareness Network. Linda Hight, the media coordinator for the Church of Scientology, also accused West of participating in mind control experiments funded by the CIA. She erroneously claimed that he had advocated for "chemical castration and implanting electrodes in people's brains." She was at least correct in saying that he held "the dubious distinction of being the first psychiatrist to kill an elephant with LSD."

West denied all of Hight's accusations. For the rest of his life, he maintained that he had "never taken part in 'mind-control' experiments funded by the CIA or anybody else." His son would later remark, "He often said and did contradictory things."

In 1998, at the age of seventy-four, West developed an aggressive cancer that metastasized throughout his entire body. He had always opposed the death penalty because it removed from a person their agency over their own life. Now that he was about to die from cancer, he decided to exercise that agency. On the night of January 2, 1999, he downed a bottle of pills and never woke up.

13

Prison Experiments

James "Whitey" Bulger waved two pistols in the air. "I'll shoot the first one who moves!" he yelled inside the Hoosier State Bank. On his instructions, the nervous tellers emptied their tills and handed him $12,612, then he sprinted out the door.

The cops were quick on his trail. On March 4, 1956, as Bulger left a nightclub north of Boston, ten FBI agents surrounded him. "The arrest was effected smoothly and without incident," notes an FBI report. "Bulger was not armed at the time but indicated in his comments to the agents that, if he had not been completely surrounded, he would have made a daring attempt to flee." Three months later, he was sentenced to twenty years in prison.

Only twenty-six years old, Bulger was at the cusp of his life of crime. In time, he would become one of Boston's most notorious gangsters, someone who "could teach the devil tricks," according to a fellow mob boss. His résumé would eventually include spending time in Alcatraz, participating in at least eleven murders, and making the FBI's Ten Most Wanted Fugitives list. But before any of that, he had to serve—and survive—his incarceration at the Atlanta Federal Penitentiary.

Inside the cold stone walls of the formidable prison, Bulger faced one of the most frightening episodes of his life. "Total loss of appetite," he remembered. "Hallucinating. The room would change shape. Hours of paranoia and feeling violent. . . . Horrible periods of living nightmares and even blood coming out of the walls. Guys turning to skeletons in front of me. I saw a camera change into the head of a dog. I felt like I was going insane." He could sleep for only a few hours before inevitably waking up in a cold sweat. For decades afterward, he refused to talk about his experience, fearing that if he did he would be sent to a mental institution. "I was in prison for committing a crime, and feel they committed a worse crime on me."

In the basement of the prison hospital, pharmacologist Carl Pfeiffer was dosing the prisoners with LSD. Bulger likened Pfeiffer to "a modern-day Dr. Mengele," the Nazi doctor who performed sadistic experiments on prisoners at the Auschwitz concentration camp. So scarred was Bulger that he pledged to kill anyone selling LSD in his Boston neighborhood. He also swore to his friends that he would murder Pfeiffer if he ever got the chance.

Pfeiffer's drug experiments appear to have caused two prisoners in Atlanta to go insane. Bulger watched them being "pried loose from under their beds, growling, barking and frothing at the mouth." The guards "put them in a strip cell down the hall. I never saw or heard them again." Declassified CIA documents confirm that at least two prisoners were transferred out of the program because of mental problems.

Boston attorney Anthony Cardinale said that if he had been the defense attorney at Bulger's 2013 trial for racketeering and firearms possession (resulting in two consecutive life sentences), he would have prepared a simple defense: "Nearly two years of LSD testing fried his brain. . . . I'd have had Bulger sit there doodling and drooling." Cardinale then launched into a mock speech to the jury, beginning, "He's a victim, ladies and gentlemen, and they—the government—are the reason he did all this. . . . They put all this in his head. They damaged and manipulated him to the point they turned him into a psychotic killer."

Sidney Gottlieb first became interested in Carl Pfeiffer upon reading his academic articles, which characterize depression, schizophrenia, and other psychological disorders as biochemical imbalances in the brain that can be cured with LSD. Gottlieb became even more interested upon learning that, in 1955, Pfeiffer had gotten a job at Emory University, just down the road from the Atlanta Federal Penitentiary. Eager for access to a large pool of potential test subjects, Gottlieb recruited Pfeiffer to conduct MKULTRA drug experiments on the prisoners in Atlanta.

When Gottlieb was asked during his depositions whether he had taken any steps to ensure that Pfeiffer treated the prisoners in an ethical way, he said, "I don't think we were doing that at all. We were leaving that to him. Our reasoning was if we got . . . a reputable investigator, we would trust him to institute whatever safeguards he felt were appropriate."

Pfeiffer was indeed reputable, having authored over three hundred articles and half a dozen books. His former student Eric Braverman later wrote in an obituary of him, "Carl Pfeiffer probably healed more schizophrenics than any other doctor since Jesus Christ." Sticking to the religious theme, Braverman went on to say that Pfeiffer had "clothed the emotionally naked and visited the biochemically imprisoned."

Between 1955 and 1962, the CIA gave Pfeiffer a total of $358,323.96. To his credit, he required all of the test subjects to sign a consent form, the very first sentence of which read, "I, [blank], the undersigned applicant, hereby apply for permission to participate in an investigation designed to study the hallucinatory effect of lysergic acid diethylamide, LSD-25, and similar compounds which is being conducted by Emory University School of Medicine in cooperation with the Bureau of Prisons of the Department of Justice." The test subjects were volunteers—to an extent. Although they weren't required to participate in the experiments, they were highly incentivized to do so. In exchange for volunteering, they received three dollars per test and a flattering letter for the parole board.

Marvin Williams, an uneducated black man serving time for drug possession, began crying when remembering his experience in Atlanta. He had signed Pfeiffer's consent form, but he hadn't fully understood what he was getting himself into. "I just wanted a little extra money for personal things, like soap and cigarettes," he said. "If I'd known, I would have never in a million years jumped on board." Williams was given drugs for weeks on end. "The roof and the sky exploded. Crazy things happened. I mean really crazy, like not real, but happening. It was like I was in a jungle someplace with wild animals all around me; all these crazy beasts trying to kill me and—" He stopped, tears streaming down his face. "Never again, man, never again."

The Atlanta Federal Penitentiary wasn't the only prison to host an MKULTRA subproject. The CIA also funded drug experiments at the Addiction Research Center in Lexington, Kentucky. Founded in 1935, the Addiction Research Center occupied a wing of the U.S. Public Health Service Hospital, a federal drug rehabilitation facility for prisoners and other addicts who voluntarily committed themselves for treatment. Nicknamed the Narcotic Farm, the facility consisted of a colossal Art Deco–style brick building surrounded by pastures of grazing cows.

Pharmacologist Harris Isbell conducted the drug experiments in Lexington. Like Pfeiffer, he administered LSD to his test subjects, but he also administered over eight hundred other compounds that Gottlieb sent to him, including opiates, barbiturates, amphetamines, and tranquilizers. One of the test subjects described an "extremely potent" substance in the cannabinol family as some of the best marijuana that he had ever tried. Side effects included mental relaxation and "increased appreciation of music, jokes, and other things," Isbell wrote in his notes.

Junkies in the Lexington area soon learned that whenever their supplies got low, they could commit themselves to the Narcotic Farm and volunteer for Isbell's experiments in the Addiction Research Center. This arrangement suited both parties. The junkies got their fix while Isbell got a steady supply of drug-wise guinea pigs. Not surprisingly, the Addiction Research Center became a veritable revolving door with a 90 percent return rate among test subjects. One CIA officer speaking on condition of anonymity said, "I never saw a happier bunch of people in my life." Patient Bernie Kolb agreed. "The guys on research just had a great life," he said. "They'd sit around, play cards, nod in the corner. I mean, hey, would you rather wait around for some kind of dope to be shot into you or work on the farm?"

Isbell's drug experiments were more intense than any others conducted under the MKULTRA umbrella. His main objective was to determine whether the human body could develop a tolerance to LSD. To find out, he gave seven test subjects daily administrations of LSD for up to seventy-seven days straight. The results were "the most amazing demonstrations of drug tolerance I have ever seen," he wrote. Both the mental and physical effects of the drug grew milder over time.

Isbell tried to break through the tolerance by administering double, triple, and even quadruple doses. On one occasion, he gave a test subject 532 micrograms of LSD, over seven times the amount that Frank Olson had received at Deep Creek. Whenever any of the test subjects complained about a bad reaction, Isbell ignored them because, he said, "[complaining] is to be expected with patients of this type," namely black men.

Eddie Flowers, a nineteen-year-old heroin addict from Harlem, lied about his age to join Isbell's experiments (the minimum age was twenty-one). He was eager for a high and had heard that the Addiction Research Center served better food than the rest of the Narcotic Farm anyway. As part of the program, he ate a graham cracker spiked with an unnamed drug that made him hallucinate for sixteen hours. "It was the worst shit I ever had," he said. "I was frightened. I wouldn't take it again." Others said that the graham crackers made them see elephants on the walls, bones in their hands, and even their own brains.

Flowers was at least happy to have earned his reward for participating. He walked down the hall, knocked on the drug bank window, and stuck out his arm. The attendant prepared a needle full of heroin. "If you wanted it in the vein, you got it there."

The test subjects could opt to receive a reduced prison sentence instead, but most of them chose the heroin. Isbell later defended the system, saying, "That was the custom in those days [when] the ethical codes were not so highly developed. . . . I personally think we did a very excellent job."

Although Gottlieb claimed that Isbell had always conducted his drug experiments on volunteers, one prisoner begged to differ. Before his incarceration at the Narcotic Farm, Henry Wall was a respected physician in Blakely, Georgia. Ironically, the stress of the job caused him to neglect his own health. Seeking comfort in food, his weight ballooned to over three hundred pounds. Soon he developed sores all over his body—a symptom of type 2 diabetes—and lost all but three of his teeth. To help control the pain, he started taking the narcotic Demerol.

Further contributing to his woes was the fact that Wall couldn't afford to pay his taxes because he insisted on treating his needy patients free of charge. And so the downward spiral continued. He ate even more food, developed even more sores, and took even more Demerol. One day in 1952, he overdosed on the drug. His teenage son found him passed out on the toilet, mouth agape, slumped against the wall.

Following the overdose, Wall became even more dependent on Demerol, to the point where he began writing fake prescriptions to fuel his addiction. When one of his employees notified the police, Wall was arrested and sent to the Narcotic Farm for rehabilitation.

While there, Wall became aware of Isbell's drug experiments, but he refused to participate in them. "I don't know what [the prisoners] are being given," he told his family, "but the ones that volunteer get rewarded in some way. It's really upsetting because [they] walk around like zombies or behave very strangely. Isbell's the doctor running it, and I don't mind telling you he rubs me the wrong way. I'll never know how any physician sworn to the Hippocratic Oath can treat his patients like that."

Less than a month later, Wall called home panicked. "Son," he said in a rushed whisper, "you all have to get me out of here right now! They've been giving me something, I don't know what it is, but it's made me crazier than a coot!"

"Hold on, Daddy. Did you sign up for those drug tests?"

"No . . . but they gave me something anyhow, in my food or drinks, some way or other. . . . I'd rather be in the federal pen in Atlanta than in this hellhole!"

Overcome with paranoia, Wall stopped eating and drinking anything but canned soup and water. When he returned home at the end of his sentence, he was a completely different person. Once a caring husband and father, he now exhibited violent outbursts and suicidal tendencies. During the worst such outburst, he stormed into his son's room at two in the morning and shook him awake.

"You goddamn little motherfucker," he yelled, "I'll show you! I'll give you what you deserve! Goddamn you, you little bastard! You motherfucking son of a bitch!"

His son was in shock, never having heard his father curse before. "Wait, Daddy! Wait! Hold on! What's this about?"

"Don't think you can't fool me! I know the filthy things you and your mother got up to while I was gone!"

Wall apparently thought that his own son had been having sex with his wife behind his back. Afterward, when he came to his senses, he blamed the outburst on Isbell's drug experiments, as did his son:

> To put it plainly, what Harris Isbell did to my father was to assault him with a poison that permanently damaged his brain. . . . Can you imagine yourself a respectable, middle-aged, recently prominent, heretofore sane, professional man, being told god knows what as the walls undulate around you, the drab hospital room glows with psychedelic light, the air hums with unearthly vibrations, and the faces of those around you constantly shift from human to animal to gargoyles and back to human again? It's scarcely imaginable, but that was what happened to Daddy.

14

Subprojects

In total, MKULTRA consisted of 149 subprojects, including those run by George White, Charles Geschickter, Ewen Cameron, Maitland Baldwin, Jolly West, Carl Pfeiffer, and Harris Isbell. The rest of the subprojects involved a broad range of unusual activities: performing concussion studies on human cadavers, testing chemicals for their "sobering up" abilities, analyzing the relationship between body type and temperament, studying Yoruba witchcraft to better understand non-Western approaches to psychiatry, investigating whether certain people have extrasensory perception, and administering truth drugs to criminal sexual psychopaths. Although many of the official files for the subprojects were destroyed, there still exists enough information from other sources—memos, letters, receipts, interviews, depositions—to reconstruct much of what happened.

One of the strangest MKULTRA subprojects involved polygraphs, or lie detectors. The CIA had been conducting polygraph tests since 1948, mostly on prospective employees to determine whether they had lied on their applications. (Over half of them had, usually about their past employment or ideological affiliation.) Polygraphs, which measure changes in blood pressure, chest expansion, and skin conductivity, are prone to errors and rely on the skill of the interrogator as much as the efficacy of the technology. Subproject 86 sought to build miniature polygraphs that were much more reliable.

What makes this subproject strange isn't the polygraphs but the way in which they were to be used. The CIA was worried that once it sent an agent abroad, it might not receive the same agent back. What if the Soviets replaced him with an identical imposter? The miniature polygraphs were meant for interrogating returning agents and confirming their identities. The CIA also contemplated creating a database of agent fingerprints, blood types, and bodily dimensions to compare against returning agents. One CIA-affiliated doctor even proposed embedding agents with distinctive radioactive markers for verification purposes.

Even stranger was Subproject 94. Inspired by the work of Swedish psychologist Valdemar Fellenius, who had trained seals to attach explosives to submarines during World War II, the anonymous researcher running this subproject implanted electrodes into the brains of rats, cats, dogs, monkeys, donkeys, and literal guinea pigs in an attempt to remotely control their movements. By stimulating the pleasure center of the brain, he hoped to steer the animals via positive feedback. Interestingly, it worked. A summary report confirms that "remote control of activities including speed and direction of movement has been demonstrated by limited laboratory and field trials." During one field trial, the researcher got a dog to walk along an invisible path with "relative ease." In fact, his biggest challenge had been finding an isolated field away from public view where he could conduct the experiment in secret.

Rats were just as easy to control. The researcher wrote, "If a change in direction was desired, or if the rat veered off course, stimulation was terminated. The rat remained stationary in the absence of stimulation and 'sought' the new direction by means of . . . head movement. In a short period of time, good control over the rat's free-field behavior was established." The researcher had to be careful not to "overdo the pleasure reaction" because it would cause immobilization. As for stimulating the "punishment" center of the brain to steer the animals via negative feedback, "in all cases [it] caused panic reaction and was not useful."

According to a series of heavily redacted documents whose remaining text is littered with euphemisms, the CIA planned to attach "payloads of interest" to these "guidance systems" for use in "direct executive action type operations." What were the "payloads of interest"? Deadly chemical and biological materials. What was "direct executive action"? Assassination. In other words, the CIA planned to create a fleet of remote-controlled animal assassins. And what animals did the CIA most want to serve in this role? Apparently yaks and bears, which "are capable of carrying heavy payloads over great distances under adverse climatic conditions." The ultimate goal, however, was "the application of selected elements of these techniques to man." Nothing else is known about the subproject.

All combined, the MKULTRA subprojects tested an exhaustive number of drugs, including LSD, cocaine, peyote, marijuana, and "reject drugs" that pharmaceutical companies had discarded because of untoward costs or side effects. Highly addictive substances like heroin were of particular interest. If the CIA could induce an addiction in a captured enemy agent, then it could use the withdrawal symptoms as leverage in an interrogation.

Sidney Gottlieb sent researchers around the world to gather new drugs, or as one memo put it, to "enrich our knowledge in hidden treasures." Subproject 70 involved catching ticks and milking their salivary glands for a "neurotropic toxic substance" that could serve as an effective knockout drug. Another subproject involved collecting thousands of Caribbean botanical specimens that possessed toxic, narcotic, sedative, poisonous, disinfectant, intoxicating, psychogenic, and stupefacient properties. At one point, a scientist in the CIA requested that the researchers stop sending back samples because he was "swamped" with deliveries.

One of the more interesting specimens that Gottlieb hoped to acquire was a crocodile gall bladder from Lake Tanganyika in Central Africa. The medicinal qualities of crocodile gall bladders have long been touted. In the thirteenth century, Venetian explorer Marco Polo noted how hunters in Asia risked their lives to obtain the organ: "They draw the gall from the belly and sell it very dear. It is much prized because great medicine is made of it, for if a man is bitten by a mad dog, and one gives him a little . . . he is healed immediately. And again, when a lady cannot give birth and has pain and cries aloud, then they give her a little of that serpent's gall in drink, and then the lady gives birth immediately." Gottlieb, who had a deep fascination for all things esoteric, wanted to test Polo's claims.

To acquire the specimen, he could either hire someone to kill a crocodile, remove the gall bladder, and ship it to him directly, or he could pay a licensed collector to buy a live crocodile—the going rate was $200—and ship the entire animal to an unnamed zoo, where he could dissect it himself. The anonymous author of a memo weighing these two options favored the latter approach because it was less susceptible to "poor refrigeration conditions," but the surviving record doesn't reveal what happened.

Gottlieb once sent a scientist to Mexico in search of the plant piule, described in a letter to Morse Allen as "a sort of truth serum." While the scientist was there, the locals told him about a rare mushroom called "God's flesh" that grew in the remote canyons south of Mexico City during the wet summer months. The Aztecs had apparently used it in their religious ceremonies to produce hallucinations and, intriguingly, confessions.

Upon hearing this tantalizing piece of information, Gottlieb hired a young chemist at the University of Delaware named James Moore to find the so-called "magic" mushroom. Unbeknownst to Gottlieb, amateur mycologist Gordon Wasson, the vice president of J. P. Morgan, had already found it. On a 1955 trip to Oaxaca, he spotted a large colony of the mushrooms sprouting in a ravine, grabbed a few handfuls, and brought them to Maria Sabina, a local spiritual leader known as the "Wise One." Inside her thatched-roof adobe home, she guided Wasson through a traditional ceremony involving the consumption of the mushrooms, marking the first time that an outsider had eaten them. Wasson later said that they tasted bad and had a "rancid odor," but they indeed produced hallucinations, in his case "gardens of ineffable beauty."

James Moore soon learned of Wasson's trip and asked to accompany him on the next one. As an incentive to say yes, Moore mentioned that he knew of a foundation—the Geschickter Fund—that was willing to pay their way.

In 1956, Moore, Wasson, and a support crew left for Mexico. Moore quickly developed diarrhea and lost fifteen pounds. He recalled, "I had a terribly bad cold, we damned near starved to death, and I itched all over." To the annoyance of everyone else, he complained the whole time. Wasson likened him to "a landlubber at sea."

The group visited Maria Sabina and underwent the mushroom ceremony. Wasson described his experience as "ecstasy." Moore, on the other hand, said, "There was all this chanting in the dialect. Then they passed the mushrooms around, and we chewed them up. I did feel the hallucinogenic effect, although 'disoriented' would be a better word to describe my reaction."

Gottlieb wanted to keep the existence of the "magic" mushroom a secret, but that hope quickly vanished when Wasson published a seventeen-page spread of his Mexican adventures in *Life* magazine. Afterward, Albert Hofmann, the chemist who had first synthesized LSD, isolated the mushroom's active ingredient, psilocybin.

Even though the secret was out, Gottlieb nevertheless sent samples of psilocybin to Harris Isbell so that he could test it on nine "negro males" at the Addiction Research Center in Lexington. Isbell mixed the substance with raspberry syrup to offset the bitter taste. "After thirty minutes," he wrote in a summary report, "anxiety became quite definite and was expressed as consisting of fear that something evil was going to happen, fear of insanity, or of death." A few of the test subjects burst into "almost continuous gales of laughter."

Psilocybin wasn't the only substance that Gottlieb got from mushrooms. In later testimony before the Senate, Charles Geschickter said that the CIA had spent "$107,667 buying mushrooms from Africa. And these things were then shipped down—"

Senator Richard Schweiker interrupted, "We grow mushrooms in Pennsylvania. Why did we have to bring them in from Africa?"

"These are poison mushrooms," Geschickter said.

"What did they do with the poison mushrooms once they had them?"

"They sent [them] down to—I will not name the university—to analyze them for toxic substances, but they apparently would poison somebody. I do not know what they did with them. I have not gotten the follow up on that one."

By any reasonable assessment, many of the MKULTRA subprojects were unethical. That's not to say that everyone associated with them was unethical. Most of the people involved had good intentions. In their minds, they were advancing the state of medicine or helping the United States win the Cold War. Few did it simply for fun, George White being the main exception. Still, even good intentions can lead to bad consequences.

In 1957, Lyman Kirkpatrick, the polio-stricken inspector general who had conducted the investigation into the death of Frank Olson, conducted another investigation into MKULTRA. In his final report, after briefly describing the cutout mechanism and a few of the more scandalous subprojects, he concluded, "Some of the activities are considered to be professionally unethical and in some instances border on the illegal." Yet even he recommended that they continue. "Much more testing must be conducted before the behavior program can be considered to have accomplished its objective."

Gottlieb acknowledged in his depositions that the reports of the inspector general were often "attended to by a lot of headaches."

"Well," said attorney Thomas Maddox, "with regard to the MKULTRA project in 1957, isn't it true that the Inspector General brought to your [attention] that what was going on in part was unethical and illegal?"

"I wouldn't put it that—" Gottlieb stuttered, "in those words. But I remember something like that happening. I would have to reread it."

Maddox asked, "Did you disagree with the conclusion that there was some unethical and illegal things going on, or just felt that national security overrode—"

Gottlieb jumped in, "I think something like the latter part of your statement is what we believed."

National security overrode ethical and legal qualms.

15

Assassination

Between 1953 and 1957, Sidney Gottlieb led the Chemical Branch of the CIA's Technical Services Staff. He had held this position during the Frank Olson incident, during the height of Operation Midnight Climax, and for the duration of many other MKULTRA subprojects. In the fall of 1957, he switched jobs within the CIA and moved overseas for two years. He was "engaged in operational work," he said in his depositions, but he refused to disclose anything else about his time abroad. "I think that was a classified matter. I'm not sure what I'm allowed to say about it. It had to do with an operational job."

Attorney Joseph Rauh asked him point blank, "What were your duties?"

"I am not at liberty to say that."

"Who was your superior?"

"I am not at liberty to say that either."

"What was your chain of command?"

CIA attorney Lee Strickland interjected to say that the information was off-limits.

Fortunately, some of the answers can be gleaned from the historical record.

In early 1957, veteran CIA agent William Hood became concerned that Gottlieb was too insulated from "the boonies" where actual CIA operations occurred. Hood propositioned Gottlieb, "If I get a job overseas, why don't you come along and look at it from the inside out?" Gottlieb, always willing to try something new, accepted the offer. That September, he and his family followed Hood to a base in Munich, Germany. The only project that Gottlieb is known to have worked on in Munich involved a man who had defected from East Germany and claimed to be a chemist. The CIA wanted to know whether the man was a genuine defector telling the truth or an enemy plant lying to gain favor. Gottlieb interrogated him, asking questions that only a chemist would know the answers to, and determined that he was indeed a chemist and genuine defector.

Gottlieb took two major trips while stationed abroad. First, he took his wife to Paris for a romantic holiday. Second, he returned to CIA headquarters for reasons unknown. While there, he gave a speech to an incoming class of recruits, one of whom remembered thinking that Gottlieb was "a strange person, someone who was beyond the pale, doing all sorts of strange things." The recruit further described Gottlieb as "low key, a little grey man. An hour after his appearance before you, you'd have trouble recognizing him in a crowd. He was the sort of esoteric scientist so far removed from the practicalities of real life that you had trouble taking him seriously. But you couldn't dismiss him entirely."

Despite his years of service, Gottlieb was still considered an outsider in the CIA. He had been, and would be, an outsider his whole life.

One other notable event happened while Gottlieb was living in Munich. Within weeks of his arrival, Lev Rebet, a prominent Ukrainian anti-Communist, suddenly died. Doctors concluded that Rebet had suffered a heart attack, but the real story wouldn't emerge until four years later when Soviet agent Bogdan Stashinsky defected to West Germany and confessed to murdering Rebet on orders from the Kremlin. (He had used a special spray gun that shot out a jet of cyanide.) Stashinsky's confession proved that the Soviets were still in the business of assassinations. With Gottlieb's help, the Americans wouldn't be far behind.

In 1959, Gottlieb moved back to the United States and became the science advisor to Richard Bissell, head of the CIA's Directorate of Plans (formerly the Office of Policy Coordination).

Attorney Joseph Rauh asked Gottlieb during his depositions, "Is this the period in which you were giving advice on assassinations?"

Before Gottlieb could answer, CIA attorney Lee Strickland began whispering in his ear.

Rauh grew frustrated and announced, "I think the record should show that Mr. Strickland has been whispering for 30 seconds to the witness and that is absolutely uncalled for."

Strickland protested, "I don't have the right to consult?"

"If he wants to ask for the right to consult, you can consult. He didn't make the slightest move toward you. You just whispered him an answer. That was direct coaching and absolutely wrong."

Gottlieb asked Rauh to repeat the question.

Rauh started, "If Mr. Strickland had not intervened—"

Strickland intervened, "I will intervene anyplace I want."

"That is the way the CIA acts," Rauh quipped.

Tensions were on the rise inside the small meeting room of the Boxwood House Motel. The two attorneys loathed each other, and the fireworks would only get more spectacular throughout the day.

Gottlieb finally addressed Rauh's question about assassinations. He said that within two or three years of returning from Munich, "Mr. Bissell would ask me what the possibilities in this area might be."

"Will you list the ones he asked you about and what your advice was?"

"I need to consult with my attorney."

Strickland again began whispering to Gottlieb. A minute later, he explained that Gottlieb couldn't answer the question because it would require him to divulge classified information.

Rauh was livid. "I am going to ask the question, go ahead and object. This idea that [the] CIA should represent an individual is an obvious conflict of interest. You are trying to think of what is best for your case and not what is best for Dr. Gottlieb to tell the truth and get clean at last. You got a direct conflict of interest at this table." Rauh then started his next question, "Will you state the names of—"

"Mr. Rauh," Strickland exclaimed, "if you do not apologize for that outburst to Dr. Gottlieb, I will terminate this right now."

Rauh may have been a septuagenarian hobbled by an arthritic hip, but he wasn't about to back down. He had finished first in his class at Harvard Law, served on General Douglas MacArthur's staff during World War II, fought against McCarthyism during the Red Scare, and marched on Washington beside Martin Luther King, Jr. His rugged, wrinkled face was a testament to a lifetime of challenging authority. "You may terminate right here," he said. "What I said I will repeat. You have a conflict of interest, Mr. Strickland.

You are thinking of the Agency. . . . Dr. Gottlieb's interest will be in telling the whole story and getting it over with and get his [conscience] clear. You are interested in winning this case. They are totally different things."

For the rest of the deposition, Strickland kept disrupting the questions. From Rauh's perspective, Strickland was purposefully wasting time. The CIA could certainly afford to drag out the case; not so much Rauh's law firm.

"You recognize that you may be able to break me before the end of this," Rauh told Strickland. "I am not sure whether you will be able to or not. I will certainly go to mortgaging my house before I let the CIA break me."

The two attorneys continued bickering, but they eventually moved forward.

"Dr. Gottlieb," Rauh said, "you were authorized by Mr. Strickland to give a general description of the work in the assassinations field without bringing in the names of the people to be assassinated or considered to be assassinated. Will you do so?"

Gottlieb reluctantly responded, "Mr. Bissell on some very infrequent occasions, and I don't remember the number of them, would ask my advice as to whether it was feasible to, I don't think the word 'assassination' was used, but to kill somebody in various technical ways."

"Did you ever give him advice that it was feasible to kill somebody?"

"Did I ever give advice that it was feasible? I think my advice would be couched in terms of it was possible to do this if he wanted to."

"Now, you personally took vial poisons to the Congo for the purpose of assassinating Patrice Lumumba; isn't that correct?"

In June 1960, Patrice Lumumba became the first democratically elected prime minister of the Republic of the Congo. Given that the Congo had recently rid itself of Belgian colonialism, it represented an important barometer for African sentiment in the Cold War. Would it choose to align with the United States or the Soviet Union?

When two Congolese provinces attempted to secede from the country, Lumumba turned to the Soviet Union for help. As far as the United States was concerned, he had chosen his side. Director of Central Intelligence Allen Dulles called Lumumba another Fidel Castro, "or worse." The United States naturally supported the Congolese factions that opposed Lumumba and, by proxy, the Soviet Union.

At a subsequent meeting of the National Security Council, President

Dwight Eisenhower told Dulles to "eliminate" Lumumba. The meeting's notetaker later said that after Eisenhower gave the order, "there was stunned silence for about 15 seconds and the meeting continued."

The next week, CIA representative Thomas Parrott asked Gordon Gray, Eisenhower's special assistant for national security, what to do about Lumumba. Gray informed Parrott that his "associates," a euphemism for Eisenhower that preserved the president's plausible deniability, "had expressed extremely strong feelings on the necessity for very straightforward action." Richard Bissell later clarified what Gray meant: "You don't use language of that kind except to mean, in effect, the Director [of Central Intelligence] is being told, get rid of the guy, and if you have to use extreme means up to and including assassination, go ahead."

In September 1960, Lumumba was ousted as prime minister of the Congo, but the Eisenhower administration still considered him dangerous. That same week, Eisenhower expressed to a British foreign secretary his wish that Lumumba would "fall into a river full of crocodiles." Meanwhile, the order to assassinate Lumumba had made its way from Eisenhower to Dulles to Bissell and finally to the CIA's foremost practitioner of the dark arts, Sidney Gottlieb.

During Gottlieb's depositions, attorney Joseph Rauh pulled out a report by the Church Committee, a Senate committee created in 1975 to investigate past abuses of the intelligence community, and asked whether Gottlieb was the man referred to as "Joseph Scheider." In testimony before the Church Committee, "Scheider" had admitted to delivering deadly biological materials to the Congo for the purpose of assassinating Lumumba.

Lee Strickland, Rauh's nemesis, was anxious. This was an extremely sensitive topic. He didn't want Gottlieb to say anything that could damage the CIA. Rather than let Gottlieb answer the question, he asked to confer with him alone outside.

There was a brief recess. When everyone returned to the room, Gottlieb sat down and said that he was ready to go back on the record.

Rauh began, "My question, Dr. Gottlieb, are you the Scheider referred to?"
"Yes."

As soon as the word escaped his mouth, Strickland yelled, "Objection."
Rauh looked at Gottlieb in disbelief. "What did you say?"
"Objection," Strickland repeated.

Gottlieb quickly corrected himself, "I am not at liberty to answer that question."

Rauh was still in shock. "I thought I heard you say 'yes'?"

"I never said yes," Gottlieb insisted, despite the record showing otherwise.

Strickland was on edge. What would Gottlieb say next? He eventually resorted to pinching Gottlieb whenever he didn't want him to answer a question. Rauh was in the middle of asking one when he saw it happen.

"I think we should have that on the record, that every time Mr. Strickland hears some question that he doesn't want Dr. Gottlieb to answer, he pinches him on the side. I think that ought to stop. If you got something to say, say it, quit tipping the witness with pressuring him on the side."

Strickland bickered, "First of all, there was no question on the floor that I know of. Secondly, I only touched Dr. Gottlieb's leg in order for him not to become riled at your entirely inappropriate conduct. I will let you have your say and you can go on. I was just having Dr. Gottlieb remain calm in light of your questioning which is not very gentlemanly."

Rauh shot back, "You use that technique over and over again of touching Dr. Gottlieb when you want him to turn and talk to you."

"I will continue to if that is what I think is necessary."

Rauh turned to face Gottlieb, "Will you please answer the question I asked?"

Strickland interjected, "Is there one on the floor?"

"There has been one on the floor for quite a length of time."

"Only because your questioning was so inept."

At 12:54, the group took a much-needed lunch break to calm down. Gottlieb used the time to look through the Church Committee report and jog his memory. Strickland contacted the appropriate officials at the CIA to see whether Gottlieb had permission to discuss his role in assassination attempts. The group reconvened at 2:15 in the same room of the Boxwood House Motel.

"What is the response, Mr. Strickland?" Rauh asked.

Through gritted teeth, Strickland said, "They have authorized Dr. Gottlieb to testify about those matters."

Finally Rauh felt a surge of hope. Without wasting a moment, he asked Gottlieb, "Are you the Joseph Scheider referred to in the report?"

"Yes."

This time there was no objection. Rauh's foot was in the door.

"Will you tell us all you know about the . . . CIA's action in connection with Patrice Lumumba?"

"Well, I will try," Gottlieb said. "I was asked by Mr. Bissell to consider what might be positioned in a forward overseas sense should the decision be made to assassinate Patrice Lumumba. And what we finally ended up with was a material called anthrax. And it was not clear in what way, if this was ever used, it would be administered, but several possibilities were talked about."

"Did you work on the possibilities?"

"I don't know what you mean by 'work' on them."

"Were you in on the consideration and discussion of the possibilities?"

"Yes. One of them was to put some of it on a toothbrush that he used and another was to use some kind of material that he might scratch himself with. And when that was discussed, I was then asked to actually carry some materials with me and get them placed in Léopoldville . . . And I proceeded to do that."

"You took the anthrax to Léopoldville?"

"Yes."

"You gave it to a CIA agent there?"

"Yes."

When asked what anthrax does to a person, Gottlieb said, "It produces a debilitating to lethal disease in humans. It is usually a disease that is picked up from domestic animals and [is] endemic in the Congo," making it the perfect way to kill Lumumba. Nobody would suspect a thing.

"Where did you obtain it, in the Congo or here in the United States?"

"We had an arrangement with another government agency to procure materials like that for us."

"Was this kept at Ft. Detrick?"

Gottlieb briefly conferred with Strickland, then answered, "Yes."

"And it was held by Special Operations?"

"Yes."

Fort Detrick was the successor to Camp Detrick, the biological weapons facility where Frank Olson had worked. Gottlieb was still collaborating with the scientists in its Special Operations Division and had gotten the anthrax from them.

Gottlieb placed a syringe, a surgical mask, a pair of rubber gloves, and a vial of anthrax inside a diplomatic pouch and caught a flight to Léopoldville, the Congolese capital. The plan was to inject the anthrax into a tube of toothpaste, which would quietly make its way into Lumumba's bathroom. Apparently nobody at the CIA knew that Lumumba rarely brushed his teeth because he feared being poisoned. The running joke among his friends was the he preferred bad breath to no breath at all.

Under the alias "Sid from Paris," Gottlieb arranged to meet Lawrence Devlin, the CIA station chief in Léopoldville, inside a private room of a high-rise apartment building. Once the door behind them was locked, Gottlieb handed over the pouch and told Devlin what it was for.

"Jesus H. Christ!" Devlin exclaimed. "Isn't this unusual?" He asked Gottlieb who had authorized the assassination.

"President Eisenhower," Gottlieb said. "I wasn't there when he approved it, but Dick Bissell said that Eisenhower wanted Lumumba removed."

Devlin nervously lit a cigarette and looked down at the floor. He had moral reservations about the operation, but he feared the consequences should he refuse to participate.

Gottlieb implored him, "It's your responsibility to carry out the operation, you alone. The details are up to you, but it's got to be clean—nothing can be traced backed to the U.S. government."

Devlin was stuck between a rock and a hard place, unsure of whether to stay loyal to his conscience or his country. In the short term, his country appears to have won out. He soon wrote to CIA headquarters requesting a "high powered foreign made rifle with telescopic scope and silencer. Hunting good here when lights are right." The new plan was to shoot Lumumba, or so it seemed. Devlin later said that he had requested the rifle to placate his superiors while he stalled. He figured that if he could delay the assassination long enough, then a rival political faction would likely kill Lumumba before the CIA did.

Sensing Devlin's reluctance to strike, Richard Bissell asked seasoned CIA officer Justin O'Donnell to assassinate Lumumba. O'Donnell refused on both religious and legal grounds, warning Bissell that the conspiracy to commit murder was against federal law. Bissell, unfazed, told him to at least talk to Gottlieb before making a decision.

O'Donnell indeed talked to Gottlieb, who mentioned that "there were four or five lethal means of disposing of Lumumba." Afterward, O'Donnell marched back to Bissell's office and made it clear that he would have nothing to do with the "murder attempt."

O'Donnell nevertheless agreed to lure Lumumba out of his home so that the Congolese authorities could arrest him. Doing so would undoubtedly lead to Lumumba's death, but O'Donnell didn't object because "it would have been a Congolese being judged by Congolese for Congolese crimes." When he arrived in Léopoldville, Lawrence Devlin informed him that there was "a virus in the safe." O'Donnell didn't know that the "virus" was the anthrax bacteria that Gottlieb had delivered, but, he later joked, "I knew it wasn't for somebody to get his polio shot up to date." Steadfast in his opposition to assassinating Lumumba, he told Devlin that he wouldn't need the anthrax. A relieved Devlin subsequently threw it into the Congo River.

O'Donnell failed to lure Lumumba out of his home, but others got to him anyway. In late 1960, Congolese soldiers captured Lumumba and sent him to a prison in the city of Elisabethville. The CIA station chief in Elisabethville cabled back to headquarters, "If we had known he was coming we would have baked a snake." Lumumba was tortured, beaten to within an inch of his life, executed by firing squad, and his remains were dissolved in acid. The CIA had finally gotten its wish, and without having to get its hands dirty.

Years later, O'Donnell reflected on the episode: "All the people I knew acted in good faith," even Bissell and Gottlieb. "I think they acted in light of — maybe not their consciences, but in light of their concept of patriotism." They weren't "evil people," he said. They had simply abandoned their moral compass "because the boss says it is okay."

Devlin reached the same conclusion. He said in an interview that Gottlieb "was acting under instructions from his superiors. But," he continued, "as we both know, as indicated by the boys who got hung at Nuremberg, that is no excuse."

16

Close but No Cigar

Satisfied with Gottlieb's explanation of his involvement in the attempt to assassinate Patrice Lumumba, attorney Joseph Rauh moved on to another incident.

"Could you tell us what you know about any CIA mailing of a handkerchief with poison to an Iraqi colonel?"

"I have a remembrance of that operation taking place. I can't pinpoint the time it was done, but it was not an assassination operation in any way."

"What was it?"

"It was an incapacitation attempt to get this man out of the way by giving him—I don't know the right word for it, but a kind of an incapacitating illness that was limited at the time."

"What was the purpose of incapacitating this man?"

"The purpose of it, I guess there was an operational purpose that I don't remember now. There was some reason that was useful for this government for him to be off the scene for a while."

"Did you prepare the handkerchief with the poison?"

"No. It was prepared at Ft. Detrick."

"What was your connection with this event?"

"As I remember it, I was going on an overseas trip and I mailed it from somewhere in the Far East."

"You carried it with you to the Far East and mailed it?"

"Yes."

Within the CIA, there existed a group of personnel that plotted the assassination of foreign leaders. Insiders flippantly referred to this group as the

"Health Alteration Committee." Just as flippantly, they referred to its work as "wet affairs" because it concerned the liquidation of people.

In February 1960, the chief of the CIA's Near East Division sought the help of the Health Alteration Committee. Colonel Abd al-Karim Qasim had recently overthrown the Iraqi monarchy and ordered the royal family machine-gunned to death. Once in power, Qasim established friendly diplomatic relations with the Soviet Union, a major red flag for the United States. The chief of the Near East Division didn't necessarily want to kill Qasim, but, he wrote, "we also do not object should this complication develop." Like President Eisenhower's order to assassinate Lumumba, the chief's request to "incapacitate" Qasim eventually landed on the desk of Sidney Gottlieb.

To carry out the "incapacitation" attempt, Gottlieb procured a handkerchief doused with tuberculosis from Fort Detrick, took it to what is only referred to as an "Asian country," and mailed it to Qasim. Apparently the package never reached him. Not long afterward, it didn't matter anyway. The chief of the Near East Division reported, with a touch of humor, that Qasim had "suffered a terminal illness before a firing squad in Baghdad (an event we had nothing to do with)." Who had killed Qasim to the delight of the CIA? A rival political faction called the Ba'ath Party, which ushered Saddam Hussein to power.

Nobody endured more CIA assassination attempts than Fidel Castro, the bearded, fatigue-wearing Communist leader of Cuba. Presidents Dwight Eisenhower and John F. Kennedy both conspired to topple his regime. Their most ambitious attempt, the 1961 Bay of Pigs Invasion, failed spectacularly. During the invasion, fifteen hundred CIA-trained guerilla fighters from Guatemala landed on the Cuban coast and were quickly overwhelmed by a local militia. Over one hundred of the guerillas died and another thousand were captured. Ironically, the failed invasion strengthened Castro's image as a national hero, further tightening his grip on power. Even more worrisome, it also strengthened his ties with the Soviet Union.

One year later, the world was thrust to the brink of nuclear war when an American U-2 spy plane detected a fleet of Soviet ships carrying nuclear missiles to Cuba. The shipment included forty-five one-megaton warheads, each of which carried the destructive equivalent of sixty-seven Hiroshima bombs. In a White House meeting on how to respond to the threat, Attorney General Robert F. Kennedy wondered aloud whether the United States should stage a false flag attack. The Navy could intentionally sink one of its own ships and blame it on Cuba, thereby giving the United States the pretext to invade Cuba and overthrow Castro.

President Kennedy opted for a more sensible strategy. He implemented a naval blockade around the island nation and announced that he would regard any missile launched from Cuba toward any nation in the Western Hemisphere "as an attack by the Soviet Union on the United States, requiring a full retaliatory response upon the Soviet Union."

Kennedy's resolve sobered the impulsive Soviet leader Nikita Khrushchev. During negotiations, Khrushchev agreed to remove his nuclear missiles from Cuba if Kennedy pledged not to invade Cuba in the future. Kennedy also secretly agreed to remove American Jupiter missiles from Turkey, which sat menacingly close to the Soviet border. On Christmas Day, 1962, the last Soviet ship carrying nuclear missiles left Cuba, marking an end to the Cuban Missile Crisis.

Disaster may have been averted, but the Castro problem still remained. Perhaps a cunning chemist in the CIA could help solve it.

Attorney Joseph Rauh asked Sidney Gottlieb, "Please relate each of the CIA's considerations or preparations for the harassment or assassination of Fidel Castro and your role if any in any of them."

"I really can't do that very well," Gottlieb said. "There was a good deal of that work that bypassed me and it bypassed me in the following way. Just a minute." He briefly consulted with CIA attorney Lee Strickland. "A large number of these things I was not personally involved [in]."

"You never at any time were consulted on any effort to consider or prepare for the assassination of Fidel Castro?"

"As far as the assassination goes, that is a true statement," though Gottlieb acknowledged that he had consulted on "the harassment of him in various ways."

"What [were] the items on which you were consulted involving the harassment?"

"This whole idea of feeding him a material that would make his beard drop out, I remember that coming up."

"How was that to be done?"

"I forget the name of the chemical, maybe it is thallium, an organic salt with thallium in it that is supposed to have that effect."

The plan was to dust Castro's shoes with thallium salts, which cause hair loss. The scientists in the CIA's Technical Services Division (TSD, formerly the TSS) reasoned that if Castro lost his trademark beard, then he would also lose his masculine allure, his public appeal, and, like the biblical figure of Samson, his power. "It was a pretty silly project," said former SOD scientist Gerald Yonetz. The plan ultimately fell through.

The TSD concocted several other schemes to humiliate Castro in the eyes of the Cuban people. One involved circulating doctored photos depicting him as an obese slob surrounded by food and women. The caption on the photos would read, "My ration is different."

Another involved spraying aerosolized LSD inside Castro's broadcasting studio before he delivered a big speech. Gottlieb strongly advised against it because, he said, "there was no way of controlling what went on after that, that he might do something that was inimical to the interest of the USA."

Yet another involved lacing Castro's famous Cuban cigars with LSD. Ike Feldman, the Bureau of Narcotics agent who helped George White conduct Operation Midnight Climax, was put in charge of the operation. "One of my whores was this Cuban girl," he later said, "and we were gonna send her down to see Castro with a box of LSD-soaked cigars." But by the time that everything was ready, the CIA had become less interested in humiliating Castro and more interested in killing him.

The TSD contributed to a number of attempts on Castro's life. A 1967 CIA inspector general report reveals that Ray Treichler of the TSD "contaminate[d] a box full of fifty cigars with botulin toxin" to give to Castro. Treichler did a careful "flaps-and-seals job" on the box to erase any evidence of tampering. According to the report, "he kept one of the experimental cigars and still has it. He retested it during our inquiry and found that the toxin still retained 94% of its original effectiveness. . . . Merely putting one in the mouth would do the job."

Nothing ever came of the cigars because nobody could figure out how to get them to Castro without implicating the CIA. An anonymous CIA case officer explained, "It was quite obvious that there was an explosion potential here—an explosion not in the technical sense—a flap potential, if you will." The case officer made sure to clarify his metaphorical use of the word "explosion" so as not to feed the unsubstantiated rumors that the CIA had tried to give Castro exploding cigars.

The CIA next recruited mafia members "Handsome Johnny" Roselli and his partner Sam Giancana to kill Castro. Roselli agreed to do it on the condition that the CIA provide him with a method that was "nice and clean." In accordance with his wishes, the TSD prepared several pills filled with botulinum toxin. Roselli and Giancana gave the pills to their Cuban accomplice, Juan Orta, who had access to a restaurant that Castro frequented. The plan was for Orta to slip the pills into Castro's drink, but he got cold feet and gave them back. Following the failure, Robert F. Kennedy asked one of his contacts in the CIA, "Why can't you gentlemen get things cooking the way 007 does?"

The most inventive assassination plot involved Castro's hobby of ocean diving. CIA officer Desmond Fitzgerald suggested that the TSD find an unusually beautiful shell, fill it with explosives, and place it underwater where Castro often dived. If all went according to plan, Castro would be so drawn to the shell that he would pick it up, thereby activating the explosives. Fitzgerald eventually scrapped the idea after buying a book on Caribbean shells and realizing that none of them were both large enough to carry the explosives and beautiful enough to guarantee Castro's interest.

Shortly afterward, the TSD suggested that American attorney James Donovan, who was negotiating the release of the Bay of Pigs prisoners, give Castro a diving suit coated with a fungus that causes the debilitating skin disease Madura foot. Unbeknownst to the TSD, Donovan had already given Castro a diving suit, spoiling the plot.

Finally, the TSD invented a weapon straight out of a James Bond novel: a poison pen fitted with a needle so fine that its victim wouldn't even know that they had been pricked. On November 22, 1963, the very day that President John F. Kennedy was assassinated in Dallas, Desmond Fitzgerald gave the poison pen to Cuban asset Rolando Cubela. However, Cubela didn't want to use it. Surely, he said, the CIA "could come up with something more sophisticated than that." Fitzgerald assured him that the CIA could get him anything that he wanted, including guns and money. The CIA never did, though, because upon leaving the meeting and learning of Kennedy's assassination, Fitzgerald nixed the plot.

None of the assassination plots ever came to fruition. Simply killing

Castro would have been easy enough, but killing him in a way that didn't implicate the CIA proved to be impossible. Toward the end of his life, Castro joked, "If surviving assassination attempts were an Olympic event, I would win the gold medal."

17

Disillusion and Dissolution

"Doctor Gottlieb, the agency at the time had an office of the inspector general; isn't that correct?"

"I believe so."

"And they took a look at this program; is that right?"

"Yes. I think for most units in the agency there was a procedure for trying to inspect them every seven years."

"Do you recall the report of the inspector general in 1957?"

"Yes. I have some recollection of that."

"And were you there in 1963 when that was done again?"

"Yes. I was there in 1963."

"After the report from the inspector general came out, was there some discussion among those responsible for MKULTRA about the report and what to do in light of the report?"

"There must have been, sure."

"Do you remember those discussions? Or are you just saying—"

"Not very clearly. I mean, every time the inspector general made a report and came out with recommendations, they needed to be responded to. So, there would have been a considerable amount of discussion."

"Did you make some changes as a result of those reports in 1957 and 1963?"

"I really can't remember that. Not that I remember. Not that I remember."

Sidney Gottlieb had spent two years in Germany followed by four years as the science advisor to Richard Bissell in the CIA's Directorate of Plans. Both positions broadened his duties beyond the day-to-day administration

137

of MKULTRA and exposed him to the operational side of the CIA. He hadn't completely abandoned MKULTRA, but signs of the project's inevitable demise were becoming apparent.

One major sign came in 1963 when John Earman, the CIA's new inspector general, conducted another investigation into MKULTRA. His final report echoes many of the points made by Lyman Kirkpatrick six years earlier but goes further in its condemnation. Only a single copy of the report was ever made. It begins, "The concepts involved in manipulating human behavior are found by many people both within and outside the Agency to be distasteful or unethical." By funding mind control experiments, the CIA was endangering the test subjects as well as its own reputation. As for Operation Midnight Climax, "clearly the most sensitive aspect of MKULTRA," there were "significant limitations on the effectiveness of such testing." Overall, MKULTRA raised "questions of legality," jeopardized the "rights and interests" of Americans, and needed stricter controls.

Richard Helms, Bissell's successor as head of the Directorate of Plans, emphatically disagreed with Earman's call for stricter controls of MKULTRA. He wanted the project to proceed full speed ahead, writing to his colleagues, "If we are to continue to maintain a capability for influencing human behavior, we are virtually obliged to test on unwitting humans." The Soviets, he claimed, were making "inexplicable and disturbing" progress in the field of mind control; the CIA couldn't afford to fall behind. Helms did at least admit that he had "no answer to the moral issue" that MKULTRA posed.

Aside from the CIA inspector general, did anyone else in a position of power monitor MKULTRA? Did anyone else ever pull Gottlieb aside for questioning? Did anyone else ever try rein things in?

"If you are talking about the substantive aspects of it," Gottlieb said, "the answer would probably be, no."

By the time that Earman submitted his report, Richard Condon's 1959 novel *The Manchurian Candidate* had become a bestseller and was adapted into an award-winning movie starring Frank Sinatra and Angela Lansbury. The story revolves around the concept of Communist mind control. During the Korean War, American soldier Raymond Shaw is captured by Soviet commandos, taken to a secret research facility in Manchuria, and brainwashed into becoming a sleeper agent. His posthypnotic trigger is the queen of diamonds card. Upon seeing it, he will go into a trance and kill whomever he is instructed to. The Soviets plan to have Shaw return to the United States and murder a presidential front-runner, clearing the way for a Communist puppet to assume power.

Gottlieb never succeeded where the Communists in the novel did. Neither he nor anyone else associated with MKULTRA ever created a Manchurian candidate. They had found methods to kill, confuse, and humiliate, but not to control a person like a marionette.

"Sure," Gottlieb said in his depositions, "you can make somebody's mind fuzzy, and you can make somebody say silly, unpredictable things, but if your object is to change his behavior in a very specific way, that is generally not too feasible."

Attorney Thomas Maddox asked for clarification, "Sir, would it be fair to say that your conclusion is that you can destroy his control of himself, but not superimpose your own control over his behavior?"

"That might be one way of saying it, yes. I never thought of it quite that way, but, yes."

Nor did Gottlieb ever find an effective truth drug. According to a declassified document from 1961 summarizing a conversation between two anonymous CIA officers, sodium pentothal, the "pure gravy" drug that Artichoke teams had used to interrogate foreign spies, "should not be considered more effective for elicitation than getting a man drunk." In fact, a CIA memo from February 1953—two months *before* MKULTRA was created—argues that there was "no reason for believing that drugs are reliable for obtaining truthful information."

MKULTRA was on its last legs. Over its ten-year lifespan, it had spent $10 million at eighty institutions, including three prisons, twelve hospitals, fifteen research institutes, and forty-four colleges and universities. And for what?

Gottlieb tried to put a positive spin on the negative results. When asked whether he had learned anything useful from the various MKULTRA experiments, he said, "Sure. Sure. I think [we] learned a lot of things. Most of the information was negative information, but you know, I think it established pretty clearly the limits of what you could do in surreptitiously altering a human's behavior by covert means. It was damn little."

Before its ultimate demise, MKULTRA morphed into another cryptonym: MKSEARCH. The name change signaled, at least in theory, a new beginning, but MKSEARCH mainly just continued several MKULTRA subprojects, including those run by George White, Charles Geschickter, Maitland Baldwin, and Carl Pfeiffer. Throughout the 1960s, the amount of funds dedicated to MKSEARCH dwindled until Gottlieb canceled the whole thing. He had other secret work to attend to.

18

Torture

The CIA's disillusionment with MKULTRA was made clear in February 1964 when KGB officer Yuri Nosenko defected to the United States. Nosenko brought with him valuable information from behind the Iron Curtain. He named a number of Soviet agents operating in the West, claimed that the Soviets had bugged the American embassy in Moscow, and said that the KGB file of Lee Harvey Oswald showed that the Soviet Union hadn't been involved in the assassination of President John F. Kennedy. All of these revelations were of the utmost importance—if they were true. But was Nosenko telling the truth, or was he a double agent sent by the Kremlin to mislead the United States?

James Angleton, the CIA's paranoid chief of counterintelligence, naturally distrusted Nosenko. As did Richard Helms. Both men agreed that they needed to interrogate him. But with what methods? Despite all of the money poured into MKULTRA, and despite Helms's incessant support for the project, they opted for the traditional methods of isolation, physical pain, and psychological distress.

Nosenko was placed in a concrete cell for three years. He had no privacy from the guards, no window to the outside world, and no reading material. His metal bed, which was built deliberately too small, had no sheet or pillow. He was given a dollar's worth of gruel per day to eat. There were no temperature controls in his room, nor could he turn off the lightbulb that burned day and night. In an attempt to stimulate his mind, he created a makeshift chess set out of lint. When the guards found it, they swept his cell clean.

Nosenko constantly talked to his interrogators. However, the CIA still couldn't determine whether he was telling the truth. Given his treatment, he would have said anything to make the pain stop. As one counterintelligence officer remarked, "If you have a blowtorch up someone's ass," they'll talk. The CIA abused Nosenko for information, but because of the abuse, it couldn't trust the information.

For thousands of years, people have known that torture often elicits false confessions. One chronicler from the Middle Ages told the story of Jacques de Molay, a man who confessed to spitting on the cross under pain of torture: "And he would have confessed that he had slain God Himself if they had asked that." Similarly, in 1321, Christians in France tortured dozens of lepers until the lepers confessed to poisoning wells across the country. Further torture got the lepers to confess that the Jews had paid them to do it. Even more torture got them to implicate the Muslims in the plot, despite the fact that no Muslims lived in France at the time. The Christians used the confessions as justification for killing thousands of innocent people and seizing their property. All the while, not a single well had been poisoned.

During the European witch craze of the seventeenth century, the Duke of Brunswick was so appalled by the torture methods that the Catholic Church administered to supposed witches that he invited two renowned Jesuit scholars to supervise one session, thinking that they would denounce what they saw. Instead, the Jesuits reported back, "The Inquisitors are doing their duty. They are arresting only people who have been implicated by the confession of other witches."

Not satisfied, the duke asked the Jesuits to follow him to the torture chamber. "Let me question her," he said. The Jesuits obliged.

"Now woman," said the duke in the chamber, "you are a confessed witch. I suspect these two men," the Jesuits, "of being warlocks. What do you say? Another turn of the rack, executioners."

"No, no!" shrieked the woman. "You are quite right. I have often seen them at the Sabbat. They can turn themselves into goats, wolves and other animals."

"What else do you know about them?"

"Several witches have had children by them. One woman even had eight children whom these men fathered. The children had heads like toads and legs like spiders."

The duke turned to the Jesuits. "Shall I put you to the torture until you confess, my friends?"

One of the Jesuits, Friedrich Spee, had a change of heart. In 1631, he famously wrote, "Torture has the power to create witches where none exist." And yet the practice of torture continued.

Over three hundred years later, the U.S. House Select Committee on Assassinations analyzed the case of Yuri Nosenko and concluded that his treatment had "virtually ruined him as a valid source of information." The CIA eventually determined that he was a bona fide defector, released him from custody, and paid him $80,000 in compensation.

Nosenko's treatment was especially ironic because a year before his defection to the United States, the CIA had completed a study to determine the most effective interrogation methods. The resulting report, *KUBARK Counterintelligence Interrogation* (KUBARK was the CIA's cryptonym for itself), argues that instead of resorting to physical abuse, the interrogator should build rapport to establish the "comforting awareness" that the subject "is considered as a person, not a squeezable sponge." A subject who's treated with dignity is more likely to cooperate out of respect, while a subject who's treated with cruelty is more likely to refuse to cooperate out of spite.

Regarding torture, the report reaches the same conclusion as Friedrich Spee, the Duke of Brunswick, and countless others before them: "Intense pain is quite likely to produce false confessions, concocted as a means of escaping from distress." Moreover, the report lists three additional reasons why torture is futile. First, "the threat to inflict pain . . . can trigger fears more damaging than the immediate sensation of pain." The realization of those fears—the actual infliction of pain—"is likely to come as a relief." Second, if torture is administered at the beginning of an interrogation without success, the subject will become more resistant to subsequent interrogation methods. (The Mongols knew this as far back as 1291, writing in their legal code that officials must "first use reason to analyze and surmise, and shall not impose abruptly any torture.") Third, if torture is administered at the end of an interrogation, the subject will infer that the interrogator has become desperate. "He may decide that if he can just hold out against this final assault, he will win the struggle and his freedom. And he is likely to be right."

That said, the report does suggest placing the most hostile subjects in sensory deprivation. As the recent experiments of Ewen Cameron, Donald Hebb, and Maitland Baldwin had shown, sensory deprivation heightens anxiety, and therefore a subject in sensory deprivation might come to associate a kind interrogator "with the reward of lessened anxiety, human contact, and meaningful activity." In essence, sensory deprivation serves as a psychological trick to boost the positive feelings that a subject has for an interrogator, making it more likely that the subject will cooperate.

The report also acknowledges that drugs can be useful in interrogations, just not in the way that Sidney Gottlieb had hoped. The drugs themselves can't make a subject tell the truth, but they can make it *easier* for a subject to tell the truth. That's because drugs, even placebos, can alleviate the feeling of guilt associated with talking. In the words of the report, "No one could blame him for telling his story now." Under the influence of drugs, the subject has no choice but to talk — or so he tells himself.

Hypnotism can have the same effect. The report cites the work of psychologist Martin Orne, whom the CIA funded through the SIHE cutout organization, as proof. In a paper on interrogation techniques, Orne differentiates between hypnotism and the "hypnotic situation." While hypnotism is the process of inducing a trancelike state (hypnosis) in someone, the hypnotic situation is the process of inducing the *belief* that such a state has been induced, even if it hasn't. The hypnotic situation can "relieve the individual of a feeling of responsibility for his own actions and thus lead him to reveal information."

Orne suggests that the interrogator implement the "magic room" technique to better capitalize on the hypnotic situation. To do so, the interrogator gives the subject a reason to believe that hypnotism is effective, even if it isn't. For example, the interrogator might pretend to hypnotize the subject into thinking that his hands are getting warmer. The subject, seated at a desk, will resist the hypnotism, but his hands actually will be getting warmer because of a heater concealed under the desk. As a result, the subject can be convinced that he has been hypnotized, even if he hasn't.

A similar technique requires the interrogator to give the subject a knockout drug. Whenever the subject wakes up, the interrogator reads aloud part of a conversation that they supposedly had while the subject was asleep. In reality, the interrogator has invented the conversation from whole cloth, but the subject doesn't know that. A subject who thinks that he has already talked is more likely to talk again.

Despite the *KUBARK* report, despite Orne's findings, despite the potential for blowback, and despite the Nuremberg Code, Geneva Conventions, and the Universal Declaration of Human Rights adopted by the United Nations, which says, "No one shall be subjected to torture or to cruel, inhuman or degrading treatment or punishment," the United States continued to torture people with little success. In response to the September 11, 2001, terrorist attacks, the George W. Bush administration authorized the CIA to interrogate "detainees" using beatings, waterboarding, rectal feeding, stress positions, sleep deprivation, mock executions, and physical confinement in coffinlike boxes.

The CIA, in turn, awarded psychologist James Mitchell an $81 million contract to conduct these "enhanced interrogations." Mitchell, who had never so much as witnessed an interrogation before, was a supervisor for Survival, Evasion, Resistance, and Escape (SERE) training in the military. The SERE program had been developed at the end of the Korean War to teach soldiers how to defend themselves against Communist interrogation methods. Armed with a knowledge of SERE, Mitchell reverse engineered those methods for the CIA. In his view, the key to a successful interrogation was to treat each detainee "like a dog in a cage." When an FBI agent confronted Mitchell about the fact that the detainees weren't dogs but human beings, he responded, "Science is science." An undisclosed number of detainees died as a result.

Mitchell's "*Clockwork Orange* kind of approach," as an insider described it, indeed got the detainees to talk. One of them confessed to knowing that his companions in the terrorist group al-Qaeda were plotting to blow up malls, banks, supermarkets, nuclear power plants, the Golden Gate Bridge, and the Statue of Liberty. Of course, none of the plots were real. The detainee wasn't even a member of al-Qaeda.

Mitchell later faced backlash for his actions. Trying to elicit sympathy, he once testified in court, "I cry at dog food commercials."

In 2014, the Democrats on the Senate Select Committee on Intelligence produced a 6,700-page report on the American torture program. (The Republicans refused to cooperate because they didn't want to appear soft on terrorism.) The full, unredacted report has never been made public, but the Barack Obama White House released its 500-page executive summary. "The CIA's use of its enhanced interrogation techniques," it says, "was not an effective means of acquiring intelligence or gaining cooperation from detainees." The CIA had justified the use of certain torture methods with "inaccurate claims of their effectiveness." Several detainees who provided accurate information did so "prior to, or without having been subjected to these techniques."

Given that throughout history torture has never produced reliable confessions, it's easy to understand why the CIA experimented with drugs and other esoteric interrogation methods as part of MKULTRA. The problem is that when those methods failed, the CIA, contrary to its own advice, returned to torture.

19

Technical Services

In the mid-1960s, as MKULTRA ground to a halt, Sidney Gottlieb became the director of the CIA's Technical Services Division. Under his leadership, the TSD became the CIA equivalent of James Bond's legendary Q Division, the fictional organization that created the superspy's most ingenious gadgets. TSD personnel forged bank cards, driver's licenses, and birth certificates. They put hidden cameras in pens, wristwatches, and cigarette lighters. They developed portable key-copying kits, lasers that could detect audio from windowpane vibrations, and Trojan Horse surveillance systems embedded in gifts destined for foreign diplomats—the gifts that kept on giving.

CIA officer Philip Agee wrote about other TSD inventions:

> Horrible smelling liquids in small glass vials can be hurled into meeting halls. A fine clear powder can be sprinkled in a meeting-place becoming invisible after settling but having the effect of tear-gas when stirred up by the later movement of people. An incendiary powder can be moulded around prepared tablets and when ignited the combination produces ample quantities of smoke that attacks the eyes and respiratory system much more strongly than ordinary tear-gas. A tasteless substance can be introduced to food that causes exaggerated body colour. . . . Invisible itching powder can be placed on steering wheels or toilet seats, and a slight smear of invisible ointment causes a serious burn to skin on contact. Chemically processed tobacco can be added to cigarettes and cigars to produce respiratory ailments.

These inventions were among the most guarded secrets in the entire CIA. When one officer gave a tour of CIA facilities to a visitor, he pointed to the TSD area and joked, "I can't take you through there. I don't think either one of us would emerge alive."

Gottlieb was a tough but caring boss. Whenever TSD personnel got into heated arguments, he would force the offending parties to share an office. "They may refuse to talk to each other," he would say, "but by God, they're going to sit there and look at each other all day." He also made heartfelt attempts to connect with his colleagues. He would call them on their birthdays, remember their spouses' names, and discuss their hobbies in conversation. He knew firsthand how it felt to be an outsider in the CIA, and now that he had some modicum of power, he wanted to spare others the feeling.

With Gottlieb at the helm, the TSD grew to over four hundred people. Carlos Luria, a former undercover agent in Germany, taught the new recruits lock-picking, secret writing, and other tricks of the trade. As a capstone to their education, he made them pass a field trial. They had to break into his house, disable the alarm, open a variety of envelopes, photograph the contents, reseal the envelopes, hide an audio transmitter in the telephone, reset the alarm, and relock the doors, all before his neighbors called the police for suspicious activity. If the recruits got caught, Luria said, "they might spend an uncomfortable hour or two at the local police station, but better that they make their mistakes here than in the field."

Most of the recruits passed the field trial without a problem, but there were some exceptions. One team of recruits was about to leave the house when the neighbor's daughter and her boyfriend parked in the driveway. The team was trapped inside "while the car's shock absorbers got a real workout," Luria said. In an act of desperation, the team's commander called the police to complain of "unseemly going-on—right in front of God and everyone—and on a public street, too!" When the cops arrived, lights flashing, the recruits panicked. "Man," said one of them afterward, "I thought my pants would never dry."

Perhaps the most imaginative of the TSD's inventions was the skyhook, designed to extract an agent from any location in a hurry. As part of the skyhook system, the agent would attach one end of a nylon line to a body harness and the other end to a helium balloon that he would release into the air. A capture plane equipped with thirty-foot "horns" protruding from its nose would snag the dangling line, the agent would be whisked away, and the plane's crew would use a winch to reel him into the fuselage.

Easier said than done. The first live test of the skyhook used a pig instead of a human. As soon as the capture plane snagged the line, the pig was jerked upward at 125 miles per hour. A problem with the harness caused the pig to start spinning uncontrollably, but it survived. Upon being reeled into the plane, it took a moment to regain its balance, then attacked the crew.

The CIA only ever used the skyhook once in the field. During the aptly named Operation Coldfeet, Major James Smith and Lieutenant Leonard LeSchack parachuted onto an ice floe in the Arctic Ocean to spy on an abandoned Soviet drift station. No plane could land on the ice, nor could any ship penetrate it, so when they were ready to leave, the skyhook was their only option.

After taking photographs and gathering materials, LeSchack released his balloon for pickup. Gale-force winds immediately whipped it through the air, dragging him along until he slammed into a block of ice. For a few seconds he lay there bruised and exhausted, fearing for his life. Then, without warning, the capture plane snagged his line, and he disappeared into the clouds. Now it was Smith's turn. Having watched LeSchack, he nervously released his own balloon and was similarly dragged across the ice, though he managed to stop himself by shoving the heel of his boot into a fissure. The pilot of the capture plane later remembered, "The line made contact on the outer portion of the left horn. It just hung there for what to me was an eternity." Finally the line slid into the catching mechanism. Smith was secured. Both Operation Coldfeet and the skyhook were a success.

The TSD often had to find ways to eavesdrop on private meetings. If it had sufficient warning of when and where a meeting would occur, it could usually get an agent to plant a listening device beforehand. But that wasn't always an option. For instance, the compound of one undisclosed Asian head of state was so secure that the TSD was at a loss for what to do—until someone noticed the cats. Apparently the Asian head of state had a soft spot for felines, some of which even sat in his lap during his meetings. These cats were the keys to the compound.

The TSD wanted to turn the cats into clandestine mobile listening devices. Dr. Robin Michelson, co-creator of the cochlear implant, figured out how. In a scene reminiscent of *Frankenstein*, he anesthetized a cat and inserted a microphone into its inner ear canal, hidden from view. Connected to the microphone was a small audio transmitter that he buried under the skin at the base of the cat's skull. Lastly, he wove the transmitter's long antenna into the fur running down the cat's spine.

The hour-long procedure was relatively simple compared to what came next. For the plan to succeed, the "Acoustic Kitty" would have to be trained to get within earshot of the target conversation. Otherwise, the ambient noise in the room would drown out the words.

UCLA biologist Bob Bailey was well-known for his ability to train any animal. Throughout his career, he had trained raccoons to play basketball, chickens to play tic-tac-toe, and dolphins to detect submarines. He had consulted for Walt Disney, the U.S. Navy, and now for the TSD. To train the Acoustic Kitty, he subjected it to positive and negative feedback via ultrasonic sound. "We found that we could condition the cat to listen to voices," he said. Depending on the specific voice and command used, the cat would travel forward or backward, left or right.

That's as far as the project ever went. According to former CIA officer Victor Marchetti, when the Acoustic Kitty was taken out for its first field trial, the TSD techs set it down on the street outside their van "and a taxi comes and runs him over." Meanwhile, the techs couldn't figure out why their equipment had suddenly stopped working. "There they were, sitting in the van with all those dials, and the cat was dead!"

The TSD trained a number of other animals for secret operations. In the 1960s, Bailey trained red-tailed hawks to carry cameras over enemy territory. However, the hawks were never sent abroad because of an overlooked government law restricting the transportation of birds. On another occasion, Bailey trained ravens to deposit audio transmitters onto windowsills, and this time he made sure that the birds reached their destination. He personally carried one of them on a commercial flight abroad, even though it was illegal. "[The raven] was in a map case under the front seat," he later revealed. "Every now and then [it] would make a noise," causing Bailey to squirm in his seat.

In conjunction with Fort Detrick, the TSD launched a program to update the lethal L-pill developed by the OSS R&D Branch during World War II. When bitten through its waxy outer coating, the L-pill oozed a goo of potassium cyanide that caused death within minutes—ideally. It didn't always

PROJECT MIND CONTROL

work as advertised. Sidney Gottlieb and the other scientists in the TSD wanted to develop a much more reliable suicide device.

At first they simply made the L-pill more potent. The CIA gave these improved pills to U-2 spy plane pilots in case they ever got shot down over enemy territory, but a series of close calls forced the CIA to reconsider its use of the pills. On one occasion, pilot Carmine Vito, nicknamed "The Lemon Drop Kid" because he constantly sucked on lozenges, reached into his pocket and popped what he thought was a lozenge into his mouth. As he ran his tongue over its smooth surface, he noticed that it was unusually flavorless. He spat it out only to realize that he had been sucking on his L-pill.

The TSD subsequently gave the pilots a new suicide device in the form of a needle coated with sticky brown shellfish toxin. One finger prick from the needle would deliver enough toxin to kill a grown man. To prevent any accidental pricks, the needle was stored in a narrow hole drilled into the side of a silver dollar.

The needle soon made international news when a U-2 spy plane was shot down over the Soviet Union. Its pilot, Francis Gary Powers, parachuted to safety, but the Soviet military captured him and confiscated his suicide needle.

Put on trial in Moscow for espionage, Powers confessed to intentionally violating Soviet airspace. As part of the trial, a panel of Russian scientists pricked a dog with the needle to see what would happen. The head of the panel explained to the court, "Within one minute after the prick the dog fell on his side, and a sharp slackening of the respiratory movements of the chest was observed." Three minutes later, "the heart stopped functioning and death set in."

Powers was found guilty and sentenced to three years in prison followed by seven years of hard labor. After serving less than two years, he returned to the United States as part of a prisoner exchange. The suicide needle was never again sent into the field, but the shellfish toxin that made it so deadly would dramatically impact the futures of Gottlieb, the TSD, and the entire CIA.

On November 25, 1969, President Richard Nixon announced that the United States would no longer make biological weapons for offensive military purposes. Moreover, he pledged to destroy the country's stockpile of biological weapons. Part of his motivation for doing so was a genuine concern about the dangers of such weapons, but he was also trying to boost his public image as a man of peace amid the ongoing turmoil of the Vietnam War. Regardless, Nixon's directive ushered in a massive disarmament campaign across the United States, including at Fort Detrick, where the CIA kept its stockpile of biological agents.

Gottlieb and Richard Helms, now the director of central intelligence (DCI), deliberated on what to do in light of the directive. The CIA's stockpile of biological agents included eleven grams of shellfish toxin, eight milligrams of cobra venom, and cultures of anthrax, brucellosis, encephalitis, smallpox, tuberculosis, tularemia, and valley fever. Should the CIA really destroy these rare and valuable substances? The shellfish toxin alone had been painstakingly harvested from tens of thousands of Alaskan butter clams at a cost of many millions of dollars. Even so, Gottlieb and Helms couldn't bring themselves to disobey a presidential order.

Nathan Gordon could. As chief of the TSD's Chemistry Branch, he wasn't going to stand idly by while years of hard work were flushed down the drain. When an officer from Fort Detrick called to ask about destroying the stockpile, Gordon said that he would take care of it. Unbeknownst to Gottlieb and Helms, he placed the substances in a secure eight-by-ten vault in Washington, D.C., where they sat forgotten for the next five years, waiting to be found.

20

Keeping Secrets

Sidney Gottlieb was a shadowy figure in the CIA. Few of his colleagues ever knew what he was up to, especially during the heyday of MKULTRA. He was the odd chemist, the man with the limp and stutter, the outsider left to his own devices, quite literally. Even fewer people outside of the CIA knew what he was up to. His neighbors occasionally saw him milk goats and dance to folk music, but nothing about his private life hinted at his work—or at least almost nothing did.

In the late 1960s, Gottlieb's eldest son, Peter, began dating a high school classmate, "Elizabeth," who later spoke about her experience. Having grown up in a conservative Catholic family, she found "the Gottlieb family dynamic [to be] so different from what I experienced. . . . They would have discussions about politics and what was happening in the world. They had so many more books—Sidney had a library in a den off the eating area. And they were so much more frank and open with each other than I was used to. I remember a time when one of Peter's sisters yelled, 'Oh shit! I've got my damn period again!' And I thought, 'Well, this is different.'"

Another difference was their attitude toward religion. "There was no religious feeling in that household." Gottlieb and his wife did, however, have "mystical leanings." They would talk about "esoteric subjects that never came up at my dinner table at home. I remember feeling kind of entranced by their whole dynamic as a family. It was exotic. They were very unusual people. He meditated, but they weren't wackos or anything like that. There was something I just couldn't put my finger on."

As Elizabeth became more comfortable around the Gottliebs, and as they became more comfortable around her, she began to realize what that "something" was:

> One day that summer, we were out at the house swimming. The parents had gone to the store to buy food for dinner and Peter goes, kind of conspiratorially, "Come here. I want to show you something." He takes me into his father's den, his library, and says, "Turn around." He did something—he didn't want me to see what he did—and the wall of books opened up. Behind it was all this stuff. Weapons—I couldn't tell which kind, but guns. There was other stuff back there. It was like a secret compartment. I asked him, "What is *that* for?" He closed it back up quickly and said, "You know, my father has a price on his head." I said, "Why, is he a criminal?" He said, "No, he works for the CIA." Then he said, "You know, my dad has killed people. He made toothpaste to kill someone." Later on he told me, "Don't tell anyone that you were in there, and don't ever tell anyone you know that my father kills people."

Elizabeth reflected, "You just got the sense that there were certain things they knew they had to follow, kind of unspoken protocols. You had to honk your horn when you arrived at the bottom of the driveway. Guests could come over, but only at certain times. . . . There probably was a worry about security, and someone coming after him."

Gottlieb was indeed worried about someone coming after him, especially in 1972 when news of the Watergate scandal broke. Five men with connections to the Richard Nixon White House had snuck into the headquarters of the Democratic National Committee at the Watergate complex in Washington, D.C., to photograph campaign documents and bug the phones of Nixon's political rivals. The TSD had supplied the perpetrators with disguises, false identification papers, and a voice-altering device.

In the wake of the Watergate scandal, Gottlieb was driven out of the CIA. But before he left, when the writing was on the wall, he took one of the most drastic actions of his entire career.

Throughout Gottlieb's twenty-two years in the CIA, he had tried to avoid leaving a paper trail of his actions whenever possible. He often delivered orders orally, not in writing, to give himself a degree of plausible deniability. John Earman lamented this fact in his 1963 inspector general report: "A substantial portion of the MKULTRA record appears to rest in the memories of the principal officers and is therefore almost certain to be lost with their departures."

Still, Gottlieb accumulated thousands of files over the course of his career. When asked during his depositions what he had done with them, he said, "As best I can remember, at about the end of 1972 or the beginning of 1973, they were destroyed."

"Whose idea was it to destroy them?"

"It was my recommendation to destroy them."

Gottlieb didn't arrive at the decision "hastily or impetuously, or in a flood of fright." Most of the files were highly classified and required permission from DCI Richard Helms to even move, let alone destroy.

As fate would have it, Helms, an irascible man with an intimidating underbite, was also leaving the CIA. President Nixon had just won his 1972 reelection bid and wanted to inject fresh blood into his administration. He called for the resignation of dozens of appointed officials, including Helms, whom Nixon resented for refusing to help cover up the Watergate scandal.

Sometime after Gottlieb learned that Helms was being ousted, he approached him about destroying the MKULTRA files. The exact content of their conversation is unknown, but a CIA psychologist with personal knowledge of the destruction maintained that Gottlieb had told Helms, "Let's let this die with us." Helms agreed and responded, "It was our bath, let us clean the tub."

Attorney Thomas Maddox asked Gottlieb, "After Director Helms concurred, what action did you take?"

"Probably I directed one of the security officers ... to see that these things were destroyed in whatever the normal procedure for document destruction was at that time."

On January 30, 1973, the security officer went to the CIA records center in Warrenton, Virginia, and tossed the files into an incinerator. The chief of the records center made sure to write in an exculpatory memo, "Over my stated objections the MKULTRA files were destroyed by order of the DCI (Mr. Helms) shortly before his departure from office."

In their depositions, Gottlieb and Helms gave multiple reasons for why they destroyed the files. One reason was to protect the identities of the researchers associated with MKULTRA. Attorney Joseph Rauh wasn't buying it. He pressed Helms, "The CIA doesn't give out, does it, any confidential sources? . . . Why was it necessary to destroy documents in order to keep secret the names of cooperators?"

Helms deflected, "It was suggested to me that the documents be destroyed and it seemed to me at the time that it was a sensible thing to do and so I authorized it."

"I am asking you a question," Rauh insisted. "You asserted a little earlier that one of the reasons was that you had to protect people who had confidential relations. . . . Why did you have to destroy documents to protect the confidentiality?"

"Maybe it wasn't entirely necessary to do it that way but this is the decision I was asked to make and I made it."

Rauh grew frustrated with Helms's dismissive answers. He also grew frustrated with Helms's attorney, Robert LaPrade, who kept objecting to his questions. At one point, Rauh lost his composure and told LaPrade, "I consider you one of the most insulting people I have had the misfortune to deal with."

Things went slightly better with Gottlieb. Besides claiming to have destroyed the files to protect the identities of the researchers, he said, "there was an intense drive to destroy what paper we could for economy reasons. The Agency was drowning in paper, everybody was cleaning files out of all kinds."

Rauh still wasn't buying it. He proceeded to grill Gottlieb about the destruction of the files, and then about MKULTRA in general.

CIA attorney Lee Strickland interjected, "You are badgering him. That was thirty years ago."

"I am glad you said thirty years ago," Rauh retorted with an air of righteous indignation. "It is thirty years ago because the CIA hid it for thirty years, thirty years ago because you destroyed the documents. I am not responsible for the thirty years ago."

Buckling under the weight of his conscience, Gottlieb eventually revealed that he had destroyed the files because he was "concerned that papers like that left behind could never be put in the context in which they were done and they would be misunderstood by people. It was embarrassing to people and that sort of thing. . . . I'm embarrassed by it."

Sometime before retiring, Gottlieb had realized that if the public ever learned about MKULTRA, his and the CIA's reputations would be ruined. All of that time and money and pain and suffering for so little in return. Better that nobody know what happened. Better to destroy any trace of the project.

James Schlesinger briefly replaced Helms as director of central intelligence. (The CIA would churn through a handful of directors in the coming years.) An economist by training, he announced to his new subordinates, "This is a gentleman's club, and I am no gentleman," indicating that he wasn't one of the good ol' boys who protected one another from scrutiny. He had come to shake things up.

Schlesinger immediately began instituting bold reforms, firing fourteen hundred people in the process. Whenever his assistants questioned his rationale for firing a particular person, he would say, "He's been here twenty years, that's long enough." Asked whether he should show more compassion, he grumbled, "Don't talk to me about compassion. The only compassion I've got is for the American taxpayer." Unsurprisingly, morale within the CIA sank to an all-time low.

Another of Schlesinger's reforms was to restructure the TSD. He changed its name to the Office of Technical Services and appointed a new director to replace Gottlieb. On his way out the door, Gottlieb prepared one last memo describing how, under his leadership, the TSD had assisted various government agencies:

> Department of Defense: Documents, disguise, concealment devices, secret writing, flaps and seals, counter-insurgency and counter-sabotage courses . . .
>
> Federal Bureau of Investigation: At the request of the FBI we cooperated with the Bureau in a few audio surveillance operations against sensitive foreign targets in the United States.
>
> Bureau of Narcotics and Dangerous Drugs: Beacons, cameras, audio and telephone devices for overseas operations, identity documents, car-trailing devices, SRAC [short-range agent communications], flaps and seals, and training of select personnel responsible for the use thereof . . .
>
> Immigration and Naturalization: CI [counterintelligence] analysis of foreign passports and visas, guidance in developing tamper-proof alien registration cards . . .

Department of State: Technical graphics guidance on developing a new United States Passport, analyses of foreign passports, car-armoring and personnel locators (beacons) for ambassadors. . . .

Secret Service: Gate passes, security passes, passes for presidential campaign, emblems for presidential vehicles, a secure ID photo system . . .

White House: Stationary [*sic*], special memoranda, and molds of the Great Seal have been furnished . . .

Police Representing Washington, Arlington, Fairfax, and Alexandria: During the period 1968–1969 a series of classes reflecting basic and surveillance photography, basic audio, locks and picks, counter-sabotage and surreptitious entry were given to selected members from the above-mentioned cities.

In recognition of Gottlieb's two decades of service, the CIA awarded him the Distinguished Intelligence Medal, one of its highest honors.

Two and a half years after the MKULTRA files met fire, the CIA conducted an internal investigation into their destruction. The investigators discovered that in addition to destroying the MKULTRA files, Gottlieb had ordered his secretary to destroy a safe drawer full of his personal files. The secretary couldn't remember exactly what the personal files contained, but she knew that among them were "technical journals and papers written by Dr. Gottlieb as well as files dealing with Sensitive personnel matters and some Secret Sensitive papers."

During Richard Helms's deposition, attorney Joseph Rauh asked him whether he had similarly destroyed any of his personal files.

"Yes," Helms said. "I ordered certain tapes which were part of my office equipment destroyed."

"What were those tapes about?"

"Those tapes had a variety of things. They covered all kinds of talks that I had with foreign leaders, and other material. I just thought that it would be better if they were destroyed."

"Did you have any consultation with anybody about those destructions?"

"No, I did not. They were my tapes, tapes that involved me and I felt I had the authority to destroy them."

"You say they were your tapes. They were tapes made on Government property, weren't they?"

"As I say, they were involving me. . . . They were tapes on government property but most of them involved things in which I was involved."

"You thought you had the right to destroy anything where you were involved?"

"Yes."

Helms's blunt answer gave Rauh the perfect opportunity to read aloud a CIA regulation prohibiting the unilateral destruction of files. It concludes, "The heart of this judgement is to ensure that the complete story can be reconstructed in later years." Rauh then asked, "Was your destruction of MKULTRA and/or your own tapes consistent with that?"

Before Helms could answer, CIA attorney Lee Strickland said that Helms should have a chance to read the regulation for himself. Otherwise, "We don't know what we are talking about."

"I know what I am talking about," Rauh quipped. "If you don't feel you do, I can't help it."

Once Helms finished reading the regulation, he said with surprising nonchalance, "I had the authority as director to, if you like, go beyond this instruction record. It seemed to me that it was desirable to do so."

Put another way, some people are above the law. It was the same sentiment that had led to the abuses of MKULTRA.

21

The Family Jewels

Upon leaving the CIA, Sidney Gottlieb and his wife, Margaret, sold their house, cars, and goats and embarked on a world tour. Margaret wrote in an autobiographical essay, "The children took what they wanted, and we booked ourselves onto a freighter, leaving from San Francisco and heading for Perth." During their two-year trip, they visited Australia, Africa, India, and many places in between. "We were just following our noses."

While in New Delhi, the couple spent their free time volunteering at a leper hospital. Margaret had grown up in India some fifty years earlier, yet little had changed in the intervening time. "Village life is the same," she wrote, "the dirt, the monkeys, the stray dogs, the filth, the open gutters, the people defecating and peeing wherever they happen to be, the bribery, the total contrariness of everything. Nothing makes sense—to us!" Despite the foul conditions, Gottlieb was content to toil away in relative obscurity, his controversial past squarely behind him. Or so he thought.

In 1973, the year that Gottlieb retired, DCI James Schlesinger learned that CIA personnel had broken into a psychiatrist's office and stolen the medical records of military analyst Daniel Ellsberg. The personnel wanted to discredit Ellsberg because he had leaked to the press a copy of the Pentagon Papers, which catalogued a number of lies and illegal activities that the U.S. government had perpetrated during the Vietnam War. Around the same time, Schlesinger also learned that journalist Seymour Hersh was about to publish a story on Project Azorian, the CIA's costly attempt to retrieve a sunken Soviet submarine from the bottom of the Pacific Ocean with a giant claw. Both incidents made Schlesinger wonder how many other incriminating or embarrassing skeletons lay hidden in the CIA's closet. If the press caught wind of those skeletons before he did, it could spell disaster for the intelligence community. There could be no more surprises.

William Colby, head of the CIA's Directorate of Operations (formerly the Directorate of Plans), devised a solution. He suggested that Schlesinger issue a directive to all past and present employees, from undercover agents to building janitors (sometimes one and the same), ordering them to report any illegal activities that they either knew of or had been involved in while at the CIA. Schlesinger liked the idea. "Goddamn it," he told Colby, "let's find out where the time bombs are. Find out what they all are so we don't trip over land mines."

In response to the directive, a surprising number of people submitted reports. The CIA's Office of the Inspector General compiled all of them into a secret 693-page file nicknamed the "Family Jewels." Ironically, Schlesinger had issued the directive to stay one step ahead of the press, but by forsaking compartmentalization and assembling the CIA's most sensitive secrets into one file, he made it much easier for those secrets to leak out.

Among the secrets contained in the Family Jewels were the CIA's connection to the Watergate scandal; the CIA's involvement in assassination attempts on foreign leaders; and the existence of CIA programs to open mail (HTLINGUAL), spy on antiwar protestors (MHCHAOS), and perform drug experiments on unwitting people (MKULTRA). Shortly after the Family Jewels file was compiled, Schlesinger left the CIA to become secretary of defense. Colby succeeded him as director of central intelligence.

William Colby was an owlish man with a checkered past. During the Vietnam War, he had directed the CIA's Phoenix Program that tortured and killed tens of thousands of people. According to Anthony Herbert, the most decorated combat soldier of the Vietnam War, Phoenix execution teams "wiped out entire families and tried to make it appear as though the [Viet Cong] had done the killing." Out of resentment for what the Viet Cong had supposedly done, "The villagers would then be inclined to some sort of allegiance to our side, otherwise known as the good guys."

As a devout Roman Catholic, Colby was familiar with atoning for past sins. In his first month as DCI, he issued directives that ended HTLINGUAL, limited MHCHAOS, prohibited MKULTRA-type experiments, and forbade CIA personnel from engaging in assassinations. Later summarizing the directives, he said that they essentially decreed, "Thou shalt not this, Thou shalt not that." But to his chagrin, they proved to be too little too late.

On December 9, 1974, Seymour Hersh called Colby and said, "I've got a story bigger than My Lai." Hersh had previously won a Pulitzer Prize for exposing the 1968 My Lai Massacre, in which U.S. Army soldiers murdered hundreds of unarmed South Vietnamese civilians. What might he have found now? Obviously something to do with the CIA, but that's as much as Colby knew. Over the objections of several colleagues, Colby agreed to a meeting with Hersh. A year earlier, he had convinced Hersh to delay publishing his story on Project Azorian. Maybe he could do it again.

During the meeting, an anxious Colby listened while Hersh explained that he knew of several illegal CIA programs. It soon became clear that Hersh had somehow acquired the Family Jewels, likely from a disgruntled ex-employee who had been fired in Schlesinger's purge of personnel. Colby was shocked. He acknowledged that a year earlier, Schlesinger had ordered all past and present employees to report any illegal activities that they either knew of or had been involved in while at the CIA. "We got a few blips," he said. So Hersh had heard. After the meeting, Colby told his assistant, "The SOB has sources that are absolutely beyond comparison."

Colby didn't have any luck silencing Hersh this time. On December 22, 1974, the front page of *The New York Times* proclaimed in bold letters, "Huge C.I.A. Operation Reported in U.S. Against Antiwar Forces, Other Dissidents in Nixon Years." The story revealed that the CIA had spied on thousands of antiwar protestors despite the fact that the CIA's charter forbade it from operating within the United States.

Secretary of State Henry Kissinger said that Hersh's story had the effect of tossing "a burning match in a gasoline depot." It painted the CIA as an American Gestapo, an abuser of civil rights, not a protector of them. To make matters worse, Kissinger suspected—correctly—that Hersh hadn't exposed all of the CIA's skeletons. The story was just the tip of the iceberg.

Colby soon gave Kissinger a written summary of what else the Family Jewels contained that hadn't yet been exposed. The summary included the drug experiments on unwitting people and the assassination attempts on foreign leaders. In other words, it included much of what Sidney Gottlieb had done throughout his career.

Since President Nixon had recently resigned from office because of the

Watergate scandal, Kissinger relayed the summary to Nixon's successor, Gerald Ford. He told Ford that some of the activities mentioned in the summary "clearly were illegal, while others—though not technically illegal—raise profound moral questions." Ford realized that Hersh's story would likely lead to a congressional investigation of the CIA and therefore to the exposure of the rest of the Family Jewels—unless he took action.

In a bout of quick thinking, Ford's deputy chief of staff, Dick Cheney, developed a plan to forestall a congressional investigation of the CIA. What if Ford established his own investigation? That way, Congress would be dissuaded from launching a duplicate investigation, and the executive branch would have control over what got released. Ford jumped at the idea. On January 4, 1975, he established the United States President's Commission on CIA Activities within the United States, otherwise known as the Rockefeller Commission, named after its head, Vice President Nelson Rockefeller.

Ironically, Ford would be the one to let slip the biggest secret of all. On January 16, he held a White House luncheon for the top editors of *The New York Times*. At the end of the hour-long event, one of the editors asked Ford how he expected the Rockefeller Commission to win public trust when many of its members were hard-line conservatives. Ford, in a moment of unexpected honesty, admitted that he had staffed the Rockefeller Commission with people who would allow some of the CIA's skeletons to stay hidden.

"Like what?" asked one of the editors.

"Like assassinations," said Ford.

As soon as the words left his lips, the gravity of what he had said, and to whom he had said it, dawned on him. "That's off the record!" he barked.

Afterward, the editors of *The New York Times* deliberated on whether to publish the fact that the CIA's closet might contain literal skeletons. They ultimately agreed that they were morally obliged to stay quiet, though they didn't stay quiet enough. Word of what happened somehow reached CBS News correspondent Daniel Schorr. Through his aggressive journalism, Schorr had made a habit of antagonizing government officials. President Lyndon Johnson once called him a "prize son-of-a-bitch," and President Nixon put him on his list of enemies. If anyone was going to break the story of CIA assassinations, it was him.

On February 27, Schorr sat down to interview DCI William Colby. In the middle of the interview, Schorr mentioned that he had heard about Ford's gaffe. Colby fell silent.

"Has the CIA ever killed anybody in this country?" Schorr asked in his blunt manner.

"Not in this country," Colby said.

"Not in this country!" Schorr was astounded by the implication that the CIA had killed people *out* of the country. "Who?" he demanded.

"I can't talk about it."

"Hammarskjöld?" a United Nations secretary general who had died in a mysterious plane crash.

"No, of course not!"

"Lumumba?"

At this suggestion, Colby ended the discussion. "I can't go down any list with you, sorry."

The next day, Schorr taped a news segment for CBS that began, "President Ford has reportedly warned associates that if current investigations go too far they could uncover several assassinations of foreign officials involving the CIA." The cat was out of the bag. Ford now had no choice but to tell the Rockefeller Commission to add assassinations to its list of CIA activities to investigate, the very activity that the commission had been created to conceal.

Former DCI Richard Helms was furious that the CIA's secrets—the very secrets that he had spent his career protecting—were now being flaunted in the press. And from his perspective, nobody bore more blame than Colby. It was Colby who had been responsible for collecting the Family Jewels, which had led to Hersh's story in *The New York Times*, which had led to the creation of the Rockefeller Commission, which had led to Ford's gaffe. As far as Helms was concerned, Colby had betrayed the CIA, and Daniel Schorr was his accomplice.

On April 28, 1975, Helms, now the U.S. ambassador to Iran, privately testified before the Rockefeller Commission. A group of journalists, including Schorr, waited outside the room to question him. When he emerged from behind the door, his face was ashen and he looked fatigued. The testimony had obviously been a grueling process.

"Welcome back," Schorr said.

Helms couldn't contain his blind rage. "You son of a bitch!" he shouted.

"You killer! You cocksucker!" He strung together every expletive imaginable before softening his tone. "Mr. Schorr, I didn't like what you had to say on some of your broadcasts on this subject. And I don't think it was fair, and I don't think it was right. As far as I know, the CIA was never responsible for assassinating any foreign leader."

A journalist in the group spoke up, "Were there discussions about possible assassinations?"

"I don't know whether I stopped beating my wife," Helms said, indicating that the reporter was asking a loaded question. "There are always discussions about practically everything under the sun."

"Of assassinations?"

"Of everything under the sun."

"But you never answered my question," noted the journalist.

"Well, I'm not trying to answer your question."

During one of Colby's own appearances before the Rockefeller Commission, he acknowledged that the CIA had previously attempted to assassinate foreign leaders. Vice President Nelson Rockefeller pulled him aside and whispered, "Bill, do you really have to present all this material to us? We realize that there are secrets that you fellows need to keep." The other members of the Rockefeller Commission weren't so obsequious. They produced an eighty-six-page section on CIA assassination plots for the commission's final report, but Henry Kissinger and Dick Cheney led a successful effort to remove it before publication.

The section has since been declassified. It mostly contains interviews of government officials, among them Richard Bissell, McGeorge Bundy, Richard Helms, Edward Lansdale, John McCone, Walt Rostow, and Maxwell Taylor. Most claimed never to have participated in any conversations about assassinations. Some claimed that even if the conversations had occurred, they couldn't remember them.

In June 1975, the Rockefeller Commission issued its final report. Along with substantiating the allegations in Seymour Hersh's *New York Times* story, it revealed many other disturbing facts. For one, it confirmed that the CIA was capable of forging birth certificates, driver's licenses, and Social Security cards. More importantly, the report contains the first public acknowledgment of MKULTRA. In a section on science and technology, it says:

The Agency has tested some of its new scientific and technological developments in the United States. One such program included the testing of certain behavior-influencing drugs. . . . Some tests were directed against unsuspecting subjects, most of whom were U.S. citizens. . . . The drug program was part of a much larger CIA program to study possible means for controlling human behavior. Other studies explored the effects of radiation, electric-shock, psychology, psychiatry, sociology and harassment substances. . . . Unfortunately, only limited records of the testing conducted in these drug programs are now available. . . . It was clearly illegal to test potentially dangerous drugs on unsuspecting United States citizens.

The Rockefeller Commission discovered little of substance about MK-ULTRA because Gottlieb had destroyed the relevant files. However, the report does describe one important incident from 1953:

LSD was administered to an employee of the Department of the Army without his knowledge while he was attending a meeting with CIA personnel working on the drug project. . . . This individual was not made aware that he had been given LSD until about 20 minutes after it had been administered. He developed serious side effects and was sent to New York with a CIA escort for psychiatric treatment. Several days later, he jumped from a tenth-floor window of his room and died as a result.

The truth was finally coming out.

Frank Olson's death had caused his wife, Alice, and their three children, Eric, Nils, and Lisa, immense grief. Alice turned to the bottle for solace. She became an alcoholic, frequently locking herself in the bathroom to escape her responsibilities. Her kids would often come home from school and find her passed out at the kitchen table. One Christmas Eve, she was arrested for driving while intoxicated. "Sometimes she was a mean drunk," Eric said. "For a long time, the subject of my father was strictly taboo in our house." Nils added, "The most innocent of questions about my father would set her off. She would fly into a rage and burst into tears."

Not until over twenty years after Olson died did his family learn what had really happened to him. On June 11, 1975, Eric received a phone call from his brother-in-law, whose voice was loud and rushed.

"Have you seen today's *Washington Post*?"

"No," Eric said. "Why?"

"There's a story in it that you need to read right away. It's about your father."

"My father? What about my father?"

"Go out and get a copy. Then call me back."

Eric ran down the street and grabbed the newspaper from a kiosk. "Suicide Revealed," read the headline, in reference to the Rockefeller Commission report. "A civilian employee of the Department of the Army unwittingly took LSD as part of a Central Intelligence Agency test, then jumped 10 floors to his death less than a week later."

Eric stood there silently, transfixed by the story. Two paragraphs in, his hands began to shake. He thought to himself, "At long last, after all this time, some sort of news arrives." He had finally gotten confirmation of what he had long suspected, that there was more to his father's death than what he had been told.

The Olsons prepared to file a lawsuit against the CIA. The Ford administration, fearing a public relations nightmare, invited them to the White House for a personal meeting with the president, during which Ford issued a formal apology on behalf of the United States government. Eric later said that he only accepted the apology because the grandeur of the Oval Office clouded his thinking: "You go into that sacred place, that oval, and you're really in a special charmed circle and you can't think straight. It works. It really works."

While in Washington, D.C., the Olsons also met with DCI William Colby. He likewise apologized to them, saying, "This is a terrible thing. It never should have happened. Some of our people were out of control in those days." Before they left, he handed them a packet of declassified documents containing everything that the CIA could find regarding the death of Frank Olson.

The CIA eventually paid the Olsons $750,000 in exchange for their agreement not to file a lawsuit. From the CIA's perspective, disaster had been averted. But more revelations were lurking just around the corner.

22

The Investigations

The public wouldn't have to wait long to learn additional details about MKULTRA. In the coming years, a flood of information would pour forth from the spigot of congressional investigations.

Prior to these investigations, congressional oversight of the intelligence community had been careless at best. Some critics joked that Congress was a "blind and toothless watchdog." Throughout the 1950s, the Senate subcommittee responsible for monitoring the CIA met less than once per year. The equivalent subcommittee in the House of Representatives met once per year for two hours, during which "we accomplished virtually nothing," said one member. The CIA was perfectly happy with the arrangement. No oversight meant no accountability. Allen Dulles, the longest-serving director of central intelligence (1953–1961), once said that he felt an obligation to inform only one person of the CIA's activities: the president of the United States, and only if he asked.

DCI William Colby later acknowledged the dangers of Dulles's philosophy. "The old tradition," he told a reporter for the *Chicago Tribune*, "was a consensus that intelligence was apart from the rules. That day is over. I'm glad it's over. Because I think that was the reason we did step over the line in a few cases, largely because no one was watching. No one was there to say 'Don't do that.'"

President Ford had established the Rockefeller Commission to prevent a congressional investigation of the intelligence community, but its revelations only whetted the appetites of congressmen eager to gain notoriety by exposing other skeletons. In 1975, the Senate created a select committee to investigate the past abuses of the CIA, NSA, FBI, and IRS. Chaired by an ambitious senator named Frank Church, the Church Committee, as it came to be known, uncovered a number of activities that it deemed "massive wrong-doing." These included HTLINGUAL, MHCHAOS, MKULTRA, the CIA's participation in assassination attempts, the NSA's secret monitoring of telecommunications traffic, and the FBI's COINTELPRO (*Counter Intelligence Program*), an analogue to MHCHAOS that spied on and harassed political organizations and civil rights activists. Regarding MKULTRA, the Church Committee said that the project demonstrated "a fundamental disregard for the value of human life." Senator Church famously called the CIA "a rogue elephant on a rampage." To many Americans, the intelligence community seemed to have become a version of the authoritarian state that it had sworn to protect them against.

Unlike the Rockefeller Commission, the Church Committee interviewed CIA personnel associated with MKULTRA, including Sidney Gottlieb. The itinerant chemist and his wife had just left India to take an overland bus tour of the Middle East when he received a letter from the Church Committee summoning him to the United States for questioning.

As soon as Gottlieb landed in Washington, D.C., he called attorney Terry Lenzner to ask for legal representation. Lenzner, the former chief counsel for the Senate Watergate Committee, later remembered talking to Gottlieb on the phone for the first time: "[His] husky voice had a pronounced stutter, but he came across as confident, not nervous." Soon after the call, they met in person. "As I sat waiting on a park bench, a man with a limp came toward me. He was casually dressed, his clubfoot dragging behind him." Gottlieb approached cautiously, "casting furtive glances around him—subtly enough that it was clear to me he had been well trained in the art of countersurveillance."

At the meeting, Gottlieb asked Lenzner for a sample of his handwriting, explaining, "I have someone at the agency who can analyze it and tell me whether I should trust you." Lenzner jotted down some random words onto a scrap piece of paper. A few days later, Gottlieb called him. "You checked out," he said. "No character defects." Gottlieb had, in fact, made a wise choice of attorney. Lenzner was able to secure a deal whereby Gottlieb was granted immunity for anything that he discussed during his testimony.

A complete transcript of Gottlieb's testimony has never been released, but Lenzner wrote a firsthand account of what happened. Gottlieb apparently defended the CIA "as the guardian of the country's security" and argued that MKULTRA had been necessary to help win the Cold War.

The testimony took a turn when Senator Richard Schweiker produced a heavily redacted memo labeled "Health Alteration Committee."

"Dr. Gottlieb," Schweiker said, "can you tell me what this memo is about?"

Gottlieb became visibly flustered.

Lenzner covered the microphone. "What's up, Sid?"

Gottlieb whispered, "I need to talk to you about this."

Lenzner asked for a brief recess. He and Gottlieb then fled to a small office and closed the door behind them. Gottlieb had gone pale and was panting for breath. He started doing Tai Chi to calm his nerves.

Lenzner was confused. "Sid, help me out here. What's in the memo?"

"That's the one. The one that worked."

The memo concerned Abd al-Karim Qasim, the Iraqi colonel to whom Gottlieb had mailed a handkerchief doused with tuberculosis. Gottlieb mistakenly believed that the tuberculosis had indeed killed Qasim. Lenzner, thinking quickly, suggested that Gottlieb give a vague explanation for the memo and hope that the senators lost interest.

And that's exactly what happened. Gottlieb testified that the handkerchief had been "treated with some kind of material for the purpose of harassing that person who received it." According to Lenzner, "The senators didn't know enough to ask the right follow-up questions, and Sid made it through the hearing relatively unscathed."

Afterward, Lenzner threatened to sue the government if Gottlieb's name appeared in the Church Committee's final report. The Church Committee reluctantly agreed to use the pseudonym "Joseph Scheider" instead.

Back when James Schlesinger and William Colby were collecting the Family Jewels, an unnamed officer recommended that they investigate the CIA's connection to Fort Detrick. A subsequent investigation led to the discovery of a storage vault in Washington, D.C., that contained the shellfish toxin, cobra venom, and nineteen other "lethal substances" that Nathan Gordon had secretly stashed away in defiance of President Nixon's directive to destroy the country's stockpile of biological weapons. The vault also contained narcotics and hallucinogenic drugs, or what Colby called "the residue of a number of different CIA programs."

Like Gottlieb, Gordon testified before the Church Committee. During his testimony, he rationalized his insubordination in two ways. First, he argued that the shellfish toxin wasn't technically a living organism, and therefore it hadn't been subject to Nixon's directive to destroy *biological* weapons. Second, he claimed that Nixon's directive applied to the Department of Defense, not the CIA.

Gordon's arguments weren't convincing. Senator Walter Mondale chastised him, "As far as I'm concerned, based upon your testimony, the only conceivable way that the President could have his order executed was to have you over to dinner and plead with you." Even former DCI Richard Helms told the Church Committee that Nixon's directive "certainly" applied to the CIA. Nixon had "wanted these things got rid of and whether they were in the Army or the CIA, he wanted them disposed of."

In a televised session of the Church Committee, DCI William Colby explained that the CIA had collected the shellfish toxin to develop a new suicide device for U-2 spy plane pilots. Senator Frank Church, sensing that there was more to the story, pointed to the existence of CIA dart guns as an indication that there was also a desire to use the toxin for assassinations.

"You mention suicides," Church said. "Well, I do not think a suicide is usually accomplished with a dart, particularly a gun that can place the dart in a human heart in such a way that he does not even know that he has been hit."

Colby could only agree. "There is no question about it. It was also for offensive reasons. No question about it."

The Church Committee was eager to hear Colby elaborate on CIA assassination plots, especially because three months earlier, on June 19, 1975, Chicago mobster Sam Giancana was murdered the day before he was supposed to testify about his connection to a CIA plot to assassinate Fidel Castro. Giancana had been shot in the back of the head while frying sausages in his basement kitchen. The killer then turned over his body and shot him six more times in the face. Colby was quick to tell reporters, "We had nothing to do with it."

During Colby's testimony, Senator Church asked with a hint of excitement, "Have you brought with you some of those devices which would have enabled the CIA to use this [shellfish toxin] for killing people?"

"We have, indeed."

In front of the awestruck audience, Colby unveiled a battery-powered dart gun fitted with a telescopic sight. It shot a frozen dart of shellfish toxin that would melt inside of the victim's body, eliminating any trace of the crime. The CIA called the weapon a "non-discernable microbioinoculator." Colby walked it over to Senator Church, who joked, "Don't point it at me."

The dart gun had never been used to assassinate anyone, but it had been tested on sheep. Army weapons specialist Charles Baronian remembered watching one of the tests. The sheep "didn't bleat. It didn't move. It just fell dead. You couldn't help but be impressed."

When Senator Howard Baker questioned Colby, he asked, "Mr. Colby, it is clear to me from the evidence at hand that somebody authorized the formulation, the development and the retention of these toxic materials. Can you tell me who did that?"

"The development," Colby stammered, "the research and development, I think, was begun in the sixties, the early sixties. I cannot tell you specifically who authorized it."

"Is there a record that would tell us who did it?"

"The records are very incomplete, as you know, sir."

"Why are they incomplete?"

"Some of them apparently have been destroyed."

"Do you know who destroyed them?"

"I do. I have a report that one set was destroyed by the Chief of the Division in question before his retirement."

"Do you know who that was?"

"Mr. Gottlieb."

"Is that Mr. Sidney Gottlieb?"

"Yes."

On live television, Colby and the Church Committee associated one name with the suspicious activities of the CIA's past: Sidney Gottlieb. The public was eager to learn more about this mysterious figure whom newspapers quickly dubbed "Dr. Death."

One month after the Senate created the Church Committee, the House of Representatives similarly created the Pike Committee to investigate the past abuses of the intelligence community. Representative Otis Pike, the committee's silver-haired and silver-tongued chairman, argued that he should have access to all relevant CIA documents. Otherwise, the executive branch would have dictatorial control over those documents, undermining the constitutional system of checks and balances between the separate branches of government.

The CIA refused to comply. Donald Gregg, the CIA officer responsible for responding to the Pike Committee's requests for documents, said that the experience "made my tour in Vietnam seem like a picnic. I would vastly prefer to fight the Viet Cong than deal with a polemical investigation by a Congressional committee." When a White House attorney accidentally left a notebook containing classified information in Pike's office, Pike couldn't help but highlight the hypocrisy of the situation. The executive branch was refusing to share classified documents because it claimed that doing so would jeopardize national security, yet its employees were losing those very documents. Pike returned the notebook to President Ford with a snide cover letter saying, "If he loses it again, it's O.K., I have a copy."

Compared to the Church Committee, the Pike Committee was less focused on specific programs and more focused on systemic problems. It concluded that the CIA was "prejudiced by political judgments and wishful thinking" and had consistently failed to predict the outbreak of major events, such as the Tet Offensive, the Soviet invasion of Czechoslovakia, the Yom Kippur War, and India's first nuclear test. An internal CIA report agreed, calling its own predictions "simply, obviously, and starkly wrong." However, the CIA refused to say so publicly, both out of spite for Pike and a desire to save face.

The Pike Committee further concluded that the CIA wasn't quite the "rogue elephant" that Senator Frank Church portrayed it as. In many cases, the CIA had simply been following the orders of the president, not acting on its own. MKULTRA, of course, was the main exception. But even MKULTRA wasn't so much a rogue elephant as it was a rogue tentacle, a semiautonomous appendage connected to the body of a larger creature—the CIA—that swam in murky waters.

Pike's opponents in Congress prevented his committee from publishing its final report, but a copy was leaked to CBS News correspondent Daniel Schorr. Called before Congress to testify about the leak, Schorr refused to divulge his source at the risk of imprisonment. "To betray a source," he said in his opening statement, "would be for me to betray myself, my career, and my life." CBS subsequently forced him to retire.

The intelligence community had never before been so thoroughly scrutinized as it was by the Rockefeller Commission, the Church Committee, and the Pike Committee. *The New York Times* went so far as to call 1975 the "Year of Intelligence" because of the three investigations. Within the intelligence community, however, 1975 was often referred to as the annus horribilis.

In 1976, President Ford pressured DCI William Colby into resigning. Ford wanted new leadership in the CIA, especially because Colby had lost the respect of his colleagues for having collected the Family Jewels, cooperated with the Church Committee, and criticized the CIA's culture of secrecy and compartmentalization. In the eyes of many members of the intelligence community, Colby had betrayed them.

Twenty years later, in 1996, Colby's dead body was found in an offshoot of the Potomac River. His green canoe was nearby, weighed down with sand. The CIA, which had exclusive control of the death scene, said that there were no signs of foul play. The medical examiner suspected that Colby had suffered a heart attack while canoeing, fell into the water, and drowned.

Not everyone believed the official explanation. Colby's body wasn't bloated or disfigured, as is common in drowning victims. Also, the supposed time of death was around 10:00 P.M., an odd time to go canoeing. Lastly, one of Colby's neighbors had visited his home after he went missing. The door was unlocked, the radio was on, and the remnants of a meal were left sitting on the kitchen table.

23

The Hearings

On the recommendations of the Church and Pike Committees, President Ford issued executive orders that strengthened oversight of the intelligence community, prevented drug testing on unwitting people, and banned government employees from engaging in, or conspiring to engage in, "political" assassinations. The second of these orders was in direct response to MKULTRA. Even so, the public still knew relatively little about the project. If more were to be learned, there would need to be another congressional investigation. Fortunately, in August 1977, the Senate Select Committee on Intelligence and the Subcommittee on Health and Scientific Research agreed to hold a joint hearing on "Project MKULTRA: The CIA's Program of Research in Behavioral Modification."

Given that Sidney Gottlieb had destroyed the MKULTRA files, the members of the two committees originally thought that they would have to conduct interviews to obtain any new information. That is until former State Department official John Marks filed a Freedom of Information Act (FOIA) request for any and all extant files related to MKULTRA. An initial search of the CIA records center found nothing, but archivist Frank Laubinger led a second search and found seven boxes of MKULTRA files hidden away in the obscure Budget and Fiscal section. Unbeknownst to Gottlieb, these boxes had been sent to the records center in 1970 for safekeeping. They contained thousands of pages of material, none of which were thought to have survived. Most of the files concerned meticulous financial matters — including one acknowledgment of a receipt for $0.05 — but in aggregate they painted the clearest picture yet of MKULTRA.

The CIA could have easily lied about the existence of the files. Or it could have issued the famous *Glomar* response, "We can neither confirm nor deny . . ." Or it could have refused to release the files under the pretense that doing so would jeopardize national security. Instead, Admiral Stansfield Turner, the new director of central intelligence, wanted the files released. Ever since the Year of Intelligence, journalists and congressional committees had been airing out the CIA's dirty laundry. Better, he thought, to add these files to the heap and bear the inevitable backlash now rather than later.

The files played a pivotal role in the joint hearing on MKULTRA, mainly because they demonstrated the depravity of Operation Midnight Climax. At one point, Senator Edward Kennedy asked Turner about what conclusions could be drawn from the fact that the inventory list for the San Francisco safe house included surveillance equipment. Turner feigned ignorance and said that there were none. The court reporter was kind enough to record "general laughter" in the audience.

Kennedy followed up, "Is it plausible that Dr. Gottlieb would not understand the full range of activities in those particular safe houses?"

"Let me say it is unlikely," Turner replied. "I don't know Mr. Gottlieb."

"Has anybody in the Agency talked with Mr. Gottlieb to find out about this?"

"Not since this revelation [about the files] has come out."

"Not since this revelation? Well, why not?"

"He has left our employ, Senator."

"Does that mean that anybody who leaves is, you know, covered for lifetime?"

"No, sir."

Senator Kennedy was baffled. "Why wouldn't you talk with him and find out? You have new information about this program. It has been a matter of considerable interest both to our committee and to the Intelligence Committee. Why wouldn't you talk to Mr. Gottlieb?"

Turner didn't have an answer other than to say, "We would be happy to contact Dr. Gottlieb."

"Well, it's amazing to me," Kennedy said in exasperation. "Every single document that the staff reviews has Mr. Gottlieb's name on it and you come to tell us that . . . Mr. Gottlieb has not been talked to?"

Kennedy had raised a good point. Gottlieb's name appears on a large number of the documents released under the FOIA request. Curiously, most of the other names on the documents were redacted. By leaving Gottlieb's name and redacting the rest, the CIA was attempting to portray MKULTRA as the product of a lone, rogue employee. Gottlieb, the outsider, was to blame for what had happened, not the CIA's lack of oversight and culture of compartmentalization.

Gottlieb later said that he felt "victimized and appalled" by the CIA's decision to make him a scapegoat. Richard Helms sympathized with his old friend. "Ah—poor Sid Gottlieb," he said. "The nation just saw something they didn't like and blasted it, and he took the blame."

In September 1977, the Senate Subcommittee on Health and Scientific Research cajoled Gottlieb and the other principal figures of MKULTRA into testifying at a second hearing, this one specifically on "Human Drug Testing by the CIA." Gottlieb and Margaret had since returned from India and were living in San Francisco near their daughter and grandchildren. A lifelong stutterer, Gottlieb was taking classes at San Jose State University to earn a master's degree in speech pathology. "Sid is going to school two days a week and getting all A's," Margaret wrote in a letter to her relatives:

> He is going to start sailing lessons today, and gracious knows what that will lead to. We go to various kinds of dances four or five times a week and, to top it off, we got a 5' by 9' rug which we are hooking together. . . . We go wine tasting in the Santa Clara Valley. We have been hiking with the Sierra Club once or twice, we have been down to Monterey and Carmel a couple of times, we drove up to the Napa Valley, and we have friends from our college days in San Francisco whom we visit once in a while.

Before testifying at the hearing, Gottlieb claimed to have developed a heart condition that prevented him from speaking in front of large audiences. He was therefore allowed to testify in a private anteroom, thus eluding the throng of reporters that had gathered for the occasion. The reporters nevertheless caught a glimpse of him as he walked to the anteroom. One of them described him as "distinguished-looking . . . with thinning gray hair." Another managed to snap his photo, which appeared on the front page of *The New York Times*. It shows an aging man in a suit and tie, his hands clasped together, his head hung somberly as if contemplating his past—or perhaps his future.

Gottlieb's attorney, Terry Lenzner, knew that the morning newspapers would likely skewer anyone associated with MKULTRA. In a last-ditch effort to salvage his client's reputation, he asked Gottlieb, "Is there anything you can add to your opening statement that the reporters can focus on? Anything that would make news?" Lenzner's goal was to distract the press.

"Well, there is one thing," Gottlieb said. "I think that it's classified, though."

"What is it?"

Gottlieb told Lenzner a brief story.

Lenzner smiled. "We are going to declassify it right now."

Senator Edward Kennedy banged his gavel to bring the hearing to order. Gottlieb was sworn in. During his opening statement, he stammered through a brief history of MKULTRA and concluded with a plea for understanding, "I would like this committee to know that I considered all this work—at the time it was done and in the context of circumstances that were extant in that period—to be extremely unpleasant, extremely difficult, extremely sensitive but, above all, to be extremely urgent and important."

When he finished reading his prepared comments, he asked if he could describe an additional incident that he had forgotten to mention. This was the distraction.

"Fine," Kennedy said.

Gottlieb proceeded to explain how several years earlier, President Richard Nixon had visited a "potentially hostile country." Upon returning to the United States, the physician accompanying Nixon "reported some—I do not quite know how to describe it—some unusual feelings."

Kennedy wanted clarification. "Are you suggesting that at least these people, the Presidential party, were drugged by a foreign country?"

Gottlieb said that it was a possibility.

The press bit the bait. "Presidential Party Drugged in 1971" read a subsequent headline. Gottlieb may have been the master of dirty tricks, but Lenzner was a capable understudy.

The rest of Gottlieb's testimony covered various aspects of MKULTRA, from drugs to safe houses to cutout organizations. He complained of a bad memory throughout, almost as if he himself had been drugged. During a discussion of Operation Midnight Climax, Kennedy grew tired of his evasive answers and asked in exhaustion, "Can you tell us what was learned from the years of the operation of the safe house? Was it useful? What can you tell us?"

Gottlieb said that he had learned "more about what you could not do than what you could do. . . . I think the conclusion from all the activities was that it was very difficult to predictably manipulate human behavior in this way."

The most intense moment of the testimony came when Kennedy asked Gottlieb whether the death of Frank Olson had caused him to reconsider MKULTRA.

"It certainly did," Gottlieb said. "That was a traumatic period for us as far as I am concerned. It was a great tragedy. . . . It caused me a lot of personal anguish. I considered resigning from the CIA and going into other work because it affected me that way."

Senator John Chafee then asked whether any safeguards had been put in place following Olson's death.

Gottlieb vacillated before admitting that there hadn't been.

"You still had unwitting subjects, so best as you can recall, despite the concern that was shown over the death of Mr. Olson?"

Gottlieb sheepishly replied, "My answer would be yes."

"The decision was, don't change anything?"

"Well, the best I can respond to that, that seems to be the case."

After the hearing, Richard Helms wrote to Gottlieb expressing his sympathy. Gottlieb began a letter in response, "I wondered how confirmation of the Nixon doctors story came out so immediately after my testimony. Now I know, and I thank you for it." He went on to complain that the hearing "was run at the lowest possible level." The senators seemed to be mostly interested in "how many prostitutes one could fit on the end of a needle, and not at all on the larger and more significant issues that might conceivably be of interest to their committee."

Gottlieb wasn't entirely wrong. The hearing had only covered a few sensational aspects of MKULTRA. Still, the thirty-six pages of his testimony gave the public the most personal account of the project ever made up to that point. Yet much more would soon be revealed.

Sidney Gottlieb, the head of MKULTRA. CIA

Profile of Sidney Gottlieb. CIA

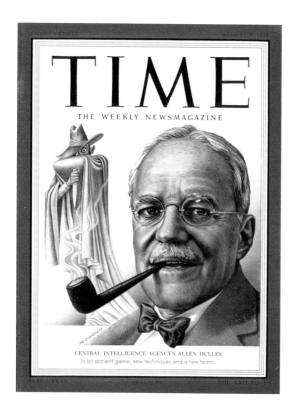

DCI Allen Dulles on the cover of *Time* magazine in 1953, the year that he established MKULTRA. WIKIMEDIA COMMONS

Frank Olson, one of the scientists
dosed with LSD at the Deep Creek
retreat. WIKIMEDIA COMMONS

The Statler Hotel in New York. Room
1018A, from which Frank Olson "fell . . .
or jumped," is circled. WIKIMEDIA COMMONS

Allen Dulles's reprimand of Sidney Gottlieb
following the Frank Olson incident. CIA

CENTRAL INTELLIGENCE AGENCY
WASHINGTON 25, D. C.

OFFICE OF THE DIRECTOR

FEB 10 1954

PERSONAL

Dr. Sidney Gottlieb
Chief, Chemical Division
Technical Services Staff

Dear Dr. Gottlieb:

I have personally reviewed the files from your
office concerning the use of a drug on an unwitting group
of individuals. In recommending the unwitting application
of the drug to your superior, you apparently did not give
sufficient emphasis to the necessity for medical collaboration and for proper consideration of the rights of the
individual to whom it was being administered. This is to
inform you that it is my opinion that you exercised poor
judgment in this case.

Sincerely,

Allen V. Dulles
Director

TOP LEFT: George White, the Bureau of Narcotics agent who ran Operation Midnight Climax. SUA

TOP RIGHT: Dr. Ewen Cameron, the psychiatrist who conducted "psychic driving" and "depatterning" experiments on his patients at the Allan Memorial Institute. McCORD STEWART MUSEUM

ABOVE: The Allan Memorial Institute in Montreal. McCORD STEWART MUSEUM

AT LEFT: Joseph Rauh, the fiery veteran attorney who conducted most of the depositions. LOC

BELOW: The drama of the depositions. Here Sidney Gottlieb slips up. LOC

1	the Church Committee Assassination Report and ask him to
2	read item "P" and then tell me if he is "Scheider" and tell
3	me if he personally took vial poison to the Congo for the
4	purpose of assassinating Patrice Lumumba.
5	(Witness perusing document.)
6	MR. STRICKLAND: May I see you outside a moment?
7	(Witness and counsel confer outside the hearing room.)
8	BY MR. RAUH:
9	Q My question, Dr. Gottlieb, are you the Scheider
10	referred to?
11	A Yes.
12	MR. STRICKLAND: Objection.
13	BY MR. RAUH:
14	Q What did you say?
15	MR. STRICKLAND: Objection.
16	THE WITNESS: I am not at liberty to answer that
17	question.
18	BY MR. RAUH:
19	Q I thought I heard you say "yes"?
20	A I never said yes.

TOP LEFT: Congolese leader Patrice Lumumba, whom Sidney Gottlieb planned to kill with anthrax. NATIONAAL ARCHIEF

TOP RIGHT: Cuban leader Fidel Castro, the target of multiple CIA assassination plots. LOC

BOTTOM LEFT: DCI Richard Helms, a champion of MKULTRA who approved the destruction of its files. NARA

BOTTOM RIGHT: DCI William Colby, a critic of MKULTRA who was involved in the collection of the CIA's "Family Jewels." NARA

DRAFT ████ — A
21 May 1953

MEMORANDUM FOR: THE RECORD

SUBJECT: Project MKULTRA, Subproject 3

1. This project will involve the realistic testing of certain research and development items of interest to CD/TSS.

2. During the course of research and development it is sometimes found that certain very necessary experiments or tests are not suited to ordinary laboratory conditions. At the same time it would be difficult, if not impossible, to conduct them as operational field tests. This project is designed to provide facilities to fill this intermediate requirement.

3. This project will be conducted by ████████████████ — C Certain support activities will be provided by CD/TSS and APD/TSS.

4. The total cost of this project for a period of one year will not exceed $8,875.00.

████████████████████████
Chemical Division/TSS — A

APPROVED: _____

████████████████████████
for SIDNEY GOTTLIEB — A
Chief, Chemical Division, TSS

PROGRAM APPROVED   APPROVED FOR
AND RECOMMENDED: OBLIGATION OF FUNDS:

████████ — A   ████████ — A
Research Chairman   Research Director

Date: MAY 2 5 1953   Date: 25 may, 1953.

Original Only.

TOP SECRET
Security Information

A declassified MKULTRA document showing how the CIA redacted most names except for Sidney Gottlieb's. CIA

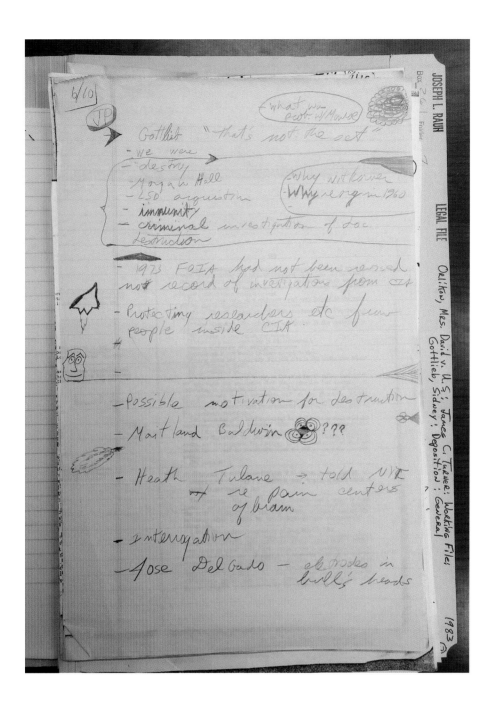

Attorney James Turner's notes for one of his depositions
with Sidney Gottlieb. LOC

Friday, December 20, 1957

354th Day—11 days to follow

CLEAR
CLOUDY
RAIN
SNOW

home flu —

X mas party Fed bldg
Press Room

The entry in George White's diary for December 20, 1957,
the day that Wayne Ritchie attended a Christmas party and
lost his mind: "Xmas party Fed bldg Press Room." SUA

24

Victims Task Force

George White, the alcoholic narcotics agent who ran Operation Midnight Climax, died in 1975, predictably from cirrhosis of the liver. The dark threads of his past, however, were only beginning to unravel. That same year, at the request of the Church Committee, the CIA created a Victims Task Force to track down White's unwitting victims and inform them that they had been guinea pigs in a secret drug experiment.

Archivist Frank Laubinger led the task force. Having found the seven boxes of MKULTRA files in the CIA records center, he was a skilled investigator. In 1979, he traveled to the West Coast to interview former CIA personnel and analyze George White's personal diary, which had been donated to the Electronics Museum at Foothill Community College in San Jose, California. "I will travel overtly as CIA," Laubinger wrote in a proposal, "use CIA credentials when and if required, and will at no time use any type of cover for these activities." To persuade former CIA personnel to talk to him, "I will assure each officer that my assignment is to attempt to identify victims, not to put former officers in jeopardy."

Laubinger made his first stop in San Jose to see White's diary. While flipping through its dingy pages of barely-legible scrawl, he spotted several references to Thomas Hansen, the former head of the U.S. Secret Service Office in San Francisco. White and Hansen had apparently been regulars at the Kuo Wah Restaurant in Chinatown. Perhaps White let slip the names of some of his victims during these drunken meals.

Laubinger decided to pay Hansen a visit. When he knocked on his front door, a woman answered. Laubinger identified himself and his purpose, prompting some "muffled conversation" behind the door. The woman then "advised me that Mr. Hansen would neither speak to me on the phone or in person. In further attempts to 'just speak to him for a moment,' I was told . . . that Mr. Hansen has been consistently and unduly bothered by representatives of various media concerning his long-time association with George White and is, therefore, 'fed up' and . . . adamantly refused to discuss the issue with anyone." Laubinger left empty-handed, but White's diary had given him plenty of other leads.

Meanwhile, Laubinger himself had unintentionally left a trail of leads for others to follow. Tracking his activity in California, journalist John Crewdson of *The New York Times* learned of the existence of White's diary. Crewdson paid an employee at the Electronics Museum seventy-five dollars a day to let him see it on a weekend when the museum was closed. A rival journalist from *The Washington Post,* sniffing a story, demanded to be let inside the museum, but the employee refused to give him similar access. It wasn't until an editor at *The Washington Post* persuaded California governor Jerry Brown to intervene (by threatening to not support his reelection campaign) that the museum finally opened its doors.

On April 26, 1979, Laubinger landed an interview with White's accomplice Ike Feldman. In his notes of the interview, Laubinger wrote that Feldman recalled once having attended a meeting with White and Allen Dulles, during which "various means of assassination were discussed." Feldman didn't reveal anything relevant to the Victims Task Force, but he said that he might be able to remember more if given total immunity. Laubinger didn't have that kind of power, so he moved on.

Four days later, Laubinger sent Sidney Gottlieb a letter full of questions about Operation Midnight Climax: Who were the victims? How many were there? Did the CIA ever follow up with them? He ended the letter, "This entire subject will soon be relegated to history." Laubinger knew that Gottlieb would be reluctant to revisit the past, and he hoped that this small bit of reassurance would lower his defenses.

When Gottlieb received the letter, he called Laubinger on the phone so that he could speak his responses rather than write them down. Not that it mattered. Gottlieb didn't remember the names of any victims, nor did he remember how many there were. In fact, he claimed not to remember much at all.

Regardless, Laubinger soon got his first big break. Sometime while interviewing former CIA personnel, he learned that one of the victims had been a young nightclub singer in San Francisco named Ruth Kelley. Laubinger refused to divulge his source, saying in a deposition, "I feel morally obliged not to directly answer that question." He had promised his interviewees that he would never reveal their identities if they helped him identify victims. "So the only real attribution is in my head. And it would be a breach of faith for me to tell you people who said it."

One night in 1960, just before Kelley was scheduled to perform at the Black Sheep, someone—Laubinger maintained that it wasn't George White—spiked her cocktail with LSD. Liz Evans, a prostitute who had worked for White, remembered, "She nearly flipped out during her set, but somehow managed to hold on. After she finished, she ran outside and got a cab to take her to the hospital." Laubinger's source told him that Kelley had since become a teetotaler and "was not going to touch alcohol again."

Laubinger next began tracking down every person mentioned in White's diary to determine whether any of them were victims of Operation Midnight Climax. One man said that he had seen White give LSD to a woman at a dinner party. The man only vaguely remembered the woman and at the time had "passed her off as some kook." He recalled thinking to himself, "Geez, where did George pick this one up?"

Laubinger had better luck visiting the addresses listed in the diary. At one house he met a woman who knew White. "She does not believe that she was ever given a dose of LSD," Laubinger wrote. She did, however, help identify two other women of interest: Barbara Smithe and Clarice Stein.

Barbara was the woman whose husband, Eliot, had been away when White drugged her with LSD, even though she was caring for her baby daughter. Following the incident, she left Eliot, moved back in with her parents, experienced acute paranoia, and spent the rest of her life in various sanitariums receiving electroshock therapy. She died six months before the creation of the Victims Task Force.

Clarice was living in New York City and agreed to talk to Laubinger over the phone. She characterized her time with White as "the worst experience of [my] life." The night of the drugging, she had taken a taxi home and couldn't sleep because colored lights kept flashing through her mind. She called White to ask him what was happening, but he was "totally unsympathetic," told her to go to sleep, and hung up the phone.

Given the sensational nature of Clarice's claims, Laubinger visited her in person to confirm her identity. When they met in August 1979, she was suffering from a rare blood disorder and wondered aloud whether the LSD had caused her condition. Laubinger considered this "exceedingly unlikely." During the meeting, Clarice and her husband "spoke favorably of [the] CIA, seemed to genuinely appreciate our efforts to find her, indicated a personal interest in intelligence activities, and asked if a tour of the Agency could be arranged for her." Laubinger informed them that CIA headquarters was closed to the public, but "in view of her unique relationship to the Agency, I would see if something could be arranged." If nothing else, "I would treat her to lunch in our Rendezvous Room."

By the time that the Victims Task Force disbanded in late 1979, Laubinger had contacted twelve of the fifteen potential unwitting victims mentioned in White's diary. Some of them insisted, "It didn't happen to me." Others told him, "Thanks, I learned that a long time ago. Please go away and leave me alone." Clarice was the only one who sued the CIA. She initially sought $150,000 in damages, but she settled for $15,000, plus the lunch.

As insignificant as her lawsuit may have seemed at the time, it was a harbinger of things to come.

25

The Lawsuits

The Victims Task Force had focused on finding the victims of Operation Midnight Climax, not the victims of the other MKULTRA subprojects. According to a CIA memo, those other subprojects had been run by "reputable, some even eminent, scientists" who bore full responsibility for their own actions. "Most of [their research] would have been done whether or not [the] CIA provided support." But even though the CIA didn't consider itself responsible for what had happened, others did, and they wanted justice.

In 1979, seven prisoners from the Atlanta Federal Penitentiary filed a lawsuit against the CIA for funding the drug experiments of Carl Pfeiffer. (The number of plaintiffs was later reduced to six because one of them escaped from prison.) Attorney Thomas Maddox represented the prisoners. As part of the lawsuit, he took the depositions of several former CIA personnel associated with MKULTRA, including Sidney Gottlieb.

Paul Figley, an attorney for the Department of Justice, accompanied Gottlieb to his deposition with Maddox. "I remember we drove up that morning," Figley said in a later interview. "It wasn't that far from D.C. I thought that Tom [Maddox] was going to rent some kind of conference room, but he just had the deposition in his hotel room, so we were sitting on the beds. It was very informal."

Before the deposition began, Figley told Gottlieb to answer the specific questions asked, nothing more: "Tell the truth. Don't volunteer. If the answer's yes, say yes and stop." For some reason, Gottlieb didn't listen. He instead spoke openly and honestly, just as he would do during his later depositions with attorneys Joseph Rauh and James Turner.

Figley, in turn, got to take the depositions of the prisoners who had filed the lawsuit. Some of them were still incarcerated at the Atlanta Federal Penitentiary; the rest were in prisons scattered across the South. Figley believed "in my heart of hearts" that only two of them had participated in Pfeiffer's drug experiments. The others, he thought, had joined the lawsuit either to make money or to get a reprieve from the monotony of prison life. "If you're in prison, anything that's different is fun."

Although Maddox and Figley were on opposite sides of the lawsuit, they remained cordial throughout the depositions, unlike Rauh and the CIA attorneys. In fact, Figley called Maddox "very professional on one level, but he was also very personable. We got along pretty well." On several occasions, "he would guide me to ask things that would be fun for the prisoners and fun for us." For example, before Don Roderick Scott's deposition, Maddox told Figley, "Ask him what he's in for, he's really proud of it." Figley obliged and asked the question.

"I was convicted of bank robbery," Scott said.

"Where was the bank?"

"Some little town in Georgia."

"How did you get caught?"

"Well, I got caught in the men's room."

Figley summarized the rest of the story, laughing as he did: "What had happened was, he and his brother had decided to break into the bank. They got a ladder and they broke into a second story window and he lowered himself down into a men's room. And he wasn't strong enough to climb the rope back out. So he went in on a Friday night and they found him on a Monday morning. He was a bank robber but he never got close to the money."

Another time, Figley walked into a room where a prisoner and a court reporter were already seated for the deposition. The prisoner "had like a mayonnaise jar of iced tea, but it wasn't. It was his spittoon. He was doing it to intimidate and gross out the attorneys that were deposing him. Didn't bother us, but the poor court reporter almost threw up when she realized what it was."

On April 29, 1983, Judge Richard Freeman ruled that the prisoners' lawsuit was invalid because the statute of limitations had expired. Figley didn't think that the lawsuit would have succeeded anyway. The prisoners didn't have any evidence proving that they had suffered damage or injury as a direct result of the drugs. Pfeiffer had conducted the experiments "very carefully by the standards of the time," Figley said. "It's not like the MKULTRA thing where they were dropping things in people's drinks at bars. It was a well-run program by independent scientists trying to do good science."

Other victims of MKULTRA experiments persisted. In 1979, Velma Orlikow, one of Dr. Ewen Cameron's patients at the Allan Memorial Institute in Montreal, filed a lawsuit against the Royal Victoria Hospital, the parent hospital of the Allan. The lawsuit was settled out of court for $50,000. Velma's husband, Canadian politician David Orlikow, then filed a separate lawsuit against the CIA on her behalf. Looking for legal representation, he contacted famed civil rights attorney Joseph Rauh and his young law partner James Turner. Rauh and Turner later remembered, "David Orlikow called our office with a horror story that bordered on the incredible." They agreed to represent Velma on a contingency basis, meaning that they would only be paid out of a future settlement. Eight more plaintiffs, including Jeannine Huard and Mary Morrow, eventually joined the lawsuit.

The legal basis of the lawsuit was the Federal Tort Claims Act of 1946, which waived sovereign immunity for negligent acts of government employees. Rauh and Turner maintained that the CIA had acted negligently by funding dangerous experiments without taking any precautions and by allowing Gottlieb to remain in charge of MKULTRA following the death of Frank Olson.

Rauh and the CIA's general counsel, Daniel Silver, immediately entered into out-of-court negotiations. When Rauh asked for $250,000 per plaintiff, Silver demurred, arguing that the CIA wasn't responsible for Cameron's actions and therefore didn't owe the plaintiffs anywhere close to that amount. An enraged Rauh responded by raising his ask to $1 million per plaintiff, which Silver predictably rejected.

If the CIA had one advantage, it was time. Rauh and the plaintiffs were all in advanced age, and so were the key witnesses whom Rauh planned to depose. The longer it took to go to trial, the better the chances were that the plaintiffs would lose steam—and numbers. In an effort to stall things, the CIA filed a motion to dismiss the lawsuit.

Months passed without a ruling on the motion. The judge in the Orlikow case, John Penn, was notoriously slow, benefitting the CIA. *The Washington Post* once described him as having "the worst record for moving cases forward" and said that he "regularly lists more than a dozen cases that have been awaiting a decision for longer than six months." But finally, on May 27, 1982, Penn denied the CIA's motion to dismiss. The case could now proceed.

By the end of 1983, Rauh and Turner had taken the depositions of Sidney Gottlieb, Richard Helms, Robert Lashbrook, and John Gittinger. Usually present at the depositions was Rauh's nemesis, CIA attorney Lee Strickland. The exchanges between these two veteran attorneys often became bitter and heated. Once when Rauh was grilling Gottlieb about assassination plots, Strickland asked what relevance it had to the Orlikow case.

Rauh replied, "What Dr. Gottlieb has done is to show a reckless disregard of human life. I can think of nothing more relevant to a reckless disregard to human life than carrying poison to someone. That is the relevance."

Strickland fumed, "That is the most outrageous thing I ever heard."

Rauh's ire wasn't confined to Strickland. He criticized every CIA attorney that crossed his path. During a single deposition, he accused one attorney of tipping the witness, called him "unethical," accused another attorney of "covering up for the CIA," and called him "an adversary of the people." He once told an entire group of attorneys, "I think you guys are disgusting." Several times he threatened physical violence. "You're almost going to get a punch in the nose," he would say.

The depositions tended to help the plaintiffs and hurt the CIA. In particular, Robert Lashbrook admitted that his colleague James Monroe had encouraged Ewen Cameron to apply for a grant from the SIHE cutout organization, pointing a finger of culpability at the CIA.

The CIA knew that the depositions were dangerous. Immediately after Rauh took Helms's deposition, CIA attorneys filed a motion to suppress it on the grounds that Helms had accidentally disclosed the location of a secret facility. (The location had, in fact, already been published in *The Washington Post*.) Rauh and Turner soon received a letter informing them that they could be prosecuted for espionage if they didn't relinquish their copies of the deposition. Yet neither of them were fazed. "We resent and reject your letter," they wrote in a joint response. "Mr. Rauh . . . refuses to kneel down before the CIA."

Rauh considered the CIA's motion to suppress the deposition nothing more than an act of intimidation, a stunt meant to make his life more difficult. In a sense, it worked. Rauh grumbled that his other cases were "rather simple" compared to this one.

The Orlikow case slowly gained momentum, especially when Rauh and Turner learned that back in 1977, the CIA had issued an official apology—orally, not in writing—to the Canadian government for funding Cameron's work. This was a veritable smoking gun of culpability. By apologizing, the CIA had essentially admitted that it had done something wrong. Rauh attempted to take the deposition of the CIA station chief in Ottawa to confirm the story, but the CIA filed a motion to stop the deposition from happening. A glacial Judge Penn eventually upheld the motion, depriving Rauh of the opportunity to secure this vital piece of evidence.

Rauh did at least get to take the deposition of John Hadwen, the Canadian foreign service officer who had received the apology. However, Hadwen's attorney, James Mabbutt, repeatedly invoked national security to prevent Hadwen from divulging any relevant information. At one point, Rauh joked that if the relevant information truly was vital to national security, "I am a red-headed Chinese." Rauh was convinced that the CIA had pressured Hadwen and Mabbutt to not cooperate.

For one of the only times in his life, Joseph Rauh felt defeated. The CIA was countering his every move with questionable, if not illegal, tactics. To make matters worse, he was old, aching, and heavily dependent on a cane to walk. In a desperate attempt to settle the case, he sat back down at the negotiating table with CIA attorney Scott Kragie and lowered his ask to $150,000 per plaintiff. Kragie made a counteroffer of $25,000. Rauh, insulted, terminated the negotiation on the spot.

Meanwhile, the CIA was involved in another lawsuit of enormous importance. Back in 1977, activists John Sims and Sidney Wolfe had submitted a FOIA request for the names of the individuals and institutions that the CIA had funded through its cutout organizations. The CIA refused to answer the request, citing a provision in the National Security Act of 1947 that made it responsible for "protecting intelligence sources and methods from unauthorized disclosure." Sims and Wolfe filed a lawsuit to force the CIA to release the names.

In a 7–2 decision, the Supreme Court sided with the CIA. The majority opinion said that only the CIA could determine whether releasing certain information would "lead to an unacceptable risk of compromising the Agency's intelligence-gathering process." In other words, the CIA was its own watchdog. The ruling substantiated a sly comment made by Richard

Helms to a group of newspaper editors: "The nation must, to a degree, take it on faith that we, too, are honorable men devoted to her service."

Furthermore, the ruling hurt the plaintiffs in the Orlikow case. Rauh said that because of it, "identities of key witnesses were concealed from us, documents were withheld." The Supreme Court had thrown a wrench into the gears of justice, preventing the case from proceeding full speed ahead.

With the Orlikow case stalling again, Rauh asked Canadian ambassador to the United States Allan Gotlieb (no relation to Sidney Gottlieb) to publicly announce his support for the plaintiffs. Gotlieb had already written David Orlikow a private letter of support, but he refused to make his views public. Rauh soon learned why. Gotlieb had recently hosted Richard Helms at the Canadian embassy and was actively trying to cultivate him for influence and connections.

Rauh next wrote a direct appeal to Canadian prime minister Brian Mulroney, confessing, "Anger wells up inside as I ask myself why I go on overtaxing my strength with cross-country trips and seven-day workweeks, and I risk bankrupting my small firm to help Canadian citizens whose own government works against them." He wrote in another letter to Mulroney, "It's a hell of a note when a 75-year-old U.S. civil liberties lawyer cares more about these injured Canadian citizens, now in the twilight of life, than their own government." The letters had little effect.

Rauh's health only deteriorated from there. In January 1987, he underwent hip replacement surgery. During the recovery, he suffered a mild heart attack and developed a bleeding ulcer. He was still as fiery as ever, but his body was failing him. Unable to satisfy the rigorous demands of the job, he decided to retire from law. "I say goodbye," he wrote to the plaintiffs, "with three cheers for your valor and with confidence that both the ultimate outcome of the case and the verdict of history will vindicate my belief . . . that neither the CIA nor any similar body can forever be above the law in a functioning democracy."

Now that Rauh was out of the picture, the CIA went on the offensive. It launched an aggressive publicity campaign to inform people that the Canadian government had also funded Cameron's experiments and was just as culpable for what had happened. Legally, the publicity campaign was an irrelevant red herring, but it succeeded in convincing the Canadian government to downplay the damage done by Cameron. After all, the plaintiffs in the Orlikow case might decide to file more lawsuits in the future. Hoping to deter such lawsuits, the Canadian government gave each of the plaintiffs an ex gratia payment of $20,000.

The buzz surrounding the Orlikow case prompted newspapers across Canada and the United States to publish articles on the plight of the plaintiffs. As a result, dozens of people began mailing in letters of support, many of which veered into the realm of conspiracy theories. One concerned citizen from Philadelphia wrote, "The CIA has resumed its brainwashing experiments under the Reagan administration. . . . I really don't know how I would fit into your case, but I am ready, willing and able to testify *against* Ronald Reagan."

The majority of the letters were from people claiming to have been, or to have known, victims of Cameron. "My mother was treated by the S.O.B.," wrote one man. "She had and still has a lousy life and we (my brother and sisters) had a lousy life too in those days." A woman in Vancouver wrote to say that she had been admitted to the Allan in 1958 for suicidal tendencies: "I remember most vividly my terror of shock treatments. I was given an injection that paralyzed me. I could not breathe or speak or move but I could hear. I would lie there, scared out of my wits while a nurse and a doctor put the jelly on my temples." Unfortunately, she couldn't join the lawsuit because she hadn't received her medical records from the Allan proving that she had been a patient there.

Attorney James Turner picked up where Joseph Rauh left off, urging Judge Penn to schedule a trial as soon as possible. Penn initially scheduled the trial for five months later, in June 1988, but the CIA stuck to its delay strategy and invoked an obscure section of the U.S. Code to convince him to postpone it until October.

Although Rauh had retired from law, he still had influence. Around this time, he wrote a personal letter to the new DCI William Webster pleading for cooperation in the Orlikow case. "Wouldn't the Agency be a stronger organization by some recognition of error?" he asked. "Is it in our nation's interest or tradition to compound the old wrong by continuing the struggle endlessly until many or most of the victims leave this earth with broken lives and without recognition or recompense?"

At last, one of Rauh's letters had the intended effect. As the October trial loomed large, Webster reopened settlement negotiations. After six rounds of offers and counteroffers, a deal was struck. The plaintiffs walked away with $750,000 to be divided among them, coincidentally the same amount of money given to the family of Frank Olson. The son of one plaintiff wondered, "Was $750,000 the CIA's fire-sale price for wrecking human lives?"

Rauh and Turner later met Webster at a reception and thanked him for his help. To their surprise, he thanked them for bringing the case to his attention, saying, "Sometimes you see the right thing to do, and you do it."

Former DCI Richard Helms, on the other hand, considered the settlement a misguided attempt by the CIA to win back public trust. While reflecting on MKULTRA, he said, "I know there's been a great hoo-hah and lawsuits and all kinds of jiggery-pokery about whether this was done legally or illegally, morally or immorally . . . but it was established that that was a legitimate function of the Agency to try and do this, and we went ahead and did it." In his view, some operations succeed, some fail. If the CIA wants the successes, it must risk having the failures. The settlement would only serve to undermine the CIA's ability to take any risks at all:

> Why is a country spending so much of its time complaining about a minor operation of this kind which has a useful function to it? Why is it that as a country we always have to wait until disaster strikes and then we want to spend billions of dollars trying to solve the problem? AIDS is a good example; cancer is a good example. We're always late in the game, trying to run to catch up. So I have no apologies for that whole affair, and I think that some of the lawsuits have been absolutely egregious, I mean ridiculous. I can't possibly explain why certain psychiatrists did the things that they did, but at least they were supposed to be reputable people at the time that they were given financing.

Much like the CIA, Sidney Gottlieb couldn't escape his troublesome past. In 1981, an artist named Stanley Glickman sued him for $30 million. Glickman claimed that almost thirty years earlier, he had been eating lunch at a café in Paris when an American man with a limp dosed him with LSD. Afterward, Glickman became a paranoid recluse and lost his girlfriend, his passion for art, and his sense of self.

Gottlieb maintained that the encounter "absolutely never happened." So did archivist Frank Laubinger, who had reviewed Gottlieb's personnel file for the Victims Task Force and didn't find any evidence that Gottlieb had traveled to Paris at the time of the supposed drugging. Laubinger also said in a deposition, "If I were in operations and looking for the worst place in the world to try something like that, it would be Paris. Any operator that did something like that in Paris would be judged an absolute idiot within the organization."

Glickman's attorney retorted, "That is a strong argument that it happened."

The case slowly dragged on for years. Everyone involved—Glickman, Gottlieb, even the judge—died before a resolution. A different judge ultimately dismissed it.

The CIA faced yet another lawsuit in 2002, this time from U.S. marshal Wayne Ritchie. In 1957, Ritchie had attended a Christmas party at a post office building in San Francisco. Within half an hour of arriving, as he sipped on his bourbon and soda, a dizzying array of kaleidoscopic colors flashed before his eyes. Confused and concerned, he went upstairs to clear his clouded head, but instead, a fog of paranoia engulfed him. "I got down to where I thought everyone was against me," he recalled. For some reason, he couldn't shake the feeling that his fellow marshals wanted him kicked off the force.

Ritchie left the party in a daze. When he stumbled into his apartment, his girlfriend told him that she was tired of living in San Francisco and wanted to move to New York. They got into an argument, and he stormed off to the Vagabond Bar for more drinks. That's where he hatched a bizarre plan to set his life back on track. He would rob a bar for enough cash to buy his girlfriend a plane ticket to New York, which would somehow fix everything.

Ritchie returned to the post office building, but not for the Christmas party. He grabbed two service revolvers from his locker and headed to an all-black bar downtown. Once inside, he pulled out the revolvers and demanded the money in the till.

The robbery was over in an instant. A quick-thinking patron hit Ritchie over the head, knocking him unconscious. The police took him to jail, where after a few hours his head finally cleared of the paranoia that had been plaguing him all night. Ashamed of what he had done, he asked an officer for a pistol and one bullet to "save the State some money."

Ritchie ultimately pled guilty to attempted armed robbery. The judge spared the rod and slapped him with a five-hundred-dollar fine. Following the ordeal, Ritchie left his job in disgrace, was regarded as a pariah by his former friends, and fought suicidal urges for the next thirty years.

In 1999, Ritchie was reading a newspaper when he came across an article describing MKULTRA. He had never heard of the project before, but two things in particular caught his eye: LSD and George White. Ritchie had known White back in the 1950s. "My God," he thought, "how could he have done that to me?"

Was Ritchie right? Had he been an unwitting victim of Operation Midnight Climax? Fortunately, White's diary offers a clue. On December 20, 1957, the night that Ritchie lost his mind at a Christmas party, the diary entry reads, "Xmas party Fed bldg Press Room."

White's accomplice Ike Feldman was still alive when Ritchie sued the CIA. During his deposition for the case, when asked whether he and White had ever followed up with any of the people whom they surreptitiously dosed with LSD, he said, "I didn't do any follow-up, period. . . . You just back away and let them worry, like this nitwit, Ritchie."

The attorney asked for clarification, "When you say 'let them worry,' you mean let them have a head full of LSD and let—"

"Let them have a full head," Feldman blurted, "like what happened with this nut [Ritchie] when he got out and got drunk."

Despite White's diary entry and Feldman's deposition, the judge dismissed the case, citing Ritchie's failure to conclusively prove that he had been drugged. A court of appeals upheld the ruling, but the judge noted, "If Ritchie's claims are true, he has paid a terrible price in the name of national security."

Indeed, and so had many others.

26

Old Wounds

Back in 1953, Sidney Gottlieb and Robert Lashbrook had visited Alice Olson following the death of her husband. Three decades later, Alice and her two sons, Eric and Nils, returned the favor. (Lisa, the Olson daughter, had tragically died in a plane crash in 1978.) Although they had already received a check from the government, an apology from the president, and a packet of documents from the CIA, they still wanted answers from the two men who had dosed Frank Olson with LSD at Deep Creek.

The Olsons first visited Lashbrook in California, where he was teaching chemistry at a local high school. By now he was old and cantankerous, with a crown of silver hair ringing his otherwise bald pate. "He sat in a rocking chair," Eric remembered, "and bobbed up and down like a jack-in-the-box, pushing himself up on his forearms, and then down again." Alice said that Lashbrook was "very uncomfortable" talking about the past.

During Lashbrook's deposition for the Orlikow case, attorney Joseph Rauh asked him, "What did [Alice Olson] say was her reason for visiting you?"

"General interest, I think. A number of points had been bothering her and, I think, her two sons, and she was hoping to clear them up."

"What were the points that had been bothering her which she was hoping to clear up?"

Lashbrook became uncomfortable. "I don't recall."

"You can't recall it two years ago?"

"I think that would be personal, and anyway, I don't recall specifically."

Rauh didn't believe him. "Are you refusing to tell me? There is no privilege that could possibly—are you refusing—"

"I'm saying I can't think of an answer to your question, no."

The deposition got even more heated when Rauh asked Lashbrook to repeat the questions that Alice had asked him.

"[There were] many of them, millions," Lashbrook said.

"Well, state one. We'll start with any one."

"I think you're being ridiculous."

"That is not the point. You have to answer the question."

"Look, I had a conversation with the woman. So what?"

CIA attorney Scott Kragie interjected to try to speed things along, "Mr. Lashbrook, to the best of your recollection, do you recall any specific questions that she asked you? Obviously they dealt with the death of her husband."

As if on cue, Lashbrook's memory came back to him. He said that Alice had asked him whether he thought that Harold Abramson, the doctor who had treated Frank Olson, was competent. Lashbrook told her that he did.

"That's one question," Rauh said. "Can you remember another question?"

"No, not immediately."

"Well, I'm willing to wait."

"I'm not," said Kragie, obviously irritated. "Do you recall any other questions that she had?"

Lashbrook said that he didn't, ending the line of inquiry.

In a deposition of her own, Alice said that she had asked Lashbrook whether someone had pushed her husband out of the hotel window. "He gave us assurances that this had not happened, that he knew nothing about such a thing."

Two weeks after visiting Lashbrook, the Olsons knocked on Sidney Gottlieb's door. He and Margaret had recently moved back to the East Coast, apparently after suffering a falling-out with their daughter, whose husband was an African affairs scholar critical of the CIA. They were now living in Boston, Virginia, where they raised chickens and goats. Their solar-powered house sat on a fifty-acre plot of land at the end of a long dirt road in the shadow of the Blue Ridge Mountains. A friend described the living situation:

> Gottlieb was fascinated by the concept of building a place to die. He
> spent a lot of time with mechanical and physical puzzles. There was

lots of area for arts projects. The homestead was essentially a duplex where there were two identical homes, one for the Gottlieb couple and one for a younger couple who would take more and more responsibility for the older couple as they neared their death. There was a common room where the couples would dine together. But the concept didn't work out in practice. Even though Gottlieb gave the younger couple a deed to part of the house, they did not get along.

Gottlieb was working as a speech pathologist, treating children and stroke victims. He belonged to a Zen spiritual group, volunteered at the local hospice, and acted in the annual Christmas play. He was well-liked by everyone in the community, except, apparently, his cohabitants.

When Gottlieb opened his front door on that sunny day in 1984, he eyed the Olsons for a silent moment, checking to see if they were carrying any weapons. Relieved that they weren't, he said, "I had a dream last night in which I opened this same door and you pulled a gun and shot me." Eric Olson, who had gotten a PhD in psychology from Harvard, considered the comment a disarming mechanism. By mentioning the dream, Gottlieb had put the Olsons in a position to reassure him that they meant no harm. Eric later said, "He was not the master of mind control for nothing. . . . You felt like you were playing cat-and-mouse and he was way ahead of you." Nils agreed, adding, "I felt kind of brainwashed by the guy."

Gottlieb began the conversation by distancing himself from his past: "The former Gottlieb did some things that I'm not proud of. But I'm not him. I can't answer for some of the things he did because I just don't recognize him anymore." He then explained what he remembered about the events surrounding the death of Frank Olson. Not satisfied, Eric pressed him for more information, causing Gottlieb to become defensive. "Your father and I went into this type of work because we were patriotic. We cared about our country and its survival in the face of aggressive Communism." He paused before adding, "Maybe we both went too far."

Neither party came away happy. The Olsons wanted to revisit the past while Gottlieb wanted to move beyond it. Before they left, he pulled Eric aside and asked, "Have you ever considered getting into a therapy group for people whose parents have committed suicide?"

From that moment on, Eric maintained that his father had been murdered. He mentioned his hunch to Nils, who immediately responded, "Did you know that our old friend Jim Starrs [is] a forensic scientist who specializes in exhuming bodies to resolve historical cases?"

Eric stood there dumbfounded. "You don't say?"

Eric and Nils decided to have their father exhumed and analyzed for signs of foul play. On June 2, 1994, over forty years after his burial, Frank Olson was lifted from the earth. The forensic team, led by Starrs, spent a month running a battery of tests on Olson's shriveled brown corpse. Starrs also interviewed multiple people connected to the Olson incident, including Gottlieb. He later recalled:

> I was emboldened to ask how he could so recklessly and cavalierly have jeopardized the lives of so many of his own men by the Deep Creek Lodge experiment with LSD. "Professor," he said without mincing a word, "you just do not understand. I had the security of the country in my hands." He did not say more, nor need he have done so. Nor did I, dumb-founded, offer a rejoinder. The means-end message was pellucidly clear. Risking the lives of the unwitting victims of the Deep Creek experiment was simply the necessary means to a greater good, the protection of the national security.

Gottlieb gave his own account of the interview:

> [Starrs] was an interesting man, so properly poised, yet rigid, in the style of some English manor lord or such. . . . His discomfort was infectious. I was surprised later to note that his questions were so reflective of what I had already been asked many times over. I assume he hadn't looked at the extant records before we met. Had I been in his place, I would have taken another course of inquiry.

At the end of the forensic investigation, Starrs made a shocking announcement: Frank Olson had received "a stunning blow to the head by some person or instrument prior to his exiting through the window of room 1018A." Olson was "intentionally, deliberately, with malice aforethought, thrown out of that window."

But Starrs's conclusion wasn't definitive. Another member of the forensic team maintained that the blow to Olson's head was consistent with

PROJECT MIND CONTROL

him hitting the window on the way out. Yet another member of the team complained that Starrs "tends to relish the spotlight more than he does the details" and "sometimes he overlooks, or tends to brush aside, pertinent facts, or evidence, in favor of his opinions or theories." Starrs had reached the conclusion that he had wanted to.

Nevertheless, it's an interesting coincidence that in 1997, the CIA declassified a short primer written in 1953—the year that Olson died—titled "A Study of Assassination." The primer describes seven different methods of assassination: drugs, manual, edge weapons, blunt weapons, firearms, explosives, and accidents. For manual methods, the primer says that simple tools are often "the most efficient means" available. "A hammer, axe, wrench, screw driver, fire poker, kitchen knife, lamp stand, or anything hard, heavy and handy will suffice. A length of rope or wire or a belt will do if the assassin is strong and agile." The problem with manual methods—as well as most other methods—is that they leave behind evidence of the crime. An "accident," on the other hand, "causes little excitement and is only casually investigated." The most effective "accident," according to the primer, "is a fall of 75 feet or more onto a hard surface. Elevator shafts, stair wells, unscreened windows and bridges will serve. . . . If the assassin immediately sets up an outcry, playing the 'horrified witness,' no alibi or surreptitious withdrawal is necessary."

The existence of the primer has caused much speculation about the Olson incident, but there's little reason to think it describes what happened. For one, Olson went through the window blinds, which the primer discourages. Additionally, Lashbrook didn't make an "outcry" or play the "horrified witness." Lastly, the primer specifically advises against creating a "wound or condition not attributable to the fall," which wouldn't have been the case if Olson had been bludgeoned in the head, as Starrs claimed.

Journalist Seymour Hersh visited Gottlieb in the late 1990s when MK-ULTRA was receiving renewed attention because of Starrs's investigation. "It was very strange," Hersh said of the encounter. "Gottlieb was living as if he was in an ashram in India. . . . He was trying to absolve himself, to expiate. If he'd been Catholic, he would have gone to a monastery. He was a destroyed man, riddled with guilt." Others close to Gottlieb reached the same conclusion. Rose Ann Sharp, a preschool teacher who volunteered with him, said, "A lot of Sid's later life was spent atoning, whether he needed to or not, for how he had been exposed publicly as some sort of evil scientist."

Gottlieb came to deeply regret MKULTRA, to the point where he completely lost his peace of mind. The project that had ruined so many lives finally claimed its last victim. In that sense, Gottlieb "was not a monster but a man," his friend Lois Manookian reminded the world. "He was, and is, us, and we didn't want to see it."

Sidney Gottlieb died on March 6, 1999, from pneumonia and congestive heart failure. Fittingly enough, his funeral service was private.

27

The Vicious Cycle of Secrecy

The motivations that led to MKULTRA, however flawed, aren't difficult to understand. Allen Dulles, Richard Helms, Sidney Gottlieb, and others feared that the Soviets, Chinese, and potentially other Communist powers possessed methods of mind control. The United States therefore needed its own mind control project to compete in what could become the next arms race.

What's much more difficult to understand is why nobody in the CIA ever tried to stop MKULTRA. Not everyone approved of the project, but three systemic problems prevented internal oversight: compartmentalization, bad recordkeeping practices, and the impotence of the CIA inspector general.

Compartmentalization is the "need-to-know" policy whereby CIA personnel were prevented from discussing their work with anyone other than their immediate colleagues. This policy was necessary, to a degree, to prevent sensitive information from falling into the wrong hands, but it also had the adverse effect of preventing oversight. Former DCI Stansfield Turner acknowledged as much in his book *Secrecy and Democracy*:

> In all professions it is easy to get so close to your work that you fail to realize you are not using good judgment. To prevent that, you need someone with a detached viewpoint to take an occasional look at where you are going. The CIA, with its natural emphasis on secrecy, had no internal system to provide an objective, critical review.... Something was inherently wrong when a Gottlieb or an Angleton had so much freedom to do so much harm—and all to no advantage

to the United States. The more I probed, the more I blamed these and other abuses on a practice that in the jargon of intelligence is called "compartment[aliz]ation."

Not even the CIA's Office of Medical Services, which had an obligation to protect the health of the people under its jurisdiction, knew the extent of MKULTRA. "We had offered to assist [the] TSD with medical support and guidance," said medical officer Edward Gunn, "but it was 'thank you very much.' . . . We did not know what they were doing." When asked to speculate on why the TSD had kept the Office of Medical Services in the dark, Gunn said that it was because "the medical officers might well have disapproved of their approach."

Besides compartmentalization, CIA personnel engaged in bad record-keeping practices, something that Allen Dulles had legitimized when he exempted MKULTRA from normal reporting requirements. Like compartmentalization, these recordkeeping practices—or lack thereof—were necessary, to a degree, to prevent sensitive information from falling into the wrong hands, but they also had the adverse effect of preventing oversight. In his 1963 inspector general report on MKULTRA, John Earman wrote, "Files are notably incomplete, poorly organized, and lacking in evaluative statements." This was by design so that nobody could follow the paper trail back to its source. Sometimes the actions of CIA personnel were preserved in nothing more than memories, and given the nature of MKULTRA, not even those were always safe.

Yet even when a paper trail did exist, it could be destroyed without consequence, as demonstrated by Gottlieb's destruction of the MKULTRA files. And even when a paper trail survived the destruction, it could be hidden behind the stamp of secrecy, as demonstrated by the Army's concealment of Harold Blauer's medical records. In the words of nuclear physicist Leo Szilard, "The 'secret' stamp is the most powerful weapon ever invented." And who wielded that weapon? Following the Orlikow case, the CIA appointed attorney Lee Strickland, Joseph Rauh's nemesis, to head its Freedom of Information Office.

In theory, the CIA inspector general had the ability to penetrate compartmentalization, conduct interviews when a paper trail went cold, and hold personnel accountable for their actions. In practice, however, the inspector general was largely impotent. The CIA's first inspector general,

PROJECT MIND CONTROL

Stuart Hedden, was specifically denied access to the Directorate of Plans, the division most in need of oversight. Hedden's successor, Lyman Kirkpatrick, later admitted that even though he had found evidence of negligence and wrongdoing in the CIA, he hesitated to do anything about it because he feared retaliation: "I was trying to determine what the tolerable limits were of what I could do and still keep my job." Several successive inspectors general weren't even aware of the activities mentioned in the Family Jewels.

These three systemic problems weren't unique to the CIA. A similar culture in the FBI led to similar abuses. When the FBI's assistant director, William Sullivan, was asked whether anyone in the organization had ever objected to its harassment of civil rights leaders, including Martin Luther King, Jr., he said, "Never once did I hear anybody, including myself, raise the question, 'Is this course of action which we have agreed upon lawful, is it legal, is it ethical or moral?' We never gave any thought to this realm of reasoning."

The inherent flaw of intelligence agencies is that they must keep secrets for legitimate reasons of national security, but the secrecy that they are afforded can just as easily be used to avoid accountability. In such agencies, a vicious cycle tends to emerge: secrecy leads to plausible deniability, plausible deniability leads to reckless behavior, reckless behavior leads to embarrassment, and embarrassment leads to secrecy. MKULTRA is a case study in the vicious cycle of secrecy. Compartmentalization and bad recordkeeping practices (secrecy) emboldened the perpetrators (plausible deniability) to conduct unethical experiments (reckless behavior), and the fear of exposure (embarrassment) prompted them to destroy the files (secrecy).

One can't simply "take it on faith," as Richard Helms suggested, that the CIA or any other intelligence agency won't abuse its power. Instead, Helms's eventual successor as DCI, William Colby, got it right: "The separate constitutional structure, the separation of powers. That's what's going to protect you from me." He wisely added, "And the press." To break the vicious cycle of secrecy, meaningful *external* oversight must exist. As James Madison observed at the beginning of the American experiment, humans are not angels, and therefore "auxiliary precautions" are required to keep their ambitions in check.

Daniel Schorr, the CBS News correspondent who broke the story of CIA assassination attempts, once said that there had always been two great urges in the United States, "one toward security, one toward liberty. The pendulum constantly swings between them." Before 1975, the pendulum swung toward security. The CIA abused people (violated their liberties), ostensibly to protect them from an outside threat (in the name of security).

In the CIA's defense, there can be legitimate reasons to elevate security over liberty. The Supreme Court acknowledged as much in the majority opinion for *Kennedy v. Mendoza-Martinez* (1963): "While the Constitution protects against invasions of individual rights, it is not a suicide pact." In other words, the violation of liberties is justified when doing so would prevent the greater violation of those liberties. The problem, of course, is that nobody knows the future. Anyone can use this rationale to justify abuse in the present, which is exactly what the CIA did. And the CIA was emboldened to do so because, for most of the Cold War, Congress failed to provide meaningful external oversight of the intelligence community.

The failure of congressional oversight was largely the result of a historical quirk. During World War II, the existence of the Manhattan Project was kept hidden from Congress out of fear that Congress would shut it down for wasting taxpayer money. After the United States dropped the atomic bombs on Japan, ending the war, many members of Congress were glad that they hadn't been told about the Manhattan Project, a mindset that they carried over into the Cold War. Perhaps they shouldn't peer into the dark recesses of government where secret weapons, gadgets, and schemes were being developed.

Senator Mike Mansfield took the opposite perspective. In 1956, he proposed that Congress create a watchdog committee to monitor the CIA. "Everything about [the] CIA is clothed in secrecy," he told his fellow senators. "Once secrecy becomes sacrosanct, it invites abuse." Mansfield didn't know about MKULTRA, but he intuited that something like it might be going on behind closed doors. His proposed watchdog committee would review the CIA's documents as necessary to prevent any abuse of power or people.

Others balked at the proposal. Senator Richard Russell protested, "It would be more desirable to abolish the CIA and close it up, lock, stock and barrel, than to adopt any such theory as that all the Members of the Congress . . . are entitled to know the details of all the activities of this far-flung organization." Allen Dulles predictably opposed the creation of the watchdog committee, as did President Dwight Eisenhower, who said that the proposal would pass "over my dead body." Between them, enough strings were pulled to ensure that it failed.

For the next two decades, Congress buried its head in the sand. Former DCI James Schlesinger once told of a time when he tried to inform Congress about the CIA's activities. "Mr. Chairman," he said to Senator John Stennis, "I want to tell you about some of our programs."

"No, no, my boy," Stennis replied, "don't tell me. Just go ahead and do it, but I don't want to know!"

The CIA was happy to oblige. Between 1963 and 1973, it engaged in thirty-three covert operations in Chile alone with the goal of overthrowing the country's democratically elected leader. Only six of the operations were reported to Congress.

Beginning in 1975, the "Year of Intelligence," the pendulum between security and liberty reversed course. First, President Gerald Ford issued the executive orders that prevented drug testing on unwitting people and banned government employees from engaging in, or conspiring to engage in, "political" assassinations. Congress then passed the Hughes-Ryan Amendment to the Foreign Assistance Act, which required the president to officially approve all CIA covert operations, thus eliminating the president's plausible deniability. The Hughes-Ryan Amendment also required the president to disclose all CIA covert operations to multiple congressional committees. Although Congress couldn't nix a covert operation itself, it could pressure the CIA not to pursue one by threatening to reduce its budget. Finally, and most importantly, Congress created the Senate Select Committee on Intelligence (SSCI, pronounced "sis-see") and the House Permanent Select Committee on Intelligence (HPSCI, pronounced "hip-see") to monitor the intelligence community.

In theory, these measures would prevent the intelligence community from performing illegal, ill-conceived, and unethical actions. In reality, however, they didn't work as intended, partly because most members of Congress spent more time raising money for their reelection campaigns than they did on actual committee work. Moreover, the mandatory briefings that the intelligence community was required to give to SSCI and HPSCI were often more akin to wining and dining sessions than actual briefings.

The failure of congressional oversight was made clear in the 1980s. During President Ronald Reagan's administration, DCI William Casey, a former OSS officer still clinging to the freewheeling approach of a bygone era, ignored the rule of law and refused to inform SSCI and HPSCI about covert operations. (1. Secrecy leads to plausible deniability.) Meanwhile, members of the Reagan administration, aided by the CIA, illegally sold weapons to Iran, then illegally funneled the proceeds to the Contras in Nicaragua to help overthrow the socialist Sandinista government. (2. Plausible deniability leads to reckless behavior.) A leak to the press exposed this Iran-Contra scandal. (3. Reckless behavior leads to embarrassment.) Unsurprisingly, Oliver North, one of the main perpetrators, started destroying pertinent White House documents. (4. Embarrassment leads to secrecy.)

In the wake of the Iran-Contra scandal, despite fierce opposition from the CIA, Congress passed legislation requiring each CIA inspector general to undergo a Senate confirmation hearing, to meet with SSCI and HPSCI on a regular basis, and to report any potential violations of federal criminal law to the attorney general. The embarrassment of scandals—MKULTRA, Watergate, Iran-Contra—had compelled Congress to act. Soon, however, another event would send the pendulum swinging toward security.

On September 11, 2001, nineteen members of al-Qaeda hijacked four commercial airliners and flew them into the World Trade Center towers in New York and the Pentagon building in Virginia (the fourth plane crashed in a field in Pennsylvania). Nearly three thousand people died, making it the deadliest terrorist attack in history. The George W. Bush administration subsequently launched wars in Afghanistan and, controversially, Iraq, which had no connection to the attack.

On the domestic front, Congress passed the Patriot Act, which dramatically increased the government's surveillance capabilities without meaningful oversight from the judiciary. (1. Secrecy leads to plausible deniability.) On Vice President Dick Cheney's advice, Bush ordered the NSA to illegally bypass certain warrant requirements when collecting internet and telecommunications metadata. (2. Plausible deniability leads to reckless behavior.) In 2005, *The New York Times* exposed this mass surveillance program after having sat on the story for a year because the Bush administration argued that its release would jeopardize national security. (3. Reckless behavior leads to embarrassment.) Michael Hayden, director of the NSA, inaccurately testified to Congress about the program's legality and effectiveness. (4. Embarrassment leads to secrecy.)

Meanwhile, the Bush administration was covertly abducting suspected terrorists from foreign countries and locking them up in secret prisons abroad. (1. Secrecy leads to plausible deniability.) It then let the CIA torture these detainees. (2. Plausible deniability leads to reckless behavior.) In 2003, SSCI and HPSCI learned that the CIA had recorded some of the torture sessions, prompting Congress to issue a preservation order for the recordings. Not long afterward, *The Washington Post* revealed the existence of the secret prisons where the torture had occurred. (3. Reckless behavior leads to embarrassment.) In response, Jose Rodriguez, Jr., head of the CIA's Directorate of Operations, destroyed the recordings of the torture sessions despite the preservation order from Congress. (4. Embarrassment leads to secrecy.) Michael Hayden, who had since left the NSA to become director of the CIA, then inaccurately testified again by saying that the torture amounted to mere "tummy slapping," even though it had caused multiple deaths. He also instructed his subordinates to inaccurately testify to Congress about the number of detainees held at the Guantanamo Bay military prison in Cuba.

The pendulum swung back. In 2005, Congress passed the Detainee Treatment Act, which prohibited the use of torture in interrogations. Ten years later, following whistleblower Edward Snowden's further revelations about the government's mass surveillance programs, Congress passed the USA Freedom Act, which imposed limits on the bulk collection of internet and telecommunications metadata.

As the previous examples show, MKULTRA was not a fluke. Rather, it was the norm in a system that lacks meaningful external oversight and lets perpetrators of abuses avoid accountability for their actions, a system in which the vicious cycle of secrecy pushes the pendulum too far toward security at the expense of liberty.

How can the American people enact meaningful external oversight of the intelligence community and hold perpetrators of abuses accountable for their actions? There are two straightforward solutions. The first is to support free speech that speaks truth to power and a free press that exposes abuses. The second is to realign the incentives of elected representatives so that they take seriously their role as overseers. Gerrymandering, closed primaries, plurality voting, and winner-take-all elections currently incentivize these representatives to engage in political theater at the expense of actual governance. If the

American people can implement some combination of redistricting reform, open primaries, ranked voting, and proportional representation, then they can create a system that better prioritizes service over selfishness.

Humans are not angels. The fact that the pendulum swings between security and liberty is a testament to the fact that the system is capable of self-correction; it's proof that the checks and balances built into the Constitution are working as intended. While it may be necessary to lower its amplitude, the swinging pendulum is a sign of a healthy society. Dread the day when the press sings nothing but the praises of those in power and Congress claims that there are no abuses to investigate. At that point, when the pendulum appears still, both security and liberty will have been lost.

28

History Loves Irony

The consequences of MKULTRA went beyond just the damage that it did, especially when LSD slipped out of the CIA's hands and into those of the counterculture movement. The drug gave the Beat Generation of writers a new definition of what it meant to be "acid-tongued." Ken Kesey once participated in an MKULTRA subproject and said that the experience led him to pen *One Flew Over the Cuckoo's Nest*. Robert Hunter participated in another subproject and credited LSD with inspiring him to write many of the Grateful Dead's most popular songs.

Allen Ginsberg reflected on the irony of the situation: "Am I, Allen Ginsberg, the product of one of the CIA's lamentable, ill-advised, or triumphantly successful experiments in mind control? Had they, by conscious plan or inadvertent Pandora's Box, let loose the whole LSD fad on the US and the world?" Counterculture icon Timothy Leary thought so. "I wouldn't be here now without the foresight of CIA scientists," he said. John Lennon, the legendary singer-songwriter for the Beatles, put it most elegantly in a 1980 *Playboy* interview: "We must always remember to thank the CIA and the Army for LSD. That's what people forget. . . . They invented LSD to control people and what they did was give us freedom."

At the outset of MKULTRA, Sidney Gottlieb had wanted to use drugs to bend people to his will, but he ended up fueling the rebellion of an entire generation.

Perhaps the most important consequence of MKULTRA was the inspiration that it gave to conspiracy theorists. Donald Bain's book *The Control of Candy Jones*, published in 1976, introduced one of the first conspiracy theories based on MKULTRA. It describes how the CIA supposedly turned a model named Candy Jones into a hypnotic courier. John Marks, the former State Department official who had filed the FOIA request leading to the discovery of the surviving MKULTRA files, investigated the claims in the book, but none of them survived his scrutiny. He realized that Jones's husband had invented the entire story. "I couldn't get one cross reference that worked!" Marks said. "The whole thing was bullshit."

Nineteen years later, Cathy O'Brien published the most outrageous MKULTRA conspiracy theory. In her 1995 book *Trance Formation of America,* coauthored with her husband, Mark Phillips, she claims that when she was a child in the 1960s, her father filmed pornography with her, made her perform bestiality with dogs, and struck a deal with the CIA to groom her for an MKULTRA subproject called Project Monarch (which doesn't exist). According to O'Brien, Project Monarch was an effort to recruit "multigenerational incest abused children with Multiple Personality Disorder for its genetic mind control studies."

O'Brien claims that when her MKULTRA mind-control programming was complete, her father prostituted her to tourists, Masons, mobsters, Satanists, drug dealers, police officers, a school principal, a guidance counselor, and members of the U.S. Coast Guard. He then sold her to a senator in exchange for a lucrative military contract. Under the senator's control, O'Brien was sexually abused by governors, congressmen, presidents, vice presidents, a first lady, foreign leaders, baseball players, a White House chief of staff, a secretary of education (and his brother), a who's who of country music stars, unnamed leaders of the New World Order, lines of military personnel ranging from three to twenty at a time, and other high-profile individuals "too numerous" to name. After each incident, her memories were erased with "cryptoamnesia scrambling." Here O'Brien appears to have misread or deliberately altered the word *cryptomnesia,* which is a separate phenomenon related to memory.

The accusations in the book get even more absurd. O'Brien claims that she served as a drug mule and hypnotic courier to governors, presidents, and foreign leaders. She claims that one president could control her actions with different colored jellybeans. She claims that she had once known more statistical data about baseball "than would ever be in print." She claims that multiple government officials, including a president and a vice president, hunted her for sport inside a military enclosure. She claims that the

North American Free Trade Agreement "routed U.S. traumatized, robotic, mind controlled children to Saudi Arabia" to serve as "sex slaves and camel jockeys." She claims that one vice president activated "a hologram of the lizard-like 'alien' which provided the illusion of [him] transforming like a chameleon before my eyes." She claims that a CIA agent repeatedly impregnated her, aborted the fetuses, ate some of them, and preserved the others in jars to sell in his "interstate occult body parts business." Finally, she claims that she was scheduled for ritual sacrifice, but a heroic intelligence officer named Mark Phillips (her future husband and coauthor), rescued her before it could happen. Phillips then helped O'Brien "recover" her memories by subjecting her to lengthy bouts of hypnotism, a technique that had already become notorious for producing false memories of physical and sexual abuse during the Satanic Panic social contagion of the 1980s.

In fact, the fraudulent book that sparked the Satanic Panic, *Michelle Remembers* (1980), foreshadows much of O'Brien's own story. It describes the memories that Michelle Smith "recovered" when the devout Catholic psychiatrist Lawrence Pazder (her future husband and coauthor) subjected her to lengthy bouts of hypnotism. Smith claims that Satanists beat and molested her, smeared her with feces, buried her alive in a cemetery, and forced her to participate in human and animal sacrifices. She provides no corroborating evidence, nor has anyone found the relevant police reports and hospital records that supposedly exist. Her family, friends, teachers, and neighbors all deny the allegations. There are even yearbook pictures of Smith in school during the time when she claims that Satanists were holding her captive. Nevertheless, the book sold hundreds of thousands of copies — the Catholic Church even tried to finance a promotional tour to inspire church attendance — demonstrating how lucrative such claims could be.

It should come as no surprise that Cathy O'Brien's husband, Mark Phillips, was a member of the International Society for the Study of Dissociation, a pseudoscientific organization responsible for spreading Satanic Panic conspiracy theories. One of its cofounders, Bennett Braun, argued that devil-worshiping cults performed ancient "transgenerational" rituals to give children multiple personality disorder, not unlike O'Brien's later claims about Project Monarch. In 1995, a former patient sued Braun for falsely convincing her that she had been raped by her father and that she had engaged in cannibalism and infanticide. She received a $10.6 million settlement while Braun lost his medical license. Phillips, it seems, similarly victimized O'Brien without her realizing it. He even credited Braun with teaching him how to "recover" memories.

O'Brien insists that her memories must be true because of how vivid and traumatic they are, but vivid and traumatic memories are just as susceptible to being false as any others. Psychologists Ulric Neisser and Nicole Harsch demonstrated as much nearly a decade before O'Brien published her book. On January 28, 1986, the day after the space shuttle *Challenger* exploded, they asked over a hundred students at Emory University to describe how they had heard about the disaster. Two and a half years later, Neisser and Harsch tracked down forty-four of those students and asked them to do the same thing. The results? A quarter of the students got every significant detail wrong (where they were, what they were doing, who had told them, etc.), and over half of the students got a majority of the significant details wrong. There was "no relation between confidence and accuracy at all." Even when shown their original responses, many of the students insisted that their present "memories" were the correct ones. Other experiments have shown just how easy it is to implant false memories in people through leading questions. In some cases, simply getting someone to imagine a scenario is enough to make them develop false memories of having experienced it, hence the unreliability of memories "recovered" through hypnotism.

Just as ridiculous as the claims in O'Brien's book is the wordplay that permeates it: "trance-form," "perpeTraitors," "soul property." In the most groanworthy example, one service entrance sign at NASA headquarters is referred to as "Serve-us En-Trance." The goal of such writing is to trick gullible readers into believing that these superficial, coincidental linguistic patterns are indicative of some deeper truth. This is the lazy person's approach to evidence, equivalent to spotting faces on burnt toast or animal shapes in the clouds.

The book is a collage of conspiracies, a fever dream of malice and misinformation. No doubt O'Brien sincerely believes that these things happened to her, but that doesn't mean that anyone else should. None of the sources that she cites support her claims, nor do the "documents" (mostly just business cards) provided in a photo section. Even though there are "literally thousands of files of documentation that support much of what I am reporting," O'Brien doesn't show any of them because, she says, they're still classified.

And while it's true that the absence of evidence isn't necessarily evidence of absence, neither is it evidence of existence. All claims need *some* empirical support to have any credibility. Yet in the twisted world of conspiracy theories, an absence of evidence is itself evidence of a cover-up. Nothing is proven, nothing can be disproven.

In 1956, psychologists Leon Festinger, Henry Riecken, and Stanley Schachter described a similar phenomenon after observing an apocalyptic cult predict that God would soon destroy the world in a massive flood. When the date of destruction came and went without so much as a light rain, rather than acknowledge their mistake, many of the cult members found creative ways to reconcile their cognitive dissonance between faith and fact. Some of them suggested that God had destroyed the world in a figurative, not literal, sense. When this explanation failed to persuade everyone, others suggested that God had spared the world *because* they had believed in its destruction so fervently; he had rewarded them for their unquestioning devotion to him. Amazingly, this explanation won out, even though to the outside world it was clearly just a nonfalsifiable post hoc rationalization. The cult members became convinced that their failed prediction was actually confirmation of their worldview. The fact that nothing had happened was proof that they had been right to believe that something would. Afterward, they exhibited *more* confidence in their beliefs and *more* enthusiasm for proselytizing to others. "I've given up just about everything," said one cult member in a surprisingly candid moment. "I've cut every tie. I've burned every bridge. I've turned my back on the world. I can't afford to doubt. I have to believe." It's hard not to believe something when your identity depends upon it being true.

Vincent Bugliosi, the attorney who prosecuted cult leader Charles Manson, identified several other errors in reasoning common to conspiracy theorists:

> The conspiracy community regularly seizes on one slip of the tongue, misunderstanding, or slight discrepancy to defeat 20 pieces of solid evidence; accepts one witness of theirs, even if he or she is a provable nut, as being far more credible than 10 normal witnesses on the other side; treats rumors, even questions, as the equivalent of proof; . . . and insists, as the late lawyer Louis Nizer once observed, that the failure to explain everything perfectly negates all that is explained.

Moreover, conspiracy theorists tend to adopt grand, sweeping explanations. To them, everything is always connected. Nothing is ever a mistake, or an anomaly, or a coincidence. For instance, some conspiracy theorists argue that a cabal of elites—the Deep State, the Freemasons, the Bilderbergers, the Illuminati, the New World Order, the Elders of Zion—is responsible for orchestrating wars, mass shootings, "natural" disasters, economic depressions, and other of society's ills. In reality, the world is a much more nuanced and complicated place; the devil truly is in the details. Every event is the result of a combination of causes that are often hard to discern. There is no master plan. There are no evil geniuses in charge of everything. The inmates are running the asylum.

O'Brien employs most of the aforementioned errors in her book. Still, some people believed her, spawning innumerable other MKULTRA conspiracy theories in the process. Particularly popular are those that involve sex slaves, celebrities, pedophilia, cannibalism, ritual sacrifice, and other classic conspiratorial tropes. Like McCarthyism during the Red Scare, these sensational claims generate fear, which generates coverage, which generates converts. Ironically, the conspiracy theorists have managed to manipulate more people than MKULTRA ever did.

The CIA remains conspicuously quiet about the spread of MKULTRA conspiracy theories. One CIA officer speaking on conditions of anonymity gave a surprising reason as to why:

> The Agency, over the past several decades, has done a large amount of work at creating, fostering, and adding to a lot of selected conspiracy theories with the object of what it terms "off-balancing" the public's mind set. . . . Put succinctly, it's in the Agency's best interest to have as many so-called kooks as possible out there. . . . That so many intelligent and sincere theorists have been pigeonholed as "fruit loops" is an intended byproduct.

This tactic, pioneered by the Russian government, is known as "censorship through noise," famously summarized by President Donald Trump's senior strategist Steve Bannon, who said that the best way to deal with opposition is to "flood the zone with shit." The CIA, if the anonymous officer is correct, encourages the "kooks" to proliferate their nonsense in hopes that the legitimate researchers who expose the CIA's past misdeeds will be lumped in with the "kooks" and dismissed as crazy. If people don't know who to trust, maybe they won't trust anyone at all, even those who speak the truth. In yet another bit of irony, the conspiracy theorists have become pawns in an actual conspiracy.

While the propagation of conspiracy theories can delegitimize the truth (as in censorship through noise), the propagation of the truth can legitimize conspiracy theories. The fact that the government conducted unethical programs such as MKULTRA, "enhanced interrogations," involuntary sterilizations, human radiation experiments, and others of a similar nature, combined with the fact that the government *has* engaged in cover-ups, gives credence to conspiracy theories. If the government did something as scandalous as MK-ULTRA, the logic goes, then what else might it have done—or be doing? This thought process opens the door to disinformation campaigns that trick people into believing lies that sound plausible. Operation Denver (also known as Operation Infektion) is one such example.

The groundwork for Operation Denver began on July 16, 1983, when the Indian newspaper *Patriot,* a KGB-funded mouthpiece of Soviet propaganda, published an article with the headline "AIDS May Invade India: Mystery Disease Caused by US Experiments." The article itself claims to have been written by a "well-known American scientist and anthropologist," but the KGB actually wrote it. Regardless, many of the other claims in the article were true: AIDS contaminated blood donations, it had no effective cure, it was likely caused by a virus, and its first major outbreak had occurred in the United States.

The article also correctly notes that the U.S. military sprayed "dummy germ warfare agents and weakened micro-organisms" in major American cities. Additionally, the CIA "repeatedly tested viruses of dangerous diseases, narcotics and psychotropics, using volunteers, prisoners and drug addicts as guinea-pigs." Lastly, the article says, "Fort Detrick is notorious as a place where biological weapons are being developed in laboratories and where in the past they were repeatedly tested at its proving grounds." All of these claims were true, which made it easier for readers to swallow the lie that came next: "It is fairly safe to conclude that experts at Fort Detrick have developed one more type of biological weapon," AIDS.

To further bolster the lie that American scientists created AIDS at Fort Detrick, the KGB published similar articles in newspapers around the world.

In a carousel of lies, some of those articles cited the *Patriot* article as proof that other independent newspapers had reached the same conclusion, making the story seem more credible.

Many people believed the AIDS lie. A RAND study from 2005 found that over 50 percent of African Americans believed that AIDS was man-made, 25 percent believed that it was created in a government laboratory, and 12 percent believed that it was spread by the CIA. They believed the lie because, given what the government had done in the past, it sounded like the sort of thing that the government *would* do. This is the slippery slope that leads people to believe disinformation.

Nathaniel Lehrman was one of the believers. In 1985, he read a story in *The New York Times* about Sidney Gottlieb's attempt to assassinate Patrice Lumumba with a biological substance (now known to be anthrax) that had been procured from Fort Detrick. If the story was true, Lehrman reasoned, then surely the CIA had experimented with other biological substances from Fort Detrick. And on whom was the CIA known to experiment? "Western homosexuals, drug addicts, and African Americans," he concluded. And which groups of people were experiencing the worst outbreaks of AIDS? Western homosexuals, drug addicts, and African Americans. Coincidence? Yes, but that didn't stop Lehrman—and, predictably, Cathy O'Brien—from connecting the dots anyway.

The best lies are based on the truth. Perhaps the simplest way to combat conspiracy theories and disinformation campaigns is to act with moral integrity, thereby undermining any claims to the contrary.

History is only as good as its sources. Sidney Gottlieb destroyed most of the MKULTRA files, an act that necessarily invites suspicion and speculation. As a result, a complete picture of the project will never be painted. Had those files survived, they undoubtedly would have revealed additional unsavory facts, but facts nonetheless.

That said, MKULTRA is surprisingly well documented. Primary sources about the project include notes, memos, letters, receipts, memoirs, diaries, interviews, depositions, government reports, institutional records, and a trove of declassified documents. Yet given Gottlieb's destruction of the files, it's easy to create a conspiracy theory about MKULTRA. Anyone can fill in the gaps in the record with their wildest imagination. MKULTRA can be misconstrued as a project that traffics child sex slaves, controls pop star

Britney Spears, or hosts human hunting expeditions for government officials. And if you don't believe the conspiracy theories, some will argue, then maybe it's because you're a victim of just such a project. Maybe you've been conditioned not to ask questions. Maybe you've been drugged through the vaccines. Maybe through the drinking water. Maybe through the airplane contrails in the sky.

Once shrouded in euphemisms to hide its actions, MKULTRA has ironically become a euphemism for the very action that it failed to uncover: mind control.

Epilogue

Sidney Gottlieb may not have developed methods of mind control, but mind control is nevertheless possible. People can be manipulated into thinking and doing astonishing things. They can be turned into Pavlovian animals—automatons of muscle memory—stimulated in just the right way to blindly follow a command. They can be stripped of their former sense of self and given a new persona in its place, à la Dr. Ewen Cameron. The most obvious place where this happens is within cults.

How do cults get people to spread lies, submit to abuse, disconnect from their families, and commit horrifying acts that have included murder, suicide, terrorism, and cutting off one's own genitals? Steven Hassan, a mental health professional and former member of the Unification Church "Moonie" cult, has developed a helpful explanation: the BITE (Behavior, Information, Thought, Emotion) model. Cults typically employ these four methods of control to manipulate their members.

Behavior control involves dictating what someone can do, such as what they can eat, when they can sleep, how they can dress, where they can go, and with whom they can associate.

Information control involves restricting what someone can know, usually by preventing them from accessing—and teaching them to distrust—noncult sources of information, all the while feeding them a steady diet of cult propaganda.

Thought control involves reinforcing what someone has been told to believe, usually through a combination of taking oaths, saying prayers, singing songs, reciting mantras, performing rituals, discouraging dissent, elevating faith over evidence, insisting on the infallibility of scripture, and inculcating a tribal mentality of "us versus them" or "good versus evil." To help achieve this tribal mentality, cult members often refer to each other in familial terms ("brother," "sister," "father," "mother") and sometimes will even give each other new names to erase their former identities and strengthen their sense of kinship. They also tend to develop a unique vocabulary that further differentiates themselves from the outside world.

Emotion control involves instilling in someone certain feelings to make them beholden to the cult: guilt, fear, shame, anger, loyalty, dependence. The mandatory confession of sins, donation of money, and proselytizing to others are common, as are the ideas that apostates should be shunned, deserve severe punishment, and are solely responsible for their failures. Moreover, cult members often experience extreme emotional highs and lows from being "love bombed" one moment to being chastised the next.

All groups fall on a spectrum from benign to manipulative. The groups toward the benign end—most schools, sports teams, and corporations— may have a small sampling of the aforementioned characteristics without being cults. However, the more of these characteristics that a group has, the more likely it is to be a cult that unduly controls the beliefs and behaviors of its members.

Take the CIA, for example. In its quest to develop methods of mind control, it exhibited many of these cultish characteristics. One internal review of secrecy practices unintentionally makes the point by describing how the CIA "has its initiation, its oaths, its esoteric phrases, its sequestered areas, its secrets within secrets. And in place of passwords and hand signs, there are letter designations on badges. There are in-groups and out-groups." These characteristics aren't bad in and of themselves, but in aggregate they make abuse more likely, hence the need for external oversight.

If someone is a victim of undue manipulation, the best way to help them is by showing them empathy and respect. You can't always make them change their mind by showing them evidence, but you can at least make them *want* to change their mind by showing them kindness. Philosopher David Hume was mostly right when he said that reason is the slave of the passions.

Everyone is susceptible to undue manipulation, and those who fall victim to it seldom realize that they have. To be sure that you aren't a victim, answer the following questions:

Do you believe things simply because you want them to be true?

Do you refuse to change your mind regardless of the evidence?

Do you ignore or rationalize away evidence that contradicts your beliefs?

Do you reject the consensus of experts?

Do you talk only to people who share your beliefs?

Do you find it difficult to empathize with people who disagree with you?

Do you let your group define your identity?

Do you (or does your group) have a history of making failed predictions?

Would you do something morally repugnant (lie, cheat, steal, harm) to appease your group?

Would you tolerate other members of your group doing something morally repugnant?

If a reasonable person who disagreed with your beliefs were to answer these questions on your behalf, would their answers differ from yours?

When reading the previous question, did you think to yourself, "No reasonable person could possibly disagree with my beliefs"?

If you answered "yes" to any of these questions, think hard about why that's the case.

There's one final question—the most important question—that everyone should ask themselves: What's more probable? There are always multiple ways to interpret evidence, and the goal is to find the most probable interpretation. For example, if a source claims that ten people saw an alien spaceship, one interpretation is that ten people really did see an alien spaceship. But there are far more probable interpretations. Ask yourself: Is it more probable that aliens visited Earth, or that the source lied, exaggerated, mistook what they heard, or repeated someone else's lie, exaggeration, or mistake? Heed the advice of the popular maxim, "When you hear hooves, think horses, not zebras."

The same kind of reasoning applies when you flip a coin a hundred times in a row and it lands on heads every single time. It's *possible* that you're the luckiest person ever (the odds are 1 in 1,267,650,600,228,229,401,496,703, 205,376), but it's *more probable* that someone gave you a trick coin.

To avoid being tricked, weigh the probabilities. And to be sure that you aren't tipping the scale when you do so, answer the previous list of questions.

Acknowledgments

It takes a village. I couldn't have done it without mine.

I want to thank the following institutions and organizations for their support: the American Institute of Physics, Austin Community College, the California Institute of Technology, the Clements Center for National Security, the Lone Star Historians of Science, Louisiana Tech University, the National Academy of Sciences, the National Endowment for the Humanities, Texas A&M University, the Thomas Jefferson Center for the Study of Core Texts and Ideas, the University of Texas, and the Waggonner Center for Civic Engagement and Public Policy. The views expressed in this book do not necessarily reflect the views of these institutions and organizations.

Thank you to my agent, Scott Miller, to my editor at St. Martin's Press, Marc Resnick, and to the rest of the team at St. Martin's for making this book possible. Also, thank you to the many students, teachers, colleagues, archivists, and librarians who helped me along the way, especially H. W. Brands, Bruce Hunt, Mark Lawrence, Alberto Martínez, Jeremy Mhire, Abena Osseo-Asare, Lorraine Pangle, Megan Raby, and Anthony Stranges.

I owe the largest debt of gratitude to my friends and family. Thank you to the Bonds, Lisles, and Stocktons; to Max and Sarah, Blair and Marty, and Jack, Quinn, Peter, Nolan, and Oslo; to my parents, Mike and Lanette Lisle; and to my son, Isaac, who was born during the writing of this book. Lastly, thank you to my wife, Osiris, the love of my life. This book is dedicated to you.

Appendix

The purpose of every MKULTRA subproject:

1. Studying the effects of alkaloids on the central nervous system of humans.
2. Monitoring the psychiatric field.
3. Conducting realistic tests of R&D items (George White).
4. Funding a magician for the production of a manual on trickery and deception (John Mulholland).
5. Conducting experiments in hypnosis.
6. Developing a reliable source of domestic LSD.
7. Conducting basic research into the effects of LSD (Harold Abramson).
8. Studying the biochemical, neurophysiological, sociological, and clinical psychiatric aspects of LSD and its antagonists.
9. Evaluating various sternutatory agents, narcotics, and depressants on normal and schizophrenic humans (Carl Pfeiffer).
10. Obtaining a supply of rare drugs for experimental and operational uses.
11. Isolating and investigating the active constituents in various toxic seeds.
12. Isolating and investigating the poisonous bark of *Piscidia erythrina*.
13. Funding to support Camp Detrick activities including purchasing material.
14. Reimbursing the Bureau of Narcotics for George White.
15. See Subproject 4.

16. See Subproject 3.
17. Synthesizing LSD and related compounds.
18. Authorizing a purchase of $400,000 worth of LSD from Eli Lilly.
19. See Subproject 4.
20. Synthesizing the di-Mannich derivative of Yohimbine hydrochloride.
21. See Subproject 48.
22. Isolating and investigating the intoxicating substances present in certain varieties of *Rivea corymbosa.*
23. Studying chemical agents that modify the behavior and function of the central nervous system (Charles Geschickter).
24. Funding meetings to discuss other MKULTRA subprojects.
25. See Subproject 5.
26. See Subproject 9.
27. Studying the basic properties of LSD.
28. See Subproject 9.
29. See Subproject 5.
30. See Subproject 13.
31. Supplying two kilograms of a rare, commercially unavailable chemical.
32. Screening plants for properties of interest to the CIA.
33. Providing funds to correct for a $400 error.
34. Applying magician techniques to clandestine operations.
35. Funding Georgetown Medical Center for a new research wing.
36. Funding a meeting to obtain information of interest to MKULTRA.
37. Producing and growing botanicals of interest to the CIA.
38. Studying the psychological effects of chlorpromazine, meratron, serpentine, and bulbocapnine on humans.
39. Testing interrogation techniques on criminal-sexual psychopaths.
40. Investigating aerosol delivery of psychochemicals.
41. Synthesizing rare organic chemicals not commercially available.
42. See Subproject 3.
43. Conducting psychophysiological studies of hypnosis and suggestibility (Louis West).
44. Designing laboratory methods for screening psychochemical materials.
45. Synthesizing and evaluating psychochemical and knockout compounds (Charles Geschickter).

46. See Subproject 17.
47. Testing chemicals that alter behavior (Carl Pfeiffer).
48. Creating the Society for the Investigation of Human Ecology.
49. Determining the genuineness of hypnotic states, measuring trance states, and exploring hypnosis induction techniques.
50. See Subproject 13.
51. Studying botanical materials, especially fungal species, with psychochemical effects (James Monroe).
52. Funding expeditions for collecting botanical specimens of interest to the TSS Chemical Branch (James Monroe).
53. Reviewing Russian and American pharmacological literature.
54. Studying the mechanism of brain concussions.
55. Conducting pharmacological studies of interest to the TSS.
56. Studying the effects of foodstuffs in delaying the absorption of alcohol.
57. Studying problems related to sleep and insomnia.
58. Supporting an expedition for the purpose of studying and collecting hallucinogenic species of mushrooms (Gordon Wasson).
59. Testing and evaluating certain chemical compounds of interest to the TSS.
60. Supporting the Society for the Investigation of Human Ecology.
61. Studying the role of the human brain in adaptive behavior (Harold Wolff).
62. Studying the effects of isolation techniques (Maitland Baldwin).
63. Studying alcohol as a means of manipulating human behavior.
64. Compensating Charles Geschickter for his services.
65. Studying the factors causing individuals to defect, developing ways to detect defectors, and discovering ways to induce defection.
66. See Subproject 63.
67. Conducting library searches, consultations, assessments, and evaluations of data submitted by TSS.
68. Studying the effects of repetitive verbal signals on human behavior (Ewen Cameron).
69. Interviewing Hungarian refugees to understand the sociology of the Communist system.
70. Developing knockout drugs.
71. Testing and evaluating anti-interrogation drugs.

72. Studying the effects of drugs on the central nervous system.
73. Studying whether drugs can affect susceptibility to hypnosis (Harris Isbell).
74. Funding small grants through the Society for the Investigation of Human Ecology to authenticate its cover as a CIA front.
75. Funding the publication costs of the proceedings of a symposium on psychogenic drugs.
76. Studying anti-authoritarian behavior.
77. Refining certain concepts of personality used in TSD assessment programs.
78. Providing microbiological support to meet TSD requirements.
79. Establishing the H. J. Rand Foundation as a cutout.
80. Extracting and identifying drugs, toxins, and biological entities from human tissues.
81. Studying the adjustment of Hungarian refugees.
82. Studying the adjustment of Hungarian refugees in the Netherlands.
83. Developing technical surveys on magic, psychic phenomena, hypnosis, truth serums, and graphology.
84. Studying hypnosis as it relates to changes in motivation (Martin Orne).
85. Using blood groupings to establish the true identity of individuals.
86. Designing and building miniature polygraph machines.
87. Purifying and characterizing allergens of extremely high potency.
88. Compiling material for a course on cultural appraisal.
89. Determining why Hungarian refugees voluntarily returned to Hungary.
90. Producing a descriptive model of scientists who are likely to come into contact with Americans.
91. See Subproject 70.
92. Studying the usefulness of mechanization in foreign-language training.
93. Researching bacterial and fungal toxins.
94. Investigating remote directional control of animals.
95. Supporting cross-cultural meaning systems.
96. Obtaining personality information of researchers.
97. Evaluating techniques for influencing human behavior.
98. Researching work in mass conversion.

99. Studying the optical rotatory power of solid and liquid crystals.
100. Investigating soil microorganisms and methods to obtain maximum information from soil samples.
101. Funding consulting services in the area of biophysics for the central nervous system.
102. Studying the behavior of naturally formed groups.
103. Studying nonverbal communication in children without a common language.
104. Studying ecological relations involved in the deterioration of petroleum products.
105. Investigating the determinants of virulence in *Staphylococci*.
106. Quantifying the relationship between a stimulus and the biological response to that stimulus.
107. Funding travel expenses for ten psychologists to attend a conference.
108. Studying certain characteristics of subjects with operational potential.
109. Developing psychopharmacological agents.
110. Providing a source of exotic pathogens and the capability to incorporate them into effective delivery systems.
111. Studying levels of motivation related to certain personality characteristics.
112. Studying the development of young children's understanding of occupational roles within their society.
113. Designing and manufacturing devices and systems utilizing gas-propelled sprays and aerosols.
114. Developing a series of behavioral rating categories to define behavioral characteristics.
115. Studying the interaction of the mentally disturbed and their environment.
116. Procuring chemical products not available through other channels.
117. Studying family structure and personality development.
118. Providing consulting services of a microbiologist for biological and chemical warfare detection.
119. Reviewing literature related to recording, analyzing, and interpreting biometric signals from humans and activating behavior by remote means.
120. Establishing laboratory procedures for the chemical agent program.
121. Studying Yoruba witchcraft treatments.

122. Developing a technique for preparing and characterizing purified neurokinin.
123. Studying how people of different cultural strata in three countries react to various stages of independence.
124. Measuring carbon dioxide tension and pH of body fluids in relation to certain psychophysiological variables.
125. Studying the placebo effect.
126. Studying the constructive behavior of individuals during periods of extreme stress.
127. Studying open voting records of registered voters over a fifty-year period.
128. Testing a method of rapid hypnotic induction in simulated and real operational settings.
129. Studying the computer analysis of biometric response patterns.
130. Evaluating the Wechsler assessment on hospitalized patients.
131. Funding the expenses of an undercover agent.
132. Providing personnel and a facility for operational testing of materials.
133. Studying mechanisms of mineral transformation by microorganisms.
134. Studying the relationship between body type and temperament.
135. See Subproject 70.
136. Conducting an experimental analysis of extrasensory perception.
137. Completing a psycholexicon on handwriting for assessing personality.
138. Studying phenomena with potential functions in miniature biomedical sensors.
139. Providing services in the area of technical surveillance for biological warfare activities.
140. Designing and conducting pharmacological tests on volunteers.
141. Unknown.
142. Supporting a biological program of electrical brain stimulation in cold-blooded animals.
143. Stimulating microbial deterioration of petroleum products.
144. Unknown.
145. Unknown.
146. Consulting a plant pathologist on limited anti-crop warfare.

147. Studying the development of tolerance to tetrahydrocannabinols (Harris Isbell).
148. Consulting with a professional for pharmacological and physiological information.
149. Testing certain items and delivery systems of interest to the TSD (George White).

Notes

ARCHIVES

CIT   California Institute of Technology Archives, Pasadena, California

DDEL   Dwight D. Eisenhower Presidential Library, Abilene, Kansas

GRFL   Gerald R. Ford Presidential Library, Ann Arbor, Michigan

GUA   Georgetown University Archives, Washington, D.C.

HSTL   Harry S. Truman Presidential Library, Independence, Missouri

LOC   Library of Congress, Washington, D.C.

NARA   National Archives and Records Administration, College Park, Maryland

PHS   Presbyterian Historical Society, Philadelphia, Pennsylvania

SUA   Stanford University Archives, Stanford, California

UCLA   Charles E. Young Research Library, Los Angeles, California

ABBREVIATIONS

B   Box

CCA   Commission on CIA Activities within the United States

CIA   Central Intelligence Agency

CREST   CIA Records Search Tool

DAO   Deposition of Alice Olson

DCI   Director of Central Intelligence

DDO   Deposition of David Orlikow

DDR   Deposition of David Rhodes

DFL	Deposition of Frank Laubinger
DHA	Deposition of John Hadwen
DJG	Deposition of John Gittinger
DJH	Deposition of Jeannine Huard
DKS	Deposition of Karralyn Schreck
DLG	Deposition of Robert Logie
DLH	Deposition of Lloyd Hisey
DLO	Deposition of Frederick Lowy
DMM	Deposition of Mary Morrow
DOS	Deposition of Omond Solandt
DPG	Deposition of Philip Goldman
DRC	Deposition of Robert Cleghorn
DRH	Deposition of Richard Helms
DRL	Deposition of Robert Lashbrook
DSG	Deposition of Sidney Gottlieb
DST	Deposition of Stansfield Turner
DVO	Deposition of Velma Orlikow
DVP	Doug Valentine Papers
DWP	Deposition of Walter Pasternak
E	Entry
F	Folder
FBI	Federal Bureau of Investigation
FOIA	Freedom of Information Act
FOPD	Frank Olson Project Documents
FRUS	Foreign Relations of the United States
HPSCI	House Permanent Select Committee on Intelligence
IRS	Internal Revenue Service
ISSD	International Society for the Study of Dissociation
JRP	Joseph Rauh Papers
KGB	Soviet Committee for State Security
LJWP	Louis Jolyon West Papers
MFP	Moore Family Papers
MORI	Management of Officially Released Information Identification
NASA	National Aeronautics and Space Administration
NSA	National Security Agency
OSS	Office of Strategic Services
OTS	Office of Technical Services

R&D	Research and Development
RG	Record Group
RHP	Richard Helms Papers
SCA	Select Committee on Assassinations
SCSGO	Select Committee to Study Governmental Operations
SERE	Survival, Evasion, Resistance, and Escape
SIHE	Society for the Investigation of Human Ecology
SSCI	Senate Select Committee on Intelligence
TSS	Technical Services Staff
TSD	Technical Services Division
USGPO	United States Government Printing Office

PROLOGUE

1 *"garbage money"*: Author interview with Rosanna Del Guidice.

2 *"horrible periods"*: James Bulger, "I Was a Guinea Pig for CIA Drug Experiments," *Ozy* (May 9, 2017).

2 *Another tried to kill himself*: Jack Anderson, "Lawsuit Forces CIA Confession on MK-ULTRA," *Washington Post* (August 28, 1982).

3 *"Dr. Gottlieb"*: DSG, September 25, 1980, JRP, B 243, F 7, LOC, 5–6.

3 *"a lot more"*: Author interview with Rosanna Del Guidice.

4 *"was going to tell"*: Author interview with Paul Figley.

1. THE OUTSIDER

5 *unusual quirks*: Marks, *The Search for the Manchurian Candidate*, 55; "Key Witness in C.I.A. Inquiry," *New York Times* (September 20, 1977): 83; Kinzer, *Poisoner in Chief*, 5.

5 *"a Yankee"*: Kinzer, *Poisoner in Chief*, 6, 247.

5 *"Mr. Gottlieb"*: Kinzer, *Poisoner in Chief*, 7.

6 *"If they have Each Other"*: Margaret Gottlieb, "Autobiographical Essays," MFP, B 1, F 24, PHS.

6 *"I wanted to do"*: Albarelli, *A Terrible Mistake*, 102.

6 *"became repetitive"*: Kinzer, *Poisoner in Chief*, 8.

6 *"or any of that fancy stuff"*: Margaret Gottlieb, "Autobiographical Essays," MFP, B 1, F 24, PHS.

7 *Governor Allan Shivers*: Whitfield, *The Culture of the Cold War*, 45.

7 *"couldn't find a Communist"*: Craig and Logevall, *America's Cold War*, 124. Meanwhile, the people opposed to McCarthyism were reluctant to speak out because if they did, they risked being tarred as Communist sympathizers.

8 *The CIA*: Marchetti and Marks, *The CIA and the Cult of Intelligence*, 165.

8 *"was not intended"*: Harry Truman, December 1, 1963, David Noyes Papers, B 1, F "Chronological File, 1960–65, and Undated," HSTL.

8 *"It is now clear"*: Doolittle, *Report on the Activities*, 2–3. Also see Lisle, *The Dirty Tricks Department*, 247.

9 *"For some time"*: Harry Truman, "Limit CIA Role to Intelligence," *Washington Post* (December 22, 1963): A11.

9 *"I am impatient"*: Kinzer, *Poisoner in Chief*, 102.

10 *"more classical application"*: DSG, April 19, 1983, JRP, B 222, F 7, LOC, 10.

10 *"Did [it] produce"*: DSG, September 25, 1980, JRP, B 243, F 7, LOC, 8–9.

10 *extended Pavlov's work*: One early CIA memo claims as much, saying that the Soviets had conditioned a young boy to salivate at the thought of the number four: "They asked him to divide 8 by 2, and before he could actually verbalize the number '4' he salivated." "A/B, 1, 38/8," November 10, 1955, MORI 184428.

10 *show trials in Moscow*: See Applebaum, *Gulag*, chap. 6; McCoy, *A Question of Torture*, 22–23.

10 *Yuri Pyatakov*: Streatfeild, *Brainwash*, 4–5.

10 *Cardinal József Mindszenty*: Lawrence Hinkle and Harold Wolff, "Communist Control Techniques," April 2, 1956, CREST.

11 *"Somehow they took"*: Seed, *Brainwashing*, 53.

11 *"fully authorized"*: "Subject: Attached," March 3, 1952, MORI 147392.

11 *"All of this might seem"*: DSG, September 25, 1980, JRP, B 243, F 7, LOC, 11–12.

2. BLUEBIRD AND ARTICHOKE

13 *"utilize the polygraph"*: "Project Bluebird," April 5, 1950, CREST.

13 *"sing like a bird"*: Kinzer, *Poisoner in Chief*, 38.

13 *"Can accurate information"*: "Special Research, Bluebird," 1952, MORI 140401.

14 *"has a strong, aggressive look"*: "[redacted] Interview With," February 25, 1952, MORI 140394.

14 *"hypnotize a man"*: McCoy, *A Question of Torture*, 24.

14 *"hypnotic couriers"*: George Estabrooks, "Hypnosis Comes of Age," *Science Digest* (1971).

14 *"was forced to engage"*: "[redacted] Interview With," February 25, 1952, MORI 140394. Estabrooks also told Allen fanciful tales about how his subjects had performed paranormal feats. Some of them allegedly "read from a closed book considerable distance away." "A/B, 5, 28/11," July 9, 1951, MORI 147378.

15 *"mental claustrophobia"*: "Hypnotism and Covert Operations," May 5, 1955, MORI 190713.

15 **The Black Art**: "The Black Art," MORI 149585.

15 *"She was asked to count"*: "SI and H Experimentation," July 10, 1951, MORI 190570.

15 *reliving a recent vacation*: "SI and H Experimentation," July 10, 1951, MORI 190570.

16 *"Her rage would be"*: "Hypnotic Experimentation and Research," February 10, 1954, MORI 190691.

16 *Pierre Janet*: Orne, "The Potential Uses of Hypnosis in Interrogation," 182.

16 *"There is no evidence"*: Lovell, *Of Spies and Stratagems,* 89–90.

17 *"a prominent [redacted] politician"*: "Artichoke," January 1954, MORI 149438.

17 *"whether they wish it"*: "Organization of SO Components Dealing with Artichoke," MORI 190716.

17 *"neutralizing weapon"*: "Subject: Attached," March 3, 1952, MORI 147392.

17 *"This consists of knocking"*: M. Phillips, "The Lobotomy Files: One Doctor's Legacy," *Wall Street Journal* (December 12, 2013); Caruso and Sheehan, "Psychosurgery, Ethics, and Media," 5.

18 *"its exposure would cause"*: "Subject: Attached," March 3, 1952, MORI 147392.

18 *"What in God's name"*: Albarelli, *A Terrible Mistake,* 231.

18 *"how you interrogate somebody"*: DSG, September 25, 1980, JRP, B 243, F 7, LOC, 15.

19 *"a highly controlled"*: "Artichoke Cases," July 8, 1952, MORI 149427.

19 *"remarkable regression"*: "Artichoke Techniques," June 21, 1951, MORI 184471.

19 *"great length"*: "Artichoke Techniques," June 21, 1951, MORI 184471.

19 *Camp King*: Koch and Wech, *Code Name Artichoke*; Kinzer, *Poisoner in Chief*, 40–46. On Camp King, see Silver, "Questions, Questions, Questions." The United States is known to have recruited former Nazi scientists as part of Operation Paperclip, but their connection to Camp King is tenuous.

3. THE ORIGINS OF MKULTRA

21 *"I am beginning to see"*: Enoch and Quinn, *Statements,* 5–6. Dr. Huei-lan Chung, an infectious disease expert at the University of New York, commented on the list of diseases, "The causative agents of typhus fever and malaria are Rickettsiae and Plasmodiae respectively, whereas smallpox and yellow fever are due to two different kinds of filtrable virus. It is only natural that the prisoner in question [Enoch], not being a medical man, mixed up these infectious agents with pathogenic bacteria." Enoch and Quinn, *Statements,* 4.

21 *"It is very clear"*: Enoch and Quinn, *Statements,* 12. The *Report of the*

International Scientific Commission for the Investigation of the Facts Concerning Bacterial Warfare in Korea and China substantiated the confessions, but the report itself was propaganda. For a breakdown of the errors in the report, see Clews, *The Communists' New Weapon*. Also see Regis, *The Biology of Doom*, 226–28.

22 *"containing germ-laden insects"*: "Captured US Airmen Admit Germ Warfare," *China Monthly Review* (July 1952): 27–28.

22 *Accompanying the story*: Crane, "Chemical and Biological Warfare," 69–70.

22 *To further substantiate*: John Bruning, *Crimson Sky*, 115.

22 *"If the germ-infected"*: "Depositions by Captured US Airmen," September 16, 1952, Joseph Koepfli Papers, B 2, F "Korean War Germ Warfare," CIT.

22 *"propaganda specialist"*: *Communist Psychological Warfare*, 6.

22 *Hunter published an article*: Edward Hunter, "Brain-Washing Tactics Force Chinese into Ranks of Communist Party," *Miami Daily News* (September 1950). See Melley, "Brain Warfare."

23 *Kennan tersely responded*: Gaddis, *George F. Kennan*, 469.

23 *"some drug that caused"*: Frost, "An Interview with Richard Helms," 21.

23 *"What we found"*: Marshall Berges, "Louis J. and Kathryn West," *Los Angeles Times* (October 27, 1985): H1.

23 *"It is difficult"*: SCSGO, *Foreign and Military Intelligence*, 393.

23 *"Brain Warfare"*: Allen Dulles, "Brain Warfare," April 10, 1953, CREST.

24 *"discrediting individuals"*: Scheflin and Opton, *The Mind Manipulators*, 132.

25 *"These things are not"*: DSG, September 25, 1980, JRP, B 243, F 7, LOC, 17. See Michael Langan, "The Language of Diplomacy," *Boston Globe* (April 19, 2001).

25 *"What part did you play"*: DSG, September 25, 1980, JRP, B 243, F 7, LOC, 114–15.

26 *"Very vaguely"*: Kinzer, *Poisoner in Chief*, 48.

26 *"The Lovell referred to"*: DSG, May 17, 1983, JRP, B 223, F 1, LOC, 248–49.

26 *OSS Research and Development Branch*: See Lisle, *The Dirty Tricks Department*.

27 *Lovell persuaded Allen Dulles*: Wallace and Melton, *Spycraft*, 53.

27 *"I didn't know anything"*: DSG, September 25, 1980, JRP, B 243, F 7, LOC, 82.

4. LSD

29 *"It was particularly remarkable"*: Hofmann, *LSD*, 47.

30 *In the late 1940s*: Novak, "LSD before Leary," 90.

30 *"he'd come to me"*: Vannevar Bush, MIT Oral History Interviews, 686–87.

30 *"Ergot and Lysergic Acid"*: OSI, "Development of Research in Connection with Project Artichoke," November 21, 1951, MORI 147406.

30 *"The doctors are beside themselves"*: Fuller, *The Day of St. Anthony's Fire*, 120. Also see Jesse Rhodes, "How Deadly Bread Bewitched a French Village," *Smithsonian Magazine* (October 27, 2011); Mary Blume, "France's Unsolved Mystery of the Poisoned Bread," *New York Times* (July 23, 2008).

30 *"Tasteless, odorless"*: "Subject: Attached," MORI 148093. Albert Hofmann suspected that the CIA had gotten its first batch of LSD from the U.S. Food and Drug Administration, which in turn had gotten it from Sandoz. Michael Horowitz, "Interview: Albert Hofmann," *High Times* (July 1976).

31 *"An infinitesimally small dose"*: Harris Chadwell, "Briefing for the Psychological Strategy Board," May 13, 1953, CREST.

31 *"We had thought"*: Lee and Shlain, *Acid Dreams*, 14.

31 *"War without death"*: Scheflin and Opton, *The Mind Manipulators*, 202. The U.S. Army conducted LSD tests on soldiers. See Ross, "LSD Experiments by the United States Army."

31 *birds flying overhead*: Raffi Khatchadourian, "Operation Delirium," *New Yorker* (December 10, 2012).

31 *"I was not in control"*: Raffi Khatchadourian, "Operation Delirium," *New Yorker* (December 10, 2012). Also see Ketchum, *Chemical Warfare Secrets*, 25.

31 *Psychochemical Warfare*: Raffi Khatchadourian, "Operation Delirium," *New Yorker* (December 10, 2012).

32 *"I was fascinated"*: Albarelli, *A Terrible Mistake*, 61.

32 *Influenced by Greene's arguments*: See FRUS, *The Intelligence Community*, document 244.

32 *An American military attaché*: "D-Lysergic Acid Diethylamide (LSD-25)," May 4, 1953, MORI 184428.

32 *The company had never*: "Potential Large-Scale Availability of LSD," October 26, 1954, MORI 144957. Sandoz was already losing interest in LSD because of ethical concerns, unfavorable press, and workplace accidents. A CIA report on LSD notes, "Once, in a Swiss mental hospital, a practical joker sneaked a few granules of LSD-25 into a staff nurse's coffee. The frantic girl, apparently driven to believe that she had become schizophrenic, leaped to her death from the hospital roof." Albarelli, *A Terrible Mistake*, 375.

33 *"usually with a physician"*: DSG, April 19, 1983, JRP, B 222, F 8, LOC, 151–55.

33 *"an out-of-bodyness"*: Ted Gup, "The Coldest Warrior," *Washington Post* (December 16, 2001).

33 *"I've seen all the magicians"*: Robinson, *The Magician*, 212.

33 *Mulholland gave it all up*: Michael Edwards, "The Sphinx and the Spy: The Clandestine World of John Mulholland," *Genii Magazine* (April 2001).

33 *"divulge, publish"*: Robinson, *The Magician*, 115.

34 *"He was happy"*: Albarelli, *A Terrible Mistake*, 259.

34 **Some Operational Applications**: Melton and Wallace, *The Official CIA Manual.*

34 *"couldn't pull himself"*: Marks, *The Search for the Manchurian Candidate,* 71; Lee and Shlain, *Acid Dreams,* 29.

35 *"Is that LSD"*: Nicholas Horrock, "Destruction of LSD Data Laid to C.I.A. Aide in '73," *New York Times* (July 18, 1975).

35 *if unwitting Americans were dosed*: The CIA hired psychiatrist Nick Bercel to determine how much LSD it would take to contaminate the water supply of Los Angeles. He realized that the there was enough chlorine in the water to neutralize the drug. Lee and Shlain, *Acid Dreams,* 21.

5. DEEP CREEK

37 *"We didn't know"*: Lee and Shlain, *Acid Dreams,* 38.

37 *"very apprehensive"*: *Barrett v. United States,* 660 F. Supp. 1291 (S.D.N.Y. 1987).

38 *"I'm in awful shape"*: Albarelli, *A Terrible Mistake,* 162.

38 *"lapsing into coma"*: *Barrett v. United States,* 660 F. Supp. 1291 (S.D.N.Y. 1987). Another patient was given the same substance. Her reaction was so immediate and violent that the doctors stopped the injection early. "I've been in hell," she later said. "Why did they put me in hell? They were supposed to make me feel good. I've never felt this bad before. I feel terrible."

38 *"the United States negligently"*: *Barrett v. United States,* 660 F. Supp. 1291 (S.D.N.Y. 1987). Also see *Biomedical and Behavioral Research,* 135.

38 *"My country destroyed"*: *Cold War Era Human Subject Experimentation,* 54.

38 *"After hearing of that death"*: DSG, May 17, 1983, JRP, B 223, F 1, LOC, 268.

39 *"Yes, I was identity A"*: DSG, April 19, 1983, JRP, B 222, F 8, LOC, 186–90.

40 *"a little Detrick"*: Scott Shane, "Buried Secrets of Biowarfare," *Baltimore Sun* (August 1, 2004).

40 *"We felt that"*: DSG, May 17, 1983, JRP, B 223, F 1, LOC, 249. The collaboration between the TSS and SOD was code-named MKNAOMI, apparently in reference to Harold Abramson's secretary, Naomi Busner.

40 *"suicide agents"*: Albarelli, *A Terrible Mistake,* 781.

40 *"Who put the LSD"*: DSG, April 19, 1983, JRP, B 222, F 8, LOC, 192–93.

41 *"[Lashbrook] didn't want to come"*: Joseph Rauh, "Conversation with Robert Lashbrook," March 25, 1986, JRP, B 224, F 7, LOC, 37.

41 *"Now, you were handed"*: DRL, May 14, 1986, JRP, B 224, F 7, LOC, 8.

42 *"Now, it is your testimony"*: DRL, May 14, 1986, JRP, B 224, F 7, LOC, 36–37.

42 *"There was one"*: DRL, May 14, 1986, JRP, B 224, F 7, LOC, 40–41.

43 *"most frightening experience"*: Sheffield Edwards, "Suicide of Frank Olsen [*sic*]," JRP, B 229, F 9, LOC; *Biomedical and Behavioral Research,* 139.

43 *"We dried the virus"*: Albarelli, *A Terrible Mistake,* 75.

43 *Operation Sea-Spray: Biological Testing Involving Human Subjects.* Also see Jim Carlton, "Of Microbes and Mock Attacks: Years Ago, the Military Sprayed Germs on U.S. Cities," *Wall Street Journal* (October 22, 2001); Rebecca Kreston, "Blood & Fog: The Military's Germ Warfare Tests in San Francisco," *Discover* (June 28, 2015).

43 *"He is extremely tactless"*: Albarelli, *A Terrible Mistake,* 629–31.

44 *"a totally different person"*: DAO, September 16, 1988, JRP, B 226, F 4, LOC, 12–13.

44 *"[Olson] asked me"*: Vincent Ruwet on Frank Olson, FOPD.

44 *"Jim Stubbs wanted"*: DAO, September 16, 1988, JRP, B 226, F 4, LOC, 13–16.

45 *"How did Lashbrook"*: DSG, April 19, 1983, JRP, B 222, F 8, LOC, 200.

45 *"Once there was a student"*: Albarelli, *A Terrible Mistake,* 126.

46 *"wild and crazy"*: Albarelli, *A Terrible Mistake,* 286.

46 *"was very anxious"*: Vincent Ruwet on Frank Olson, FOPD.

46 *"Many older interests"*: Harold Abramson, "Observations on Mr. Frank Olson," December 4, 1953, FOPD.

46 *"What's behind all this?"*: Vincent Ruwet on Frank Olson, FOPD.

46 *Olson stood up and left*: Vincent Ruwet on Frank Olson, FOPD.

46 *Olson snuck out*: Robert Lashbrook, "Observations on Frank Olson," FOPD.

47 *"What do you want"*: Vincent Ruwet on Frank Olson, FOPD.

47 *"came up to my house"*: DAO, September 16, 1988, JRP, B 226, F 4, LOC, 20.

47 *"talked about the incompetence"*: Sidney Gottlieb, "Observation on Dr. Frank Olson," FOPD.

47 *"giving me dope"*: Harold Abramson, "Statement by Harold Abramson," November 28, 1953, FOPD.

47 *"psychotic state"*: Harold Abramson, "Observations on Mr. Frank Olson," December 4, 1953, FOPD.

47 *plotting to "get" him*: Robert Lashbrook, "Observations on Frank Olson," FOPD.

48 *Olson then called Alice*: Albarelli, *A Terrible Mistake,* 116.

6. THE FRANK OLSON INCIDENT

49 *"Somewhere around 0230"*: Robert Lashbrook, "Observations on Frank Olson," FOPD.

49 *"We got a jumper"*: Albarelli, *A Terrible Mistake,* 17–18.

49   *"Just hold on"*: Albarelli, *A Terrible Mistake*, 18–19.

49   *"His right hand"*: Armond Pastore to Alice Olson, July 13, 1975, FOPD.

49   *Lashbrook peered out*: "Case No. 73317," December 3, 1953, FOPD.

50   *"Somebody in there?"*: Albarelli, *A Terrible Mistake*, 20–22; Sheffield
      Edwards, "Suicide of Frank Olsen [*sic*]," JRP, B 229, F 9, LOC.

50   *"It's all over"*: DAO, September 16, 1988, JRP, B 226, F 4, LOC, 34–35.
      Lashbrook acknowledged making a call to Gottlieb, but he denied saying such a thing.

50   *James McCord, Jr.*: "Case No. 73317," December 3, 1953, FOPD.

51   *"Walter"*: "Case No. 73317," December 3, 1953, FOPD.

52   *"There was some sort of accident"*: Albarelli, *A Terrible Mistake*, 34–35.

52   *"Your father had an accident"*: Kinzer, *Poisoner in Chief*, 123.

52   *"very sympathetic"*: DAO, September 16, 1988, JRP, B 226, F 4, LOC,
      17–18.

52   *Only three caches*: "Use of LSD," December 1, 1953, FOPD.

53   *"You can't have a nice"*: Albarelli, *A Terrible Mistake*, 100.

53   *"[Sheffield] Edwards and [Harris] Chadwell"*: "Kirkpatrick Diary," FOPD.

53   *"about to kill the Schwab"*: "Conversation with Gibbons," December 14,
      1953, FOPD.

53   *On a warm day in August*: Regis, *The Biology of Doom*, 117–19.

54   *"As long as I am head"*: Ted Gup, "The Coldest Warrior," *Washington
      Post* (December 16, 2001).

54   *"could seriously affect"*: Lyman Kirkpatrick, "The Suicide of Frank Olson,"
      December 18, 1953, FOPD.

54   *"It is my conclusion"*: Lawrence Houston, "Frank R. Olson," December
      9, 1953, FOPD.

54   *"I brought out his stutter"*: Marks, *The Search for the Manchurian Candi-
      date*, 83.

54   *"an injustice"*: Luis de Florez to Allen Dulles, February 2, 1954, FOPD.

54   *Gottlieb later claimed*: DSG, April 19, 1983, JRP, B 222, F 8, LOC, 221.

55   *"It is my opinion"*: Allen Dulles to Sidney Gottlieb, February 10, 1954,
      FOPD.

55   *"backstopped"*: Robert Cunningham, "Lashbrook, Doctor Robert V.,"
      January 11, 1954, FOPD; Robert Cunningham, "Lashbrook, Robert V., Dr.,"
      January 19, 1954, FOPD.

55   *negative publicity*: Moreover, the insurance company might discover that
      LSD played a role in Olson's death. The CIA wanted to downplay its interest
      in LSD lest any enemies be tempted to acquire some for themselves.

55   *"Did [Olson's death]"*: DSG, September 25, 1980, JRP, B 243, F 7, LOC, 68.

55   *"LSD is quite capable"*: "Gottlieb, Dr. Sidney," February 3, 1953, JRP,
      B 230, F 5, LOC.

55   *"I was very upset"*: DSG, April 19, 1983, JRP, B 222, F 8, LOC, 206–7.

56   *"The Olson death"*: DSG, April 19, 1983, JRP, B 222, F 8, LOC, 199.

7. OPERATION MIDNIGHT CLIMAX

57 *"There is no question"*: "Memorandum on T.D.," June 2, 1943, MORI 184373. On White and the OSS, see Lisle, *The Dirty Tricks Department,* 207–11.

58 *"You knew a George White"*: DSG, May 17, 1983, JRP, B 223, F 2, LOC, 391–93.

59 *"A couple of crew-cut"*: John Crewdson, "Abuses in Testing of Drugs by C.I.A. to be Panel Focus," *New York Times* (September 20, 1977): 85.

59 *"always armed to the teeth"*: Albarelli, *A Terrible Mistake,* 217.

59 *"a small three-room"*: DSG, May 17, 1983, JRP, B 223, F 2, LOC, 395–96.

59 *injected LSD through the cork*: DPG, August 25, 1983, JRP, B 222, F 6, LOC, 35.

59 *"Giannini, glass in his hand"*: Reid, *The Shame of New York,* 83–84.

60 *"tied him up"*: Douglas Valentine, "Sex, Drugs and the CIA," *Counter-Punch* (June 19, 2002); Valentine, *The Strength of the Wolf,* 129–30.

60 *"I was angry at George"*: Douglas Valentine, "Sex, Drugs and the CIA," *CounterPunch* (June 19, 2002).

60 *"It was obvious"*: Douglas Valentine, "Sex, Drugs and the CIA," *Counter-Punch* (June 19, 2002).

60 *Barbara exhibited a paranoia*: In another story reminiscent of Frank Olson, Edith Christensen claimed that the CIA had drugged her husband, Marine colonel Jim Christensen. After he interviewed there in 1966, she said that he "kept asking me where I bought my meat and thought the CIA was poisoning the meat he was eating." A week later, he shot himself in the head with his service revolver. The CIA denied Edith's accusation. Scheflin and Opton, *The Mind Manipulators,* 162–66. Also see "Official Agency Statement on James R. Christensen Case," May 20, 1966, CREST; "Untruthful Attacks on the Central Intelligence Agency," June 2, 1966, CREST.

60 *"Poor little bastard"*: John Jacobs, "The Diaries of a CIA Operative," *Washington Post* (September 5, 1977): A1.

61 *"What do you know"*: DSG, May 17, 1983, JRP, B 223, F 2, LOC, 399–401.

62 *"mind-bending drugs"*: Richard Stratton, "Altered States of America," *Spin Magazine* (March 1994).

62 *"the whores"*: Marks, *The Search for the Manchurian Candidate,* 91.

62 *White paid the prostitutes*: "Accountability for Certain Expenditures under Subproject 42," August 17, 1956, MORI 17440.

62 *"I always wanted"*: Richard Stratton, "Altered States of America," *Spin Magazine* (March 1994).

62 *A declassified inventory*: "Inventory of [redacted]," MORI 17440.

62 *the bedroom"*: "Colonel George Hunter White," August 5, 1953, George White FBI File.

62 *"comprehensive library"*: Kinzer, *Poisoner in Chief,* 142.

62 *CIA audit staff*: Whenever White's spending habits outpaced the rate at which the CIA could replenish his bank account, he would tersely write, "No money yet" and "Need money!" White Letters, MORIs 17411 and 17440.

63 *"handi-dandi portable toilet"*: "Inventory of [*redacted*]," MORI 17440.

63 *"A 'doorway' was constructed"*: "Discussion with [*redacted*]," August 1, 1955, MORI 17440.

63 *"that if you spilled"*: John Crewdson, "Abuse in Testing of Drugs by C.I.A. to Be Panel Focus," *New York Times* (September 20, 1977).

63 *"when people had information"*: Richard Stratton, "Altered States of America," *Spin Magazine* (March 1994).

63 *"Two men sit"*: Albarelli, *A Terrible Mistake*, 414.

64 *He claimed not to remember*: DSG, May 17, 1983, JRP, B 223, F 2, LOC, 402–03.

64 *"White used to send me"*: Richard Stratton, "Altered States of America," *Spin Magazine* (March 1994).

65 *"cock crazy"*: Kinzer, *Poisoner in Chief*, 149.

65 *"hush puppy"*: Morse Allen, "Project MKULTRA," June 9, 1954, JRP, B 230, F 4, LOC.

65 *"He always said he never"*: Richard Stratton, "Altered States of America," *Spin Magazine* (March 1994).

65 *Gottlieb estimated*: DSG, May 17, 1983, JRP, B 223, F 2, LOC, 405–7. For the checks, see MORI 17411.

65 *"I had a feeling"*: Troy Hooper, "Operation Midnight Climax: How the CIA Dosed S.F. Citizens with LSD," *SF Weekly* (March 14, 2012).

66 *secret devices*: *Human Drug Testing by the CIA*, 106–8.

66 *"C'mon, Ike"*: Richard Stratton, "Altered States of America," *Spin Magazine* (March 1994).

66 *"I was overseas"*: DSG, May 17, 1983, JRP, B 223, F 2, LOC, 395–96, 412.

66 *"showed up with a snub"*: DWP, September 17, 1982, JRP, B 226, F 9, LOC, 95–96.

66 *Things didn't go as planned*: DDR, September 1, 1982, JRP, B 227, F 5, LOC, 94.

66 *"got no effect"*: DJG, January 19, 1983, JRP, B 222, F 5, LOC, 167.

66 *"How does administering LSD"*: DSG, May 17, 1983, JRP, B 223, F 2, LOC, 404–5.

67 *"it has a tremendous effect"*: Marks, *The Search for the Manchurian Candidate*, 95.

67 *"good for the country"*: Richard Stratton, "Altered States of America," *Spin Magazine* (March 1994).

67 *"I certainly don't"*: DSG, June 28, 1983, JRP, B 223, F 3, LOC, 523.

67 *"I was a very minor"*: Marks, *The Search for the Manchurian Candidate*, 101.

8. OVERSEAS OPERATIONS

69 *"it is a fact"*: DSG, April 19, 1983, JRP, B 222, F 8, LOC, 125–28.

70 *"Mr. Sidney Gottlieb"*: Albarelli, *A Terrible Mistake,* 176.

70 *"operations-type tests"*: "Information Concerning Possible Unauthorized Operational Use of Chemicals," August 10, 1954, JRP, B 230, F 4, LOC.

70 *"Gottlieb also is reported"*: Morse Allen, "Project MKULTRA," June 9, 1954, JRP, B 230, F 4, LOC.

70 *operation in the Philippines*: Albarelli, *A Terrible Mistake,* 135.

70 *"Is that correct?"*: DSG, April 19, 1983, JRP, B 222, F 8, LOC, 184–85.

71 *MKDELTA*: *Project MKULTRA,* 72.

71 *six different drugs*: Lyman Kirkpatrick, "Excerpt from 1957 IG Inspection of TSD," 1957, MORI 146167.

71 *"an individual in conjunction"*: *Biomedical and Behavioral Research,* 261–62.

71 *"The novelty"*: Kinzer, *Poisoner in Chief,* 106–7.

9. THE CUTOUTS

73 *he was hopeful*: DSG, September 25, 1980, JRP, B 243, F 7, LOC, 28.

73 *"We had no trouble"*: DSG, September 25, 1980, JRP, B 243, F 7, LOC, 28–31.

74 *cashier's checks*: DSG, September 25, 1980, JRP, B 243, F 7, LOC, 110.

74 *plausible deniability*: DSG, September 25, 1980, JRP, B 243, F 7, LOC, 109.

74 *"We struck oil"*: *Human Drug Testing by the CIA,* 88–89; *Project MKULTRA,* 7.

74 *"Dr. Geschickter was primarily"*: DSG, June 28, 1983, JRP, B 223, F 3, LOC, 472–74.

75 *list of the compounds*: "35–4-A," May 5, 1955, MORI 17432.

75 *"maximum levels"*: Jo Thomas, "C.I.A. Data Describe Six-Year Drug Tests," *New York Times* (August 16, 1977): 18.

75 *"I can only give*: *Human Drug Testing by the CIA,* 44–45.

75 *SIHE*: The Society for the Investigation of Human Ecology was later renamed the Human Ecology Fund.

75 *studies unrelated*: One of the unrelated studies concerned circumcision and its effects on the emotional state of children. "An Exploratory Study on the Effects of Circumcision," MORI 17475.

76 *"a lot of his head"*: A. Robert Abboud, Abraham Lincoln Presidential Library Oral History, 27.

76 *Gittinger had a bad back*: DJG, January 19, 1983, JRP, B 222, F 4, LOC, 12–13.

76 *"do their bidding"*: Lawrence Hinkle and Harold Wolff, "Communist Control Techniques," April 2, 1956, CREST.

76 *"The toxins of fatigue"*: Vogeler, *I Was Stalin's Prisoner,* 141, 158, 192.

77 *"The profound boredom"*: Lawrence Hinkle and Harold Wolff, "Communist Control Techniques," April 2, 1956, CREST.

10. PSYCHIC DRIVING

79 *"Dr. Gottlieb"*: DSG, May 17, 1983, JRP, B 223, F 1, LOC, 321–22.

79 *Rudolf Hess*: Hess was acting erratically and claimed to be suffering from mental illness. The psychiatric team briefly considered giving him truth drugs to make him confess to faking his symptoms, but Robert Jackson, the lead prosecutor for the United States, argued against it. Perisco, *Nuremberg,* 148.

80 *"He was a dictator"*: DLO, May 3, 1988, JRP, B 225, F 5, LOC, 116.

80 *"He was God"*: DDO, August 12, 1988, JRP, B 226, F 5, LOC, 38.

80 *"a spooky old place"*: DVO, June 17, 1986, JRP, B 226, F 6, LOC, 63.

80 *"An overwhelming emotional"*: Sargant, *Battle for the Mind,* 112.

81 *"Give me a child"*: A similar phrase was common among the Jesuits: "Give me a child until he is seven, and I'll give you the man."

81 *Ewen Cameron adopted*: See Lemov, "Brainwashing's Avatar."

81 *a schizophrenic boy*: Gillmor, *I Swear by Apollo,* 42–43.

81 *"a blonde and sultry girl"*: Ewen Cameron, "Adventures with Repetition," JRP, B 229, F 6, LOC, 3.

81 *"If you don't keep quiet"*: Cameron, "Psychic Driving," 502; Gordon, *Journey into Madness,* 245.

82 *"I even noticed"*: Ewen Cameron, "Adventures with Repetition," JRP, B 229, F 6, LOC, 4.

82 *"Behold the Turtle"*: Luria, *Skating on the Edge.*

82 *"Well, now, let's go back"*: DJG, January 19, 1983, JRP, B 222, F 4, LOC, 47–48.

83 *"as a means of breaking down"*: "Application for Grant," January 21, 1957, MORI 17468. It's unclear whether Cameron knew that the SIHE was a cutout for the CIA.

83 *"Did you do anything"*: DJG, January 19, 1983, JRP, B 222, F 4, LOC, 36–37.

84 *twenty hours a day*: Cameron, "Psychic Driving," 503–4.

84 *"It is doubtful"*: DFL, July 20, 1983, JRP, B 225, F 1, LOC, 142–43.

84 *"Do you realize"*: Streatfeild, *Brainwash,* 218–19.

84 *he would record*: DKS, October 2, 1988, JRP, B 228, F 2, LOC, 32.

84 *"They had this machine"*: Streatfeild, *Brainwash,* 220–21.

85 *"In my mind"*: DJH, June 25, 1986, JRP, B 224, F 3, LOC, 74–75.

85 *"Lauren G."*: Marks, *The Search for the Manchurian Candidate,* 140.

85 *"Sleep Room"*: See DWL, September 9, 1988, JRP, B 224, F 5, LOC, 37.

85 *"Cerebrophone"*: On Cameron and the Cerebrophone, see DLH,

May 19, 1988, JRP, B 224, F 1, LOC, 54–56; Lemov, "Brainwashing's Avatar," 75; Streatfeild, *Brainwash,* 216.

86 *"only babbles"*: Gordon, *Journey into Madness,* 207.

86 *"You are no good"*: DJH, June 25, 1986, JRP, B 224, F 3, LOC, 61.

86 *"I think that it's on account"*: DJH, June 25, 1986, JRP, B 224, F 3, LOC, 63–64, 79.

86 *The chambers were essentially*: Weinstein, *Psychiatry and the CIA,* 118.

86 *Hebb had paid*: Woodburn Heron, "The Psychology of Boredom," *Scientific American* 196, no. 1 (January 1957): 52–54. Also see DOS, August 11, 1988, JRP, B 228, F 3, LOC. Hebb said that the "chief impetus" for the experiment "was the dismay at the kind of 'confessions' being produced at the Russian Communist trials." Solomon, *Sensory Deprivation,* 6.

87 *"markedly irritable"*: Woodburn Heron, "The Psychology of Boredom," *Scientific American* 196, no. 1 (January 1957): 54–56.

87 *Half of the students*: Gillmor, *I Swear by Apollo,* 94.

87 *"It is one thing"*: Collins, *In the Sleep Room,* 50–52.

87 *the CIA began funding*: McCoy, *A Question of Torture,* 38; McCoy, "Science in Dachau's Shadow," 406.

87 *"sobbing in a most"*: Marks, *The Search for the Manchurian Candidate,* 138.

87 *"terminal type"*: Marks, *The Search for the Manchurian Candidate,* 138, 202.

87 *His experiments on them*: MORI 17462. Throughout the 1950s, neuroscientists in the United States conducted similar experiments even without CIA funding. John Lilly attached electrodes to the brains of monkeys and discovered the seats of pain, fear, anger, anxiety, erection, and ejaculation. The CIA soon contacted Lilly for a briefing on his research, but he refused to cooperate and switched fields. His office neighbor, none other than Maitland Baldwin, was doing research on sensory deprivation that intrigued him. Lilly decided to get involved, unaware of Baldwin's connection to the CIA. In 1954, Lilly invented the first isolation tank. Again the CIA came knocking, again Lilly refused to cooperate, and again he switched fields, this time to focus on communicating with dolphins. Perhaps the CIA got the last laugh. In Project Oxygas, it trained dolphins to become "swimmer attack systems," essentially animal torpedoes that carried explosives toward enemy ships. "Project Oxygas," November 2, 1964, CREST.

88 *"rocked the heads"*: *Human Drug Testing by the CIA,* 90.

11. DEPATTERNING

89 *"he just laughed"*: DVO, June 17, 1986, JRP, B 226, F 7, LOC, 16.

89 *"didn't know what"*: DVO, June 17, 1986, JRP, B 226, F 7, LOC, 35.

89 *"What's that?"*: DVO, June 17, 1986, JRP, B 226, F 7, LOC, 61–62.

89 *"Under Cameron's theory"*: Cooper, *Opinion of George Cooper,* 15.

90 *"short of cutting"*: "Amnesia," MORI 189903.

90 *"guarantee amnesia"*: "Artichoke," December 3, 1951, MORI 146342.

90 *"Please don't talk"*: DVO, June 17, 1986, JRP, B 226, F 7, LOC, 30–31. Velma developed a kind of Stockholm syndrome for Cameron. She depended on his reassurance despite the harm that he caused her. The feeling wasn't mutual, nor did it last. When asked whether she ever talked to her husband about Cameron, she said, "The only discussions we have is what a bastard Cameron was." DVO, June 17, 1986, JRP, B 226, F 7, LOC, 96, 103.

90 *"I don't want to do it"*: DVO, June 17, 1986, JRP, B 226, F 7, LOC, 91.

90 *"It was like they were"*: Streatfeild, *Brainwash,* 214.

90 *"This will help you"*: Gordon, *Journey into Madness,* 210.

90 *"The shock treatment"*: "Dr. Ewen Cameron Destroyed Minds at Allan Memorial Hospital in Montreal," Alliance for Human Research Protection, January 18, 2015.

91 *"You have no idea"*: Klein, *The Shock Doctrine,* chap. 1; Ingrid Peritz, "Suit Alleges Infamous MD Ruined Woman," *Globe and Mail* (January 27, 2000).

91 *Mary Morrow*: DMM, June 19, 1986, JRP, B 226, F 3, LOC.

93 *"Mommy is going"*: Collins, *In the Sleep Room,* 153.

93 *prioritized her career*: When CIA attorney Scott Kragie asked Mary whether she had ever had a romantic relationship with anyone at the Allan, she refused to answer. Attorney James Turner interjected to say that Kragie would have to get an order from the judge before she would answer. Mary remained steadfast: "He'll have to choke me first." DMM, June 19, 1986, JRP, B 226, F 3, LOC, 135–36.

94 *"We tried [psychic] driving"*: Collins, *In the Sleep Room,* 189.

94 *"[Cameron] conducted these treatments"*: DLO, May 3, 1988, JRP, B 225, F 5, LOC, 97–144. Robert Cleghorn, Cameron's successor as chief psychiatrist at the Allan, concurred. "In view of the time," he said, "[Cameron] was within ethical boundaries." DRC, May 17, 1988, JRP, B 221, F 14, LOC, 22.

12. THE WILD WEST

95 *In the early morning*: "Airman Confesses to Murder of Tot," *Fort Worth Star-Telegram* (July 5, 1954): 1.

96 *"I'd give my life"*: Wray Weddell, "Accused Rapist Wishes Slaying Hadn't Happened," *Austin Statesman* (July 7, 1954): 1.

96 *"the degree to which"*: O'Neill, *Chaos,* 360–61.

97 *"So what do you do now?"*: Interrogation Transcript, LJWP, B 143, F8, UCLA.

101 *"In the last one third"*: West, "Psychiatric Reflections."

102 *"Better than some"*: Howard Hunt, "Shaver 'Truth Serum' Test Results Bared," *San Antonio Express* (September 22, 1954).

102 *"flowing, hypnotic voice"*: David Nevin, "Defense Objections Slow Trial of Shaver," *San Antonio Express* (October 1, 1954).

102 *"Your profession"*: David Nevin, "Shaver to Appeal Only Death," *San Antonio Express* (September 29, 1954).

103 *"Why don't you leave"*: Howard Hunt, "Mrs. Shaver Told: 'Get Out of Town,'" *San Antonio Express* (September 30, 1954).

103 *In a last-ditch effort*: "Death Mixup Seen as Shaver Slaying Case Goes to Jury," *San Antonio Express* (October 2, 1954).

103 *"like a man in a trance"*: Howard Hunt, "Mysterious Note Threatens Alleged Sex-Killer's Wife," *San Antonio Express* (September 30, 1954).

103 *"I will burn the bum"*: "Shaver Granted Second Trial in S.A. Rape Death," *San Antonio Express* (June 23, 1955).

103 *"I am convinced"*: "Mete Out Death Penalty to Jimmy Shaver," *Del Rio News-Herald* (April 1, 1956).

104 *"The best you can do"*: "County Jail Inmate Confesses to Slaying," *San Antonio Express* (February 5, 1958).

104 *"I'll see that you"*: "Prisoner in Shaver Case under Guard," *San Antonio Express* (February 13, 1958).

104 *Yet another prisoner*: "Shaver Asked for Lie," *San Antonio Express* (February 27, 1958).

104 *Chere Jo Horton's father*: Don Reid, "Shaver Meets Death Smiling," *San Antonio Light* (July 25, 1958).

104 *"May God bless"*: "Chair Claims Jimmy Shaver," *Fort Worth Star-Telegram* (July 25, 1958): 1.

104 *"prisoners in the local stockade"*: O'Neill, *Chaos*, 361.

105 *"I was already sick"*: Interrogation Transcript, LJWP, B 143, F8, UCLA.

105 *last names "Sa" through "St"*: O'Neill, *Chaos*, 372.

105 *"have yielded promising"*: Louis West, "Psychophysiological Studies of Hypnosis and Suggestibility," 1956, LJWP, B 133, F 6, UCLA. Also see MORI 17441.

105 *"true memories"*: Louis West, "Report on Research in Hypnosis," 1956, LJWP, B 133, F 6, UCLA.

105 *"Five minutes after"*: West, Pierce, and Thomas, "Lysergic Acid Diethylamide," 1101–2.

105 *"How in the world"*: O'Neill, *Chaos*, 376.

106 *"all the Jews"*: Louis West, "Report on Psychiatric Evaluation of Jack Ruby," April 26, 1964.

106 *"I would like some real"*: "Texas: Trying for the Truth of It," *Time* (May 8, 1964).

106 *Beavers reached the same conclusion*: O'Neill, *Chaos*, 379–80.

106 *"science-fiction psychotherapy"*: "Scientologist Response Remains True to Form," *Daily Bruin* (August 2, 1993): 12.

107 *"anti-religious activities"*: Nancy Hsu, "Church Members File Suit against Professor, Officials," *Daily Bruin* (May 17, 1993): 3.

107 *"chemical castration"*: Linda Hight, "Scientology Responds," *Daily Bruin* (July 25, 1993): 14.

107 *"He often said and did"*: West, *The Last Goodnights*, 15.

13. PRISON EXPERIMENTS

109 *"I'll shoot"*: Lehr and O'Neill, *Whitey*, 77.

109 *"The arrest was effected"*: Lehr and O'Neill, *Whitey*, 81.

109 *"could teach the devil"*: Shelley Murphy, "Gangster's Life Lures Host of Storytellers," *Boston Globe* (April 18, 2004).

109 *"Total loss of appetite"*: James Bulger, "I Was a Guinea Pig for CIA Drug Experiments," *Ozy* (May 9, 2017).

110 *"I was in prison"*: Kathy Curran, "Whitey Bulger's Notebook Chronicles LSD Prison Testing," *CBS Boston* (July 7, 2011).

110 *"pried loose"*: James Bulger, "I Was a Guinea Pig for CIA Drug Experiments," *Ozy* (May 9, 2017).

110 *"Nearly two years"*: T. J. English, "The Defense That Sank Whitey Bulger," *Daily Beast* (July 11, 2017). After the trial, one of the jurors expressed sympathy for this argument: "Had I known [about the LSD tests], I would have absolutely held off. . . . His brain may have been altered, so how could you say he was really guilty?" Michael Rezendes, "After Learning of Whitey Bulger LSD Tests, Juror Has Regrets," *Associated Press* (February 22, 2020).

110 *Sidney Gottlieb first became*: DSG, September 25, 1980, JRP, B 243, F 7, LOC, 102.

110 *"I don't think"*: DSG, September 25, 1980, JRP, B 243, F 7, LOC, 104.

111 *"Carl Pfeiffer probably healed"*: Braverman, "Memories of Carl C. Pfeiffer," 7.

111 *$358,323.96*: DSG, December 8, 1981, JRP, B 243, F 6, LOC, 45. Pfeiffer also conducted drug tests at the Bordentown Reformatory in New Jersey.

111 *"I, [blank], the undersigned"*: "Contract," *Scott v. Casey*, 562 F. 475 (N.D. Ga. 1983).

111 *"I just wanted"*: Albarelli, *A Terrible Mistake*, 302.

111 *Addiction Research Center*: See Campbell, *Discovering Addiction*, chap. 3.

112 *"extremely potent"*: Harris Isbell, "NIMH Addiction Research Center," July 14, 1954, MORI 151524. Prisoner James Childs said that the only thing he was told was that the drugs wouldn't kill him. *Biomedical and Behavioral Research*, 249.

112 *Junkies in the Lexington*: DSG, May 17, 1983, JRP, B 223, F 2, LOC, 383.

112 *"I never saw"*: DPG, August 15, 1983, JRP, B 222, F 6, LOC, 62.

112 *"The guys on research"*: Campbell, Olson, and Walden, *The Narcotic Farm*, 23.

112 *"the most amazing demonstrations"*: Harris Isbell, "NIMH Addiction Research Center," July 14, 1954, MORI 151524.

112 *"[complaining] is to be expected"*: Marks, *The Search for the Manchurian Candidate*, 63.

113 *"If you wanted it"*: Marks, *The Search for the Manchurian Candidate*, 64.

113 *"That was the custom"*: *Biomedical and Behavioral Research*, 253–54.

113 *Henry Wall*: Wall, *From Healing to Hell*.

14. SUBPROJECTS

115 *The rest of the subprojects*: See MORIs 17453, 17455, 17393, 17395, and 17436.

115 *Over half of them had*: Crawford, "The Polygraph in Agent Interrogation," 32–34.

115 *The miniature polygraphs*: "Establishing and Substantiating the 'Bona Fides' of Agent," MORI 17488; Albarelli, *A Terrible Mistake*, 293.

116 *"remote control of activities"*: "Final Report," MORI 21825; "Project MKULTRA, Subproject No. 94," November 22, 1961, MORI 17497.

116 *"If a change in direction"*: "Final Report," MORI 21825, 45.

116 *"in all cases [it] caused"*: "Meeting with Dr. [redacted]," September 25, 1968, MORI 21914.

116 *"payloads of interest"*: "Recommendations Concerning [redacted] Program," March 3, 1967, MORI 21895.

116 *"direct executive action"*: "Project MKULTRA, Subproject No. 142," May 22, 1962, MORI 17402.

116 *"are capable of carrying"*: "Meeting with Dr. [redacted]," September 25, 1968, MORI 21914.

117 *"the application of selected"*: "Proposal," MORI 17497.

117 *"reject drugs"*: DSG, September 25, 1980, JRP, B 243, F 7, LOC, 26–27.

117 *"neurotropic toxic substance"*: "The 'K' Problem," MORI 17471.

117 *Caribbean botanical specimens*: "Exploration of Potent Plant Resources in the Caribbean Region," February 7, 1956, MORI 148092.

117 *"swamped"*: "Reports; Request for from TSS," August 10, 1954, MORI 184431.

117 *"They draw the gall"*: Bergreen, *Marco Polo*, 181.

117 *"poor refrigeration conditions"*: "Crocodile Gall Bladder," February 7, 1962, MORI 184583.

118 *"a sort of truth serum"*: "Piule," November 14, 1952, MORI 147399.

118 *James Moore*: "Did I consider what would have happened if this stuff were given to unwitting people?," Moore later asked himself. "No. Particularly no." Marks, *The Search for the Manchurian Candidate,* 110–11.

118 *"rancid odor"*: R. Gordon Wasson, "Seeking the Magic Mushroom," *Life* (June 10, 1957).

118 *"I had a terribly"*: Marks, *The Search for the Manchurian Candidate,* 114–15; "Intoxicating Mushrooms of Unidentified Species," 1955, MORI 146215.

118 *"ecstasy"*: Marks, *The Search for the Manchurian Candidate,* 114–15.

118 *seventeen-page spread*: R. Gordon Wasson, "Seeking the Magic Mushroom," *Life* (June 10, 1957).

119 *"negro males"*: Harris Isbell, "Comparison of the Reactions Induced by Psilocybin and LSD-25," May 5, 1959, MORI 151875.

119 *"$107,667"*: *Human Drug Testing by the CIA,* 93.

119 *"Some of the activities"*: Donald Chamberlain, "Kennedy Committee Interest in IG Surveys of OTS," October 31, 1975, MORI 146169; Lyman Kirkpatrick, "Excerpt from 1957 IG Inspection of TSD," 1957, MORI 146167.

119 *"attended to by a lot"*: DSG, September 25, 1980, JRP, B 243, F 7, LOC, 43–44.

15. ASSASSINATION

121 *"engaged in operational work"*: DSG, September 25, 1980, JRP, B 243, F 7, LOC, 7.

121 *"I think that was a classified"*: DSG, December 8, 1981, JRP, B 243, F 6, LOC, 10.

121 *"What were your duties?"*: DSG, April 19, 1983, JRP, B 222, F 7, LOC, 16.

121 *"If I get a job"*: Ted Gup, "The Coldest Warrior," *Washington Post* (December 16, 2001).

122 *"a strange person"*: Kinzer, *Poisoner in Chief,* 162.

122 *Bogdan Stashinsky*: Andrew and Mitrokhin, *The Sword and the Shield,* 361–63.

122 *"Is this the period"*: DSG, April 19, 1983, JRP, B 222, F 7, LOC, 19–21.

123 *"Mr. Bissell would ask"*: DSG, April 19, 1983, JRP, B 222, F 7, LOC, 21–24.

124 *"You recognize that you"*: DSG, April 19, 1983, JRP, B 222, F 7, LOC, 96.

124 *"Dr. Gottlieb"*: DSG, April 19, 1983, JRP, B 222, F 7, LOC, 32–33.

124 *"or worse"*: SCSGO, *Alleged Assassination Plots,* 57. On Lumumba and the CIA, see Reid, *The Lumumba Plot.*

125 *"there was stunned silence"*: Martin Kettle, "President 'Ordered Murder' of Congo Leader," *Guardian* (August 9, 2000); SCSGO, *Alleged Assassination Plots,* 55.

125 *"had expressed extremely"*: Madeleine Kalb, "The C.I.A. and Lumumba," *New York Times* (August 2, 1981): SM18.

125 *"fall into a river"*: FRUS, *Africa*, document 221.

125 *from Eisenhower to Dulles*: SCSGO, *Alleged Assassination Plots*, 21.

125 *"Joseph Scheider"*: DSG, April 19, 1983, JRP, B 222, F 7, LOC, 33–34.

126 *"I think we should"*: DSG, April 19, 1983, JRP, B 222, F 7, LOC, 140–41.

126 *"What is the response"*: DSG, April 19, 1983, JRP, B 222, F 7, LOC, 109–13.

128 *"Sid from Paris"*: In the Church Report, the alias is changed to "Joe from Paris" to match the pseudonym Joseph Scheider.

128 *"Jesus H. Christ!"*: Devlin, *Chief of Station*, 95–97.

128 *"high powered"*: Devlin, *Chief of Station*, 96–97; SCSGO, *Alleged Assassination Plots*, 29, 32; Shane Scott, "Memories of a C.I.A. Officer Resonate in a New Era," *New York Times* (February 24, 2008): 6.

128 *Justin O'Donnell*: In the Church Report, O'Donnell is given the pseudonym Michael Mulroney.

128 *"there were four or five"*: SCSGO, *Alleged Assassination Plots*, 38.

129 *"it would have been a Congolese"*: SCSGO, *Alleged Assassination Plots*, 39–41.

129 *"If we had known"*: SCSGO, *Alleged Assassination Plots*, 51. Also see Weissman, *American Foreign Policy*, 96–99.

129 *"All the people"*: SCSGO, *Alleged Assassination Plots*, 38.

129 *"was acting under instructions"*: Ted Gup, "The Coldest Warrior," *Washington Post* (December 16, 2001).

16. CLOSE BUT NO CIGAR

131 *"Could you tell us"*: DSG, April 19, 1983, JRP, B 222, F 7, LOC, 114–15.

132 *"Health Alteration Committee"*: SCSGO, *Alleged Assassination Plots*, 181. The members included Boris Pash, Sheffield Edwards, and Richard Bissell. Albarelli, *A Terrible Mistake*, 69.

132 *"we also do not object"*: SCSGO, *Alleged Assassination Plots*, 181. Also see Powers, *The Man Who Kept the Secrets*, 128–30.

132 *Gottlieb procured a handkerchief*: Gottlieb was involved in a similar assassination attempt on Chinese premier Zhou Enlai. The plan was to sneak poison into Zhou's rice bowl. William Corson, the head of the assassination team, said that the attempt "was called off in the nick of time" because General Lucien Truscott feared exposure. Trento, *The Secret History of the CIA*, 194.

132 *"suffered a terminal illness"*: SCSGO, *Alleged Assassination Plots*, 181.

133 *false flag attack*: Fursenko and Naftali, *One Hell of a Gamble*, 226. Operation Northwoods was a similar plot to stage a false flag attack and overthrow Castro. Operation Dirty Trick was a plot to blame Castro if the Mercury spaceflight carrying astronaut John Glenn failed.

133 *"as an attack"*: Fursenko and Naftali, *One Hell of a Gamble*, 246.

133 *"Please relate each"*: DSG, April 19, 1983, JRP, B 222, F 7, LOC, 118–19.

134 *"It was a pretty silly"*: Albarelli, *A Terrible Mistake,* 339. Also see SCSGO, *Alleged Assassination Plots,* 72.

134 *"My ration is different"*: Tim Weiner, "Declassified Paper Show Anti-Castro Ideas Proposed to Kennedy," *New York Times* (November 19, 1997): A25.

134 *"there was no way"*: DSG, April 19, 1983, JRP, B 222, F 7, LOC, 121.

134 *"One of my whores"*: Richard Stratton, "Altered States of America," *Spin Magazine* (March 1994). Also see SCSGO, *Alleged Assassination Plots,* 72.

134 *"contaminate[d] a box"*: CIA, *CIA Targets Fidel,* 37.

134 *"It was quite obvious"*: "Summary of Facts," Richard B. Cheney Files, B 7, F "Intelligence—Report on CIA Assassination Plots (1)," GRFL.

135 *"nice and clean"*: SCSGO, *Alleged Assassination Plots,* 80.

135 *"Why can't you gentlemen"*: Cormac, *How to Stage a Coup,* 35.

135 *The most inventive*: CIA, *CIA Targets Fidel,* 76–77; SCSGO, *Alleged Assassination Plots,* 85–86.

135 *"could come up with something"*: SCSGO, *Alleged Assassination Plots,* 88.

136 *"If surviving assassination"*: Moore, *Fidel Castro.* Not that CIA personnel never killed anyone. "Out in the boondocks," said one former officer, murder was an unwritten rule of the game. "One of your people gets killed in a back alley somewhere. If you know who did it you go after them, you don't ask, you're just going. Nobody back in Washington would ever have to know. . . . Nothing would ever get into the files." Powers, *The Man Who Kept the Secrets,* 126.

17. DISILLUSION AND DISSOLUTION

137 *"Doctor Gottlieb"*: DSG, December 8, 1981, JRP, B 243, F 6, LOC, 44–45.

138 *"The concepts involved"*: John Earman, "Report of Inspection of MKULTRA/TSD," July 26, 1963, MORI 17748.

138 *"If we are to continue"*: Richard Helms, "Testing of Psychochemicals and Related Materials," December 17, 1963, MORI 17750; Richard Helms, "Unwitting Tests," MORI 17752.

138 *"If you are talking"*: DSG, December 8, 1981, JRP, B 243, F 6, LOC, 43.

139 *"you can make somebody's"*: DSG, September 25, 1980, JRP, B 243, F 7, LOC, 20.

139 *"should not be considered"*: "Subject," January 27, 1961, MORI 149545.

139 *"no reason for believing"*: "Communist Mental Conditioning for Confession," February 24, 1953, MORI 145896.

139 *Over its ten-year*: Project MKULTRA, 7.

139 *"Sure. Sure."*: DSG, September 25, 1980, JRP, B 243, F 7, LOC, 72.

139 *MKSEARCH*: Marks, *The Search for the Manchurian Candidate,* 197–204.

18. TORTURE

141 ***Nosenko brought with him***: SCA, *Report of the Select Committee on Assassinations*, 101–2.

141 ***traditional methods***: Nosenko maintained that he was once drugged. See Posner, *Case Closed*, 42.

141 ***Nosenko was placed***: Streatfeild, *Brainwash*, 323–32; David Stout, "Yuri Nosenko, Soviet Spy Who Defected, Dies at 81," *New York Times* (August 28, 2008): C11.

142 *"If you have a blowtorch"*: Marks, *The Search for the Manchurian Candidate*, 44.

142 *"And he would have confessed"*: Tuchman, *A Distant Mirror*, 43.

142 *"The Inquisitors are doing"*: Mannix, *The History of Torture*, 134–35.

143 *"Torture has the power"*: Spee, *Cautio Criminalis*, 419.

143 *"virtually ruined him"*: SCA, *Report of the Select Committee on Assassinations*, 102.

143 ***KUBARK***: CIA, *Kubark Counterintelligence Interrogation*, 11. A 2014 survey of professional interrogators found that "rapport and relationship-building techniques were employed most often and perceived as the most effective regardless of context and intended outcome, particularly in comparison to confrontational techniques." Redlich, Kelly, and Miller, "The Who, What, and Why of Human Intelligence Gathering."

143 *"first use reason"*: Weatherford, *Genghis Khan*, 201.

144 *"hypnotic situation"*: Orne, "The Potential Uses of Hypnosis in Interrogation," 207–9.

145 ***Bush administration authorized***: Scott Shane, "Soviet Style 'Torture' becomes 'Interrogation,'" *New York Times* (June 3, 2007).

145 *"like a dog"*: Mayer, *The Dark Side*, 156.

145 **"Clockwork Orange"**: Mayer, *The Dark Side*, 163.

145 *"I cry at dog"*: Carol Rosenberg, "He Waterboarded a Detainee. Then He Had to Get the C.I.A. to Let Him Stop," *New York Times* (January 22, 2020).

146 *"The CIA's use"*: SSCI, *Committee Study*, xi–xii. Since Congress isn't subject to the Freedom of Information Act, some Republican members of Congress have been quietly collecting the existing copies of the full report in hopes that it never sees the light of day.

19. TECHNICAL SERVICES

147 *"Horrible smelling liquids"*: Agee, *Inside the Company*, 85. For a humorous take on CIA gadgets, see Freberg, "The Shellfish-Toxin Joy Buzzer."

148 *"I can't take you"*: Miller, *Spying for America*, 392.

148 *"They may refuse"*: Wallace and Melton, *Spycraft*, 83.

148 *"they might spend"*: Luria, *Skating on the Edge,* 52.

148 *skyhook*: The Army Air Forces had developed a similar system. During its first live test, a practice sheep broke its neck. See RG 226, E A1 134, B 52, F "Pick-Up Equipment," NARA.

149 *Operation Coldfeet*: Leary, "Robert Fulton's Skyhook."

149 *undisclosed Asian head of state*: Wallace and Melton, *Spycraft,* 200–201.

150 *"We found that we could"*: Tom Vanderbilt, "The CIA's Most Highly-Trained Spies Weren't Even Human," *Smithsonian Magazine* (October 2013).

150 *"and a taxi comes"*: Richelson, *The Wizards of Langley,* 147. Also see "Views on Trained Cats," MORI 21897.

150 *red-tailed hawks*: "Wildlife Telemetry — A Potential Intelligence Collection Media," April 16, 1964, MORI 21860; Richelson, *The Wizards of Langley,* 148.

150 *"[The raven] was in a map case"*: Tom Vanderbilt, "The CIA's Most Highly-Trained Spies Weren't Even Human," *Smithsonian Magazine* (October 2013).

150 *L-pill*: See Lisle, *The Dirty Tricks Department,* 70–74.

151 *Carmine Vito*: Polmar, *Spyplane,* 103–4.

151 *Soviet military captured him*: The U.S. government, unaware that Powers had survived, issued a false statement saying that the pilot of an innocuous weather plane had lost consciousness from a lack of oxygen and accidentally strayed into Soviet airspace. In a meeting of the National Security Council, an embarrassed President Dwight Eisenhower said that the U-2 program had been bound to fail at some point, "but that it would be such a boo-boo and that we would be caught with our pants down was rather painful." George Kistiakowsky, Transcript of Diary, 1959–60, May 9, 1960, B 1, F "May 1960," DDEL.

151 *"Within one minute"*: Powers, *The Trial of the U2,* 102; *Unauthorized Storage,* 46.

152 *Nixon's directive*: See Tucker, "A Farewell to Germs," 107.

152 *The CIA's stockpile*: *Unauthorized Storage,* 96.

152 *he placed the substances*: *Unauthorized Storage,* 60–61.

20. KEEPING SECRETS

153 *"Elizabeth"*: Kinzer, *Poisoner in Chief,* 200–201. "Elizabeth" is a pseudonym.

154 *The TSD had supplied*: Richelson, *The Wizards of Langley,* 164.

155 *"A substantial portion"*: John Earman, "Report of Inspection of MKULTRA/TSD," July 26, 1963, MORI 17748, 23.

155 *"As best I can remember"*: DSG, December 8, 1981, JRP, B 243, F 6, LOC, 71.

155 *"hastily or impetuously"*: DSG, September 25, 1980, JRP, B 243, F 7, LOC, 61.

155 *whom Nixon resented*: In the "smoking gun" tape that would doom his administration, Nixon said, "We protected Helms from one hell of a lot of things" and implied that Helms should repay his debt by covering up the scandal.

155 *"Let's let this die"*: CIA, "Memo #299–75," August 19, 1975, CREST. Also see Sidney Gottlieb to Richard Helms, October 8, 1977, RHP, B 1, F 87, GUA.

155 *"After Director Helms concurred"*: DSG, December 8, 1981, JRP, B 243, F 6, LOC, 73–74.

155 *"Over my stated objections"*: "Destruction of Drug and Toxin Related Files," October 3, 1975, MORI 146170. Also see Albarelli, *A Terrible Mistake,* 451.

156 *"The CIA doesn't give"*: DRH, March 14, 1983, JRP, B 223, F 9, LOC, 156.

156 *"I consider you"*: DRH, March 14, 1983, JRP, B 223, F 9, LOC, 237–38.

156 *"there was an intense"*: DSG, June 28, 1983, JRP, B 223, F 3, LOC, 537–38.

156 *"You are badgering"*: DSG, April 19, 1983, JRP, B 222, F 7, LOC, 88.

156 *"concerned that papers"*: DSG, December 8, 1981, JRP, B 243, F 6, LOC, 72.

157 *"This is a gentleman's"*: Powers, *The Man Who Kept the Secrets,* 57.

157 *"He's been here twenty"*: Powers, *The Man Who Kept the Secrets,* 279–80. The CIA commissioned its iconic Memorial Wall in 1973 to help boost morale.

157 *"Department of Defense"*: Monje, *The Central Intelligence Agency,* 133–35.

158 *"technical journals"*: "Destruction of Drug and Toxin Related Files," October 3, 1975, MORI 146170. She had only been working for Gottlieb for six weeks and didn't yet understand proper administrative procedures, making her suggestible.

158 *"I ordered certain tapes"*: DRH, March 14, 1983, JRP, B 223, F 9, LOC, 157–60.

21. THE FAMILY JEWELS

161 *"The children took"*: Margaret Gottlieb, "Autobiographical Essays," MFP, B 1, F 24, PHS.

161 *Project Azorian*: Sharp, *The CIA's Greatest Covert Operation*; Dean, *The Taking of K-129*; "Project Azorian." Thomas Moorer, chairman of the Joint Chiefs of Staff, considered Project Azorian foolish, but because the CIA had already spent hundreds of millions of dollars on it, National Security Advisor Henry Kissinger committed the appropriately titled fallacy of sunk costs and insisted that it continue. Overall, Project Azorian was a pyrrhic victory, costing half a billion dollars and recovering only one-third of the submarine.

162 *"Goddamn it"*: Ford, *William E. Colby,* 100.

162 *"wiped out entire families"*: Herbert, *Soldier,* 105–6.

162 *"Thou shalt not this"*: Ford, *William E. Colby,* 100; Colby and Helms, "Reflections of DCIs," 40.

163 *"I've got a story"*: Woods, *Shadow Warrior,* 400.

163 *"We got a few blips"*: Ford, *William E. Colby,* 100.

163 *"The SOB"*: Woods, *Shadow Warrior,* 403.

163 *"Huge C.I.A. Operation"*: Seymour Hersh, "Huge C.I.A. Operation Reported in U.S. against Antiwar Forces, Other Dissidents in Nixon Years," *New York Times* (December 22, 1974). When President Lyndon Johnson had initially asked DCI Richard Helms to spy on the antiwar protestors, Helms warned him that it was illegal. "I'm quite aware of that," Johnson said. "What I want is for you to pursue this matter, and to do what is necessary to track down the foreign communists who are behind this intolerable interference in our domestic affairs." Helms followed orders and established MHCHAOS. He reasoned that since the program was a high priority in the eyes of the president, "it should be a high priority in the Agency," charter be damned. In the end, MHCHAOS found no connection between "foreign communists" and the antiwar protestors. Helms and Hood, *A Look over My Shoulder,* 280; Woods, *Shadow Warrior,* 341.

163 *"a burning match"*: Kissinger, *Years of Renewal,* 320.

164 *developed a plan*: Woods, *Shadow Warrior,* 406.

164 *"Like what?"*: Schorr, *Clearing the Air,* 144.

164 *"prize son-of-a-bitch"*: Olmsted, *Challenging the Secret Government,* 63.

165 *"Has the CIA ever killed"*: Schorr, *Clearing the Air,* 145.

165 *"President Ford has reportedly"*: Schorr, *Clearing the Air,* 146.

165 *"Welcome back"*: Schorr, *Clearing the Air,* 147–48. A week later, Henry Kissinger underwent a similarly grueling session before the Rockefeller Commission. When he emerged from the room, he joked to the journalists, "Where's Schorr? I have a new name for him."

166 *"Bill, do you really"*: Woods, *Shadow Warrior,* 437–38.

166 *led a successful effort*: "Gerald Ford White House Altered Rockefeller Commission Report in 1975," *National Security Archive.*

167 *"The Agency has tested"*: CCA, *The Nelson Rockefeller Report,* 226–28.

167 *"Sometimes she was a mean"*: Albarelli, *A Terrible Mistake,* 479.

168 *"Have you seen today's"*: Albarelli, *A Terrible Mistake,* 478.

168 *"Suicide Revealed"*: Thomas O'Toole, "CIA Infiltrated 17 Area Groups, Gave Out LSD," *Washington Post* (June 11, 1975): 1.

168 *"At long last"*: Albarelli, *A Terrible Mistake,* 478.

168 *"You go into that sacred"*: Ronson, *The Men Who Stare at Goats,* 217.

168 *"This is a terrible thing"*: Albarelli, *A Terrible Mistake,* 511.

22. THE INVESTIGATIONS

169 *"blind and toothless"*: Colby and Helms, "Reflections of DCIs," 50.

169 *met less than once*: Johnson, *Spy Watching,* 102–3.

169 *"The old tradition"*: Bob Wiedrich, "Watching the CIA with Fewer Eyes," *Chicago Tribune* (February 3, 1976).

170 *"massive wrong-doing"*: SCSGO, *Foreign and Military Intelligence*, 1.

170 *FBI's COINTELPRO*: FBI director J. Edgar Hoover said that COINTELPRO sought to "expose, disrupt, misdirect, discredit, or otherwise neutralize the activities of black nationalist, hate-type organizations and groupings, their leadership, spokesmen, membership, and supporters." Churchill and Wall, *The COINTELPRO Papers*, 91.

170 *"a fundamental disregard"*: SCSGO, *Foreign and Military Intelligence*, 386.

170 *"a rogue elephant"*: John Crewdson, "Church Doubts Plot Links to President," *New York Times* (July 19, 1975): 1.

170 *Terry Lenzner*: Lenzner, *The Investigator*, 190–200.

171 *"Joseph Scheider"*: "Panel to Delete Ex-Agent's Name," *Los Angeles Times* (November 19, 1975): A11.

171 *"the residue"*: *Unauthorized Storage*, 8.

172 *During his testimony*: *Unauthorized Storage*, 61.

172 *"As far as I'm concerned"*: *Unauthorized Storage*, 71, 97–102.

172 *"You mention suicides"*: *Unauthorized Storage*, 16–17.

172 *Sam Giancana*: Woods, *Shadow Warrior*, 444.

172 *"We had nothing"*: Anderson and Gibson, *Peace, War, and Politics*, 120.

172 *In front of the awestruck*: *Unauthorized Storage*, 17. Also see Helms and Hood, *A Look over My Shoulder*, 431.

173 *"Don't point it"*: The quote doesn't appear in the transcript, but it can be heard on the recording.

173 *"didn't bleat"*: Scott Shane, "Buried Secrets of Biowarfare," *Baltimore Sun* (August 1, 2004).

173 *"Mr. Colby, it is clear"*: *Unauthorized Storage*, 22.

173 *"Dr. Death"*: Lenzner, *The Investigator*, 189. Gottlieb has since been given a number of nicknames, among them "the black sorcerer," "poisoner in chief," and "the chief wizard of the CIA's magic potion division." Hollington, *Wolves, Jackals, and Foxes*, 34; Kinzer, *Poisoner in Chief*; Talbot, *The Devil's Chessboard*, 281.

173 *Pike Committee*: Representative Lucien Nedzi had chaired an earlier House committee to investigate the intelligence community, but it dissolved when *The New York Times* revealed that Nedzi had known about the Family Jewels for a year without telling his colleagues.

174 *"made my tour"*: Haines, "Looking for a Rogue Elephant," 82–84.

174 *"If he loses it again"*: Olmsted, *Challenging the Secret Government*, 125.

174 *"prejudiced by political"*: Otis Pike, *Congressional Record* (March 9, 1976), 5901; *U.S. Intelligence Agencies and Activities*, 641.

174 *"To betray a source"*: *Investigation of Publication*, 534.

175 *Colby's dead body*: Woods, *Shadow Warrior*, 2–5.

23. THE HEARINGS

177 *"political" assassinations*: This wording still allowed for the assassination of nonpolitical targets, namely terrorists, who aren't technically political enemies because they don't run sovereign states.

177 *found seven boxes*: DFL, July 20, 1983, JRP, B 225, F 1, LOC, 99–104; Project *MKULTRA*, 5; *Human Drug Testing by the CIA*, 124. John Marks wrote a book based on the files called *The Search for the Manchurian Candidate*. After reading it, Gottlieb told Marks, "I find so many inaccuracies and such a strong bias (against [the] CIA and against me personally) that it is impractical for me to comment in detail." Sidney Gottlieb to John Marks, September 24, 1978, JRP, B 261, F 9, LOC.

177 *receipt for $0.05*: "Return of Funds Under MKULTRA," June 18, 1957, MORI 17456.

178 **Glomar** *response*: The response got its name during Project Azorian when the CIA refused to confirm or deny whether it had used the *Glomar Explorer* ship to retrieve a sunken Soviet submarine. CIA veteran Walt Logan helped develop the response and said, "We'd tell the requestor that we could neither confirm nor deny the existence of any records responsive to the request, but if we *did* have any such records, they would be classified. So, either way, they're screwed!" Sharp, *The CIA's Greatest Covert Operation*, 282.

178 *wanted the files released*: See DST, December 13, 1983, JRP, B 228, F 8, LOC, 16–21.

178 *"general laughter"*: Project *MKULTRA*, 48.

178 *"Is it plausible"*: Project *MKULTRA*, 45–47.

179 *"victimized and appalled"*: *Human Drug Testing by the CIA*, 173. Also see DSG, September 25, 1980, JRP, B 243, F 7, LOC, 113.

179 *"poor Sid Gottlieb"*: Ted Gup, "The Coldest Warrior," *Washington Post* (December 16, 2001).

179 *"Sid is going to school"*: Kinzer, *Poisoner in Chief*, 246.

179 *heart condition*: Lenzner, *The Investigator*, 201.

179 *"distinguished-looking"*: "Ex-C.I.A. Aide Asks Immunity to Testify," *New York Times* (September 7, 1977): 11.

179 *It shows an aging man*: Jo Thomas, "Key Figure Testifies in Private on C.I.A. Drug Tests," *New York Times* (September 22, 1977): 1.

180 *"Is there anything"*: Lenzner, *The Investigator*, 202.

180 *opening statement*: *Human Drug Testing by the CIA*, 169–74.

180 *describe an additional incident*: *Human Drug Testing by the CIA*, 175–76.

180 *"Presidential Party"*: "Presidential Party Drugged in 1971," *San Mateo Times* (September 21, 1977): 1.

180 *"Can you tell us"*: *Human Drug Testing by the CIA*, 190. Gottlieb was evasive during his testimony, but when he did speak, he mostly told the truth.

The same can't be said of Richard Helms, who was convicted of perjury for lying to Congress about the CIA's covert attempt to stage a military coup in Chile.

181 *"It certainly did"*: *Human Drug Testing by the CIA*, 185.

181 *"You still had unwitting"*: *Human Drug Testing by the CIA*, 188.

181 *"I wondered how confirmation"*: Sidney Gottlieb to Richard Helms, October 8, 1977, RHP, B 1, F 87, GUA.

24. VICTIMS TASK FORCE

183 *"I will travel overtly"*: Frank Laubinger, "Victims Task Force," March 9, 1979, DVP.

183 *White's diary*: One diary entry mentions that journalist Herb Caen misquoted White in an article. Caen commented on the entry, "I *thought* that's what he said. It must have been something they put in that last swizzle stick." Scheflin and Opton, *The Mind Manipulators*, 140.

183 *"muffled conversation"*: Frank Laubinger, "Tom Hansen," March 27, 1979, DVP.

184 *Following his activity*: Frank Laubinger, Memo on Victims Task Force Activities, March 30, 1979, DVP.

184 *"various means of assassination"*: Frank Labinger, "Interview of Ira C. Feldman," April 26, 1979, DVP.

184 *"This entire subject"*: Frank Laubinger to Sidney Gottlieb, April 30, 1979, DVP.

184 *he called Laubinger*: Frank Laubinger, "Telephonic Response of Dr. Gottlieb," DVP.

185 *"I feel morally obliged"*: DFL, July 20, 1983, JRP, B 225, F 1, LOC, 41–42.

185 *"She nearly flipped"*: Albarelli, *A Terrible Mistake*, 290. White once drugged Evans. She later said, "I hated every minute of it. I told him if he ever did it again that would be the last time he did it to anyone." Albarelli, *A Terrible Mistake*, 290.

185 *"was not going to touch"*: DFL, July 20, 1983, JRP, B 225, F 1, LOC, 44.

185 *"passed her off"*: "MKULTRA–George White," July 20, 1979, DVP.

185 *"She does not believe"*: "MKULTRA Subprojects 3, 14, 16, 42, 132, 149 and MKSEARCH 4," DVP.

185 *"the worst experience"*: "MKULTRA Subprojects 3, 14, 16, 42, 132, 149 and MKSEARCH 4," DVP.

186 *"exceedingly unlikely"*: "Search for MKULTRA Victims/Request to Tour Agency," August 14, 1979, DVP.

186 *fifteen potential unwitting*: "MKULTRA/Notification of Unwitting Subjects," October 9, 1979, DVP.

186 *"It didn't happen"*: DFL, November 5, 1987, JRP, B 224, F 8, LOC, 71.

25. THE LAWSUITS

187 *"reputable, some even eminent"*: Frank Laubinger, April 19, 1979, DVP. The CIA did, however, notify the various institutions funded through the cutout organizations that the funds had come from the CIA. Those institutions could then inform the victims. DFL, July 20, 1983, JRP, B 225, F 1, LOC, 110–13.

187 *Paul Figley*: Author interview with Paul Figley.

188 *statute of limitations*: *Scott v. Casey*, 562 F. 475 (N.D. Ga. 1983).

189 *"David Orlikow called"*: Rauh and Turner, "Anatomy of a Public Interest Case."

189 *Eight more plaintiffs*: The nine plaintiffs were Jeannine Huard, Florence Langleben, Robert Logie, Mary Morrow, Velma Orlikow, Jean-Charles Pagé, Lyvia Stadler, Louis Weinstein, and Rita Zimmerman.

189 *The legal basis*: Rauh and Turner, "Anatomy of a Public Interest Case."

189 *out-of-court negotiations*: Collins, *In the Sleep Room*, 214–15.

189 *"the worst record"*: "D.C. Judge Mounting Backlog Poses Court Problem," *Washington Post* (January 3, 1988).

190 *"What Dr. Gottlieb"*: DSG, April 19, 1983, JRP, B 222, F 7, LOC, 44.

190 *Rauh's ire*: DHA, March 27, 1986, JRP, B 223, F 6, LOC; DLG, May 9, 1986, JRP, B 225, F 3, LOC, 14; DVO, June 17, 1986, JRP, B 226, F 7, LOC, 59.

190 *received a letter*: Charles Briggs to Joseph Rauh, May 24, 1983, JRP, B 217, F 5, LOC.

190 *"We resent and reject"*: Joseph Rauh and James Turner to Charles Briggs, May 31, 1983, JRP, B 217, F 5, LOC.

190 *"rather simple"*: Parrish, *Citizen Rauh*, 271–72.

191 *"I am a red-headed"*: DHA, March 27, 1986, JRP, B 223, F 6, LOC, 21. Also see Joseph Rauh to James Mabbutt, May 21, 1986, JRP, B 217, F 1, LOC.

191 *In a desperate attempt*: See letters between Joseph Rauh and Scott Kragie, JRP, B 217, F 5, LOC.

191 *"lead to an unacceptable risk"*: *CIA v. Sims*, 471 U.S. 159 (1985).

192 *"The nation must"*: Laurence Stern, "Justice Dept. Probes Helms Testimony," *Washington Post* (November 17, 1975): A3.

192 *Rauh soon learned why*: Rauh and Turner, "Anatomy of a Public Interest Case."

192 *"Anger wells up"*: Collins, *In the Sleep Room*, 230.

192 *"It's a hell of a note"*: Joseph Rauh to Brian Mulroney, June 2, 1986, JRP, B 217, F 1, LOC.

192 *"I say goodbye"*: Rauh to Plaintiffs, December 16, 1986, JRP, B 287, F 17, LOC.

193 *"The CIA has resumed"*: Letter to James Turner, JRP, B 217, F 7, LOC.

193 *The majority of the letters*: Letters in JRP, B 218 F 6, LOC.

193 *"Wouldn't the Agency"*: Rauh and Turner, "Anatomy of a Public Interest Case."

194 *"Was $750,000"*: Wall, *From Healing to Hell*, 209.

194 *"Sometimes you see"*: Rauh and Turner, "Anatomy of a Public Interest Case."

194 *"I know there's been"*: Colby and Helms, "Reflections of DCIs," 51–52.

194 *Stanley Glickman*: See documents in JRP, B 261, F 2, LOC.

194 *"absolutely never happened"*: Kinzer, *Poisoner in Chief*, 256.

195 *"If I were in operations"*: DFL, November 5, 1987, JRP, B 224, F 8, LOC, 175.

195 *"I got down to where"*: Troy Hooper, "Operation Midnight Climax: How the CIA Dosed S.F. Citizens with LSD," *SF Weekly* (March 14, 2012).

195 *"save the State"*: Ketchum, *Chemical Warfare Secrets*, 224.

196 *"My God"*: Troy Hooper, "Operation Midnight Climax: How the CIA Dosed S.F. Citizens with LSD," *SF Weekly* (March 14, 2012).

196 *"Xmas party"*: George White, "Daily Appointment Book, 1957," December 20, 1957, George H. White Papers, B 7, SUA.

196 *"I didn't do any follow-up"*: *Wayne Ritchie v. United States*, 451 F.3d 1019 (9th Cir. 2006).

196 *"If Ritchie's claims"*: *Wayne Ritchie v. United States*, 451 F.3d 1019 (9th Cir. 2006).

26. OLD WOUNDS

197 *"He sat in a rocking chair"*: Albarelli, *A Terrible Mistake*, 588.

197 *"very uncomfortable"*: DAO, September 16, 1988, JRP, B 226, F 4, LOC, 22.

197 *"What did [Alice Olson] say"*: DRL, May 14, 1986, JRP, B 224, F 7, LOC, 68–71.

198 *"He gave us assurances"*: DAO, September 16, 1988, JRP, B 226, F 4, LOC, 22. Also see James Turner, "Interview with Mrs. Frank Olson," June 5, 1986, JRP, B 265, F 1, LOC.

198 *"Gottlieb was fascinated"*: Kinzer, *Poisoner in Chief*, 246.

199 *Gottlieb was working*: Ted Gup, "The Coldest Warrior," *Washington Post* (December 16, 2001).

199 *"I had a dream"*: Albarelli, *A Terrible Mistake*, 593.

199 *"He was not the master"*: Ted Gup, "The Coldest Warrior," *Washington Post* (December 16, 2001).

199 *"The former Gottlieb"*: Morris, *Wormwood*.

199 *"Your father and I"*: Albarelli, *A Terrible Mistake*, 594.

199 *"Did you know"*: Morris, *Wormwood*.

200 *"I was emboldened"*: Starrs and Ramsland, *A Voice for the Dead*, 144.

200 *"[Starrs] was an interesting"*: Albarelli, *A Terrible Mistake*, 623.

200 *"a stunning blow"*: Kinzer, *Poisoner in Chief*, 250.

200 *"intentionally, deliberately"*: Michael Ignatieff, "What Did the C.I.A. Do to His Father?," *New York Times* (April 1, 2001): SM156.

201 *"tends to relish"*: Albarelli, *A Terrible Mistake*, 606.

201 *"A Study of Assassination"*: "A Study of Assassination," 1954, CREST.

201 *"It was very strange"*: Kinzer, *Poisoner in Chief*, 258.

201 *"A lot of Sid's"*: Ted Gup, "The Coldest Warrior," *Washington Post* (December 16, 2001).

202 *"He was, and is, us"*: Ted Gup, "The Coldest Warrior," *Washington Post* (December 16, 2001).

27. THE VICIOUS CYCLE OF SECRECY

203 *"In all professions"*: Turner, *Secrecy and Democracy*, 42–45. Also see CIA, *Critique of the Codeword Compartment*; Connelly, *The Declassification Engine*, chap. 5.

204 *"We had offered"*: *Biomedical and Behavioral Research*, 259–61.

204 *"Files are notably"*: John Earman, "Report of Inspection of MKULTRA/TSD," July 26, 1963, MORI 17748.

204 *"The 'secret' stamp"*: Wellerstein, *Restricted Data*, 15. Regarding the compartmentalization of the Manhattan Project, Szilard said, "We could have had [the atomic bomb] eighteen months earlier. . . . We did not put two and two together because the two twos were in a different compartment." Jones, *Manhattan*, 270–71.

205 *Stuart Hedden*: Powers, *The Man Who Kept the Secrets*, 105.

205 *"I was trying to determine"*: Marks, *The Search for the Manchurian Candidate*, 100.

205 *Several successive inspectors*: Johnson, *Spy Watching*, 107.

205 *"Never once did"*: SCSGO, *Supplementary Detailed Staff Reports*, 135. The FBI once sent King an audio tape of him having an extramarital affair. A note accompanying the tape read, "King, there is only one thing left for you to do. You know what it is. You have just 34 days in which to do it." The "it" was suicide. Olmsted, *Challenging the Secret Government*, 97–98.

205 *plausible deniability*: On the corrupting influence of plausible deniability, see Bersoff, "Why Good People."

205 *"The separate constitutional structure"*: "William Colby: A Somewhat Candid Interview with the Former Director of the CIA," *Playboy* (July 1978).

205 *"auxiliary precautions"*: James Madison, *The Federalist* no. 51.

206 *"one toward security"*: Martin Arnold, "Controversial Reporter," *New York Times* (February 27, 1976): 13.

206 *"While the Constitution"*: *Kennedy v. Mendoza-Martinez*, 372 U.S. 144 (1963).

206 *kept hidden from Congress*: Wellerstein, *Restricted Data*, 82.

206 *"Everything about [the] CIA"*: *Congressional Record* (April 9, 1956): 2930.

206 *"It would be more desirable"*: "CIA 'Watchdog' Committee," *Congressional Quarterly* (1956).

207 *"over my dead body"*: James Reston, "Washington: File and Forget," *New York Times* (July 22, 1987).

207 *"Mr. Chairman"*: Johnson, *Spy Watching*, 400–1.

207 *thirty-three covert operations*: SCSGO, *Foreign and Military Intelligence*.

207 *Hughes-Ryan Amendment*: The Intelligence Oversight Act of 1980 rolled back some of the provisions in the Hughes-Ryan Amendment.

207 *William Casey*: DCI Robert Gates later said that Casey "was guilty of contempt of Congress from the day he was sworn in as DCI. He had zero patience for what he saw as congressional meddling in operations." Gates, *From the Shadows*, 213.

208 *In the wake of the Iran-Contra*: See Check and Afsheen, "One Lantern in the Darkest Night."

208 *bypass certain warrant requirements*: Johnson, *Spy Watching*, 182. Also see Strickland, "Civil Liberties vs. Intelligence Collection."

209 *SSCI and HPSCI learned*: Johnson, *Spy Watching*, 192.

209 *Destroyed the recordings*: Rodriguez wrote in a declassified email that "the heat" of destroying the recordings "is nothing compared to what it would be if the tapes ever got into the public domain." Neither Rodriguez nor anyone else at the CIA was ever prosecuted for the destruction. Mark Mazetti and Charlie Savage, "No Criminal Charges Sought Over C.I.A. Tapes," *New York Times* (November 10, 2010): A12.

209 *"tummy slapping"*: SSCI, *Committee Study*, 14–15.

209 *straightforward solutions*: See Gehl and Porter, *The Politics Industry*; Drutman, *Breaking the Two-Party Doom Loop*.

210 *sings nothing but the praises*: Senator and sociologist Daniel Patrick Moynihan implied as much when he developed his eponymous "law": The greater the number of complaints being aired, the better protected are the rights in that country. Troy, *Moynihan's Moment*, 133.

28. HISTORY LOVES IRONY

211 *"Am I, Allen Ginsberg"*: Ginsberg, *Poems All over the Place*, 53.

211 *"I wouldn't be here"*: Lee and Shlain, *Acid Dreams*, xx.

211 *"We must always remember"*: "An Exclusive Interview: John Lennon and Yoko Ono," *Playboy* (January 1981).

212 *"I couldn't get one"*: Streatfeild, *Brainwash*, 343.

213 *notorious for producing false memories*: See McNally, *Remembering*

Trauma, chap. 8; Loftus and Ketcham, *The Myth of Repressed Memory*; Clancy et al., "Memory Distortion."

213 **Satanic Panic**: See Wright, *Remembering Satan.*

213 **She provides no**: J. Sword, "Michelle Misremembers: How a Psychiatrist and His Patient Created the Blueprint for Satanic Ritual Abuse," *Skeptical Inquirer* (December 11, 2023).

213 **"transgenerational"**: Richard Noll, "Speak Memory," *Psychiatric Times* (March 19, 2014); Youngblood, *Trance.*

213 **sued Braun**: Pendergrast, *The Repressed Memory Epidemic,* 351–52. The first president of the ISSD, George Greaves, surrendered his medical license, eliminating the need for a hearing regarding allegations that he hypnotized a patient, masturbated himself, and sexually abused her.

214 **"no relation between confidence"**: Neisser and Harsch, "Phantom Flashbulbs."

214 **imagine a scenario**: A 2006 study had students imagine that they were performing a bizarre action. Two weeks later, several students had developed memories of having actually performed it. Seamon, Philbin, and Harrison, "Do You Remember?"

214 **wordplay**: A sampling of chapter titles from O'Brien's second book include "*Soul*utions," "Mental HELLth," "*Criminal* 'Justice' System," "Federal *Warr*ant," and "The*rapists* Mistakes." O'Brien and Phillips, *Access Denied.*

214 **absence of evidence**: During World War II, Soviet physicist Georgy Flerov noticed that top American physicists had stopped publishing journal articles, leading him to deduce that they were building an atomic bomb. "This silence is not the result of an absence of research," he wrote. "In a word, the seal of silence has been imposed, and this is the best proof of the vigorous work that is going on now abroad." But even Flerov wasn't so much noticing an absence of evidence as he was a change in publishing patterns. Holloway, *Stalin and the Bomb,* 78.

215 **"I've given up"**: Festinger, Riecken, and Schachter, *When Prophecy Fails,* 168. On failed predictions in the Christian context, see Ehrman, *Armageddon.*

215 **"The conspiracy community"**: Bugliosi, *Reclaiming History,* xliii.

216 **nuanced and complicated**: See Klaas, *Fluke.*

216 **manipulate more people**: Jolly West had been prescient to write in 1963, "The most insidious domestic threat posed by 'brainwashing' is the tendency of Americans to believe in its power." Ewing and McCann, *Minds on Trial,* 38.

216 **"The Agency, over the past"**: Albarelli, *A Terrible Mistake,* 805.

216 **"flood the zone"**: Michael Lewis, "Has Anyone Seen the President?," *Bloomberg* (February 9, 2018).

217 **Operation Denver**: In 2020, following the outbreak of the COVID-19 pandemic that had originated in China, Chinese authorities launched a remarkably similar disinformation campaign claiming that COVID-19 had come from a leak at

Fort Detrick. "Wuhan Lab Leak Theory: How Fort Detrick Became a Centre for Chinese Conspiracies," *BBC News* (August 23, 2021).

217 *"AIDS May Invade"*: "AIDS May Invade India," *Patriot* 21, no. 108 (July 16, 1983).

218 *A RAND study*: Boghardt, "Soviet Bloc Intelligence," 19.

218 *a story in* **The New York Times**: Madeleine Kalb, "The C.I.A. and Lumumba," *New York Times* (August 2, 1981): SM18.

218 *"Western homosexuals"*: J. Zambga Browne, "Link AIDS to CIA Warfare," *New York Times* (November 30, 1985): 12.

EPILOGUE

221 *BITE*: For more information on the BITE model, see Hassan, *Combating Cult Mind Control.*

222 *develop a unique vocabulary*: Scientology is a prime example. See Wakefield, *Understanding Scientology,* 193.

222 *emotional highs and lows*: The BITE model also applies to abusive relationships.

222 *"has its initiation"*: CIA, *Critique of the Codeword Compartment.* Also see Marchetti and Marks, *The CIA and the Cult of Intelligence.*

223 *tribal group*: On tribalism, see Haidt, *The Righteous Mind,* 161–64.

222 *Everyone is susceptible*: For a list of tools that can help improve critical thinking, see Sagan, *The Demon-Haunted World,* chap. 12; Prothero, *Evolution,* 14–20.

APPENDIX

227 *The purpose*: See MORIs 17354–17502.

References

INTERVIEWS

Rosanna Del Guidice (January 15, 2020)
Paul Figley (April 20, 2020)

DATABASES

Black Vault: theblackvault.com
Frank Olson Project: frankolsonproject.org
HathiTrust Digital Library: hathitrust.org
Internet Archive: archive.org
Mary Ferrell Foundation: maryferrell.org
National Security Archive: nsarchive.gwu.edu

PERIODICALS

Austin Statesman
The Baltimore Sun
Bloomberg
The Boston Globe
Chicago Tribune
Congressional Quarterly
CounterPunch
Daily Bruin
Del Rio News-Herald
Discover

El Paso Herald-Post
Fort Worth Star-Telegram
Genii Magazine
The Globe and Mail
The Guardian
High Times
Life
Los Angeles Times
Miami Daily News
The New Yorker
The New York Times
Patriot
Playboy
Psychiatric Times
San Antonio Express
San Antonio Light
San Mateo Times
Science Digest
Scientific American
SF Weekly
Skeptical Inquirer
Smithsonian
Spin Magazine
Time
The Wall Street Journal
The Washington Post

HEARINGS

Biological Testing Involving Human Subjects by the Department of Defense, 1977: Hearings before the Subcommittee on Health and Scientific Research of the Committee on Human Resources, 95th Cong., 1st Sess. 1977.

Biomedical and Behavioral Research: Joint Hearings before the Subcommittee on Health of the Committee on Labor and Public Welfare and the Subcommittee on Administrative Practice and Procedure, 94th Cong., 1st Sess. 1975.

Cold War Era Human Subject Experimentation: Hearing before the Legislation and National Security Subcommittee of the Committee on Government Operations, 103rd Cong., 2nd Sess. 1994.

Communist Interrogation, Indoctrination and Exploitation of American Military and Civilian Prisoners: Hearings before the Permanent Subcommittee on Investigations of the Committee on Government Operations, 84th Cong., 2nd Sess. 1956.

Communist Psychological Warfare (Brainwashing): Consultation with Edward Hunter, Committee on Un-American Activities, 85th Cong., 2nd Sess. 1958.

Human Drug Testing by the CIA: Hearings before the Subcommittee on Health and Scientific Research of the Committee on Human Resources, 95th Cong., 1st Sess. 1977.

Investigation of Publication of Select Committee on Intelligence Report: Hearings before the Committee on Standards of Official Conduct, 94th Cong., 2nd Sess. 1976.

Project MKULTRA: The CIA's Program of Research in Behavioral Modification: Joint Hearing before the Select Committee on Intelligence and the Subcommittee on Health and Scientific Research of the Committee on Human Resources, 95th Cong., 1st Sess. 1977.

Unauthorized Storage of Toxic Agents: Hearings before the Select Committee to Study Governmental Operations with Respect to Intelligence Activities, 94th Cong., 1st Sess. 1975.

U.S. Intelligence Agencies and Activities: The Performance of the Intelligence Community: Hearings before the Select Committee on Intelligence, 94th Cong., 1st Sess. 1975.

REPORTS

CCA. *The Nelson Rockefeller Report to the President.* Manor Books, 1975.

CIA. *Kubark Counterintelligence Interrogation.* 1963.

CIA. *CIA Targets Fidel: Secret 1967 CIA Inspector General's Report on Plots to Assassinate Fidel Castro.* Ocean Press, 1996.

CIA. *Critique of the Codeword Compartment in the CIA.* 1977.

Cooper, George. *Opinion of George Cooper, Q. C., Regarding Canadian Government Funding of the Allan Memorial Institute in the 1950s and 1960s.* 1986.

Doolittle, James. *Report on the Activities of the Central Intelligence Agency.* 1954.

Enoch, Kenneth, and John Quinn. *Statements by Two Captured U.S. Air Force Officers on Their Participation in Germ Warfare in Korea.* Chinese People's Committee for World Peace, 1952.

SCA. *Report of the Select Committee on Assassinations,* H.R. Rep. No. 95–1828. 1979.

SCSGO. *Alleged Assassination Plots Involving Foreign Leaders,* S. Rep. No. 94–465. 1975.

SCSGO. *Foreign and Military Intelligence,* S. Rep. No. 94–755. 1976.

SCSGO. *Supplementary Detailed Staff Reports on Intelligence Activities and the Rights of Americans,* S. Rep. No. 94–755. 1976.

SSCI. *Committee Study of the Central Intelligence Agency's Detention and Interrogation Program,* S. Rep. No. 113–288. 2014.

ARTICLES

Bersoff, David. "Why Good People Sometimes Do Bad Things: Motivated Reasoning and Unethical Behavior." *Personality and Social Psychology Bulletin* 25, no. 1 (1999).

Bimmerle, George. "'Truth' Drugs in Interrogation." Studies in Intelligence 5, no. 2 (Spring 1961).

Boghardt, Thomas. "Soviet Bloc Intelligence and Its AIDS Disinformation Campaign." *Studies in Intelligence* 53, no. 4 (December 2009).

Braverman, Eric. "Memories of Carl C. Pfeiffer, Ph.D., M.D.: Physician, Scientist, Teacher and Philanthropist." *Journal of Orthomolecular Medicine* 4, no. 1 (1989).

Cameron, Ewen. "Psychic Driving." *American Journal of Psychiatry* 112, no. 7 (January 1956).

Caruso, James, and Jason Sheehan. "Psychosurgery, Ethics, and Media: A History of Walter Freeman and the Lobotomy." *Neurosurgical Focus* 43, no. 3 (September 2017).

Check, Ryan, and Afsheen Radsan. "One Lantern in the Darkest Night: The CIA's Inspector General." *Journal of National Security Law and Policy* 4, no. 2 (2010).

Clancy, Susan, et al. "Memory Distortion in People Reporting Abduction by Aliens." *Journal of Abnormal Psychology* 111, no. 3 (2002).

Colby, William, and Richard Helms. "Reflections of DCIs Colby and Helms on the CIA's 'Time of Troubles.'" *Studies in Intelligence* 51, no. 3 (September 2007).

Crane, Conrad. "Chemical and Biological Warfare during the Korean War: Rhetoric and Reality." *Asian Perspective* 25, no. 3 (2001).

Crawford, Chester. "The Polygraph in Agent Interrogation." *Studies in Intelligence* 4, no. 3 (Summer 1960).

Frost, David. "An Interview with Richard Helms." *Studies in Intelligence* (Fall 2000).

Haines, Gerald. "Looking for a Rogue Elephant: The Pike Committee Investigations and the CIA." *Studies in Intelligence* (Winter 1998).

Leary, William. "Robert Fulton's Skyhook and Operation Coldfeet." Studies in Intelligence 38, no. 5 (1995).

Lemov, Rebecca. "Brainwashing's Avatar: The Curious Career of Dr. Ewen Cameron." *Grey Room* 45 (Fall 2011).

Melley, Timothy. "Brain Warfare: The Covert Sphere, Terrorism, and the Legacy of the Cold War." *Grey Room* 45 (Fall 2011).

McCoy, Alfred. "Science in Dachau's Shadow: Hebb, Beecher, and the Development of a CIA Psychological Torture and Modern Medical Ethics." *Journal of the History of the Behavioral Sciences* 43, no. 4 (Fall 2007).

Murphy, Mark. "The Exploits of Agent 110: Allen Dulles in Wartime." *Studies in Intelligence* (1994).

Novak, Steven. "LSD before Leary: Sidney Cohen's Critique of 1950s Psychedelic Drug Research." *Isis* 88, no. 1 (March 1997).

"Project Azorian: The Story of the Hughes Glomar Explorer." *Studies in Intelligence* (Fall 1985).

Rauh, Joseph, and James Turner. "Anatomy of a Public Interest Case Against the CIA." Hamline *Journal of Public Law and Policy* 2, no. 2 (Fall 1990).

Redlich, Allison, Christopher Kelly, and Jeaneé Miller. "The Who, What, and Why of Human Intelligence Gathering: Self-Reported Measures of Interrogation Methods." *Applied Cognitive Psychology* 28 (2014).

Robarge, David. "DCI John McCone and the Assassination of President John F. Kennedy." *Studies in Intelligence* 57, no. 3 (September 2013).

Ross, Colin. "LSD Experiments by the United States Army." *History of Psychiatry* 28, no. 4 (December 2017).

Seamon, John, Morgan Philbin, and Liza Harrison. "Do You Remember Proposing to the Pepsi Machine? False Recollections from a Campus Walk." *Psychonomic Bulletin and Review* 13, no. 5 (2006).

Shuster, Evelyne. "Fifty Years Later: The Significance of the Nuremberg Code." *New England Journal of Medicine* 337, no. 20 (November 13, 1997).

Silver, Arnold. "Questions, Questions, Questions: Memories of Oberursel." *Intelligence and National Security* 8, no. 2 (April 1993).

Strickland, Lee. "Civil Liberties vs. Intelligence Collection: The Secret Foreign Intelligence Surveillance Act Court Speaks in Public." *Government Information Quarterly* 20 (2003).

Tsang, Steve. "Target Zhou Enlai: The 'Kashmir Princess' Incident of 1955." *China Quarterly* 139 (September 1994).

Tucker, Jonathan. "A Farewell to Germs: The U.S. Renunciation of Biological and Toxin Warfare, 1969–70." *International Security* 27, no. 1 (Summer 2002).

West, Louis. "Psychiatric Reflections on the Death Penalty." *American Journal of Orthopsychiatry* 45, no. 4 (July 1975).

West, Louis, Chester Pierce, and Warren Thomas. "Lysergic Acid Diethylamide: Its Effects on a Male Asiatic Elephant." *Science* 138, no. 3545 (December 7, 1962).

BOOKS

Agee, Philip. *Inside the Company: CIA Diary.* Stonehill, 1975.

Albarelli, H. *A Terrible Mistake: The Murder of Frank Olson and the CIA's Secret Cold War Experiments.* Trine Day, 2009.

Anderson, Jack, and Daryl Gibson. *Peace, War, and Politics: An Eyewitness Account.* Forge Books, 1999.

Andrew, Christopher, and Vasili Mitrokhin. *The Sword and the Shield: The Mitrokhin Archive and the Secret History of the KGB.* Basic Books, 1999.

Applebaum, Anne. Gulag: *A History. Anchor Books*, 2003.

Bain, Donald. *The CIA's Control of Candy Jones.* Playboy Press, 1976.

Barrett, David. *The CIA and Congress: The Untold Story from Truman to Kennedy.* University Press of Kansas, 2005.

Bergreen, Laurence. *Marco Polo: From Venice to Xanadu.* Knopf, 2007.

Breen, Benjamin. *Tripping on Utopia: Margaret Mead, the Cold War, and the Troubled Birth of Psychedelic Science.* Grand Central Publishing, 2024.

Bruning, John. *Crimson Sky: The Air Battle for Korea.* Potomac Books, 1999.

Bugliosi, Vincent. *Reclaiming History: The Assassination of President John F. Kennedy.* Norton, 2007.

Campbell, Nancy. *Discovering Addiction: The Science and Politics of Substance Abuse Research.* University of Michigan Press, 2007.

Campbell, Nancy, J. P. Olsen, and Luke Walden. *The Narcotic Farm*. Abrams, 2008.

Chase, Alston. Harvard and the Unabomber: *The Education of an American Terrorist*. Norton 2003.

Churchill, Ward, and Jim Wall. *The COINTELPRO Papers: Documents from the FBI's Secret War Against Dissent in the United States*. South End Press, 2001.

Clews, John. *The Communists' New Weapon: Germ Warfare*. Lincolns Prager, 1952.

Colby, William, and Peter Forbath. *Honorable Men: My Life in the CIA*. Simon and Schuster, 1978.

Collins, Anne. *In the Sleep Room: The Story of the CIA Brainwashing Experiments in Canada*. Lester and Orpen Dennys, 1988.

Condon, Richard. *The Manchurian Candidate*. McGraw-Hill, 1959.

Connelly, Matthew. *The Declassification Engine: What History Reveals About America's Top Secrets*. Pantheon Books, 2023.

Cormac, Rory. *How to Stage a Coup: And Ten Other Lessons from the World of Secret Statecraft*. Atlantic Books, 2022.

Craig, Campbell, and Frederik Logevall. *America's Cold War: The Politics of Insecurity*. Harvard University Press, 2009.

Dean, Josh. *The Taking of K-129: How the CIA Used Howard Hughes to Steal a Russian Sub in the Most Daring Covert Operation in History*. Dutton, 2017.

Devlin, Larry. *Chief of Station, Congo: A Memoir of 1960–67*. PublicAffairs, 2007.

Drutman, Lee. *Breaking the Two-Party Doom Loop: The Case for Multiparty Democracy in America*. Oxford University Press, 2020.

Ehrman, Bart. *Armageddon: What the Bible Really Says About the End*. Simon and Schuster, 2023.

Ewing, Charles, and Joseph McCann. *Minds on Trial: Great Cases in Law and Psychology*. Oxford University Press, 2006.

Festinger, Leon, Henry Riecken, and Stanley Schachter. *When Prophecy Fails: A Social and Psychological Study of a Modern Group that Predicted the Destruction of the World*. Harper, 2009.

Ford, Harold. William E. *Colby as Director of Central Intelligence 1973–1976*. Center for the Study of Intelligence, 1993.

Freberg, Stan. "The Shellfish-Toxin Joy Buzzer, and Other Exotic CIA Novelties." *In Lord John Ten: A Celebration*, edited by Dennis Etchison. Lord John Press, 1988.

FRUS. Africa, 1958–1960. USGPO, 1992.

FRUS. *The Intelligence Community, 1950–1955*. USGPO, 2007.

Fuller, John. *The Day of St. Anthony's Fire*. Macmillan, 1968.

Fursenko, Aleksandr, and Timothy Naftali. *One Hell of a Gamble: Khrushchev, Castro, and Kennedy, 1958–1964*. Norton, 1997.

Gaddis, John. George F. Kennan: An American Life. Penguin Press, 2011.

Gates, Robert. *From the Shadows: The Ultimate Insider's Story of Five Presidents and How They Won the Cold War*. Simon and Schuster, 2006.

Gehl, Katherine, and Michael Porter. *The Politics Industry: How Political Innovation*

Can Break Partisan Gridlock and Save Our Democracy. Harvard Business Review Press, 2020.

Gillmor, Don. *I Swear by Apollo: Dr. Ewen Cameron and the CIA-Brainwashing Experiments*. Eden Press, 1987.

Ginsberg, Allen. *Poems All over the Place: Mostly 'Seventies*. Cherry Valley Editions, 1978.

Haidt, Jonathan. *The Righteous Mind: Why Good People Are Divided by Politics and Religion*. Vintage Books, 2012.

Hassan, Steven. *Combating Cult Mind Control*. Freedom of Mind Press, 2018.

Hassan, Steven. *The Cult of Trump: A Leading Cult Expert Explains How the President Uses Mind Control*. Free Press, 2019.

Helms, Richard, and William Wood. *A Look over My Shoulder: A Life in the Central Intelligence Agency*. Random House, 2003.

Herbert, Anthony. *Soldier*. Holt, Rinehart and Winston, 1973.

Hofmann, Albert. *LSD: My Problem Child*. Translated by Jonathan Ott. MAPS, 2009.

Hollington, Kris. *Wolves, Jackals, and Foxes: The Assassins Who Changed History*. Thomas Dunne Books, 2007.

Holloway, David. *Stalin and the Bomb: The Soviet Union and Atomic Energy 1939–56*. Yale University Press, 1994.

Huxley, Aldous. *Brave New World Revisited*. Chatto and Windus, 1958.

Jeffreys-Jones, Rhodri. *A Question of Standing: The History of the CIA*. Oxford University Press, 2022.

Johnson, Loch. *Spy Watching: Intelligence Accountability in the United States*. Oxford University Press, 2018.

Jones, Vincent. *Manhattan: The Army and the Atomic Bomb. Center for Military History*, 1985.

Kaplan, Fred. *The Wizards of Armageddon*. Simon and Schuster, 1983.

Ketchum, James. *Chemical Warfare Secrets Almost Forgotten*. ChemBooks, 2006.

Kinzer, Stephen. *Poisoner in Chief: Sidney Gottlieb and the CIA Search for Mind Control*. Henry Holt and Company, 2019.

Kirkpatrick, Lyman. *The Real CIA*. Macmillan, 1968.

Kissinger, Henry. *Years of Renewal*. Touchstone, 2000.

Klaas, Brian. *Fluke: Chance, Chaos, and Why Everything We Do Matters*. Scribner, 2024.

Klein, Naomi. *The Shock Doctrine: The Rise of Disaster Capitalism*. Metropolitan Books, 2007.

Lee, Martin, and Bruce Shlain. *Acid Dreams: The CIA, LSD, and the Sixties Rebellion*. Grove Press, 1985.

Lehr, Dick, and Gerard O'Neill. *Whitey: The Life of America's Most Notorious Mob Boss*. Crown Publishers, 2013.

Lenzner, Terry. *The Investigator: Fifty Years of Uncovering the Truth*. Blue Rider Press, 2013.

Lisle, John. *The Dirty Tricks Department: Stanley Lovell, the OSS, and the Masterminds of World War II Secret Warfare*. St. Martin's Press, 2023.

Loftus, Elizabeth, and Katherine Ketcham. *The Myth of Repressed Memory: False Memories and Allegations of Sexual Abuse*. St. Martin's Press, 1994.

Lovell, Stanley. *Of Spies and Stratagems*. Prentice-Hall, 1963.

Luria, Carlos. *Skating on the Edge: A Memoir and Journey through a Metamorphosis of the CIA*. BookSurge, 2006.

Mannix, Daniel. *The History of Torture*. Sutton, 1964.

Marchetti, Victor, and John Marks. *The CIA and the Cult of Intelligence*. Knopf, 1974.

Marks, John. *The Search for the Manchurian Candidate: The CIA and Mind Control*. Times Books, 1979.

Mayer, Jane. *The Dark Side: The Inside Story of How the War on Terror Turned into a War on American Ideals*. Anchor Books, 2008.

McCoy, Alfred. *A Question of Torture: CIA Interrogation, from the Cold War to the War on Terror*. Metropolitan Books, 2006.

McNally, Richard. *Remembering Trauma*. Harvard University Press, 2003.

Melton, H. Keith, and Robert Wallace. *The Official CIA Manual of Trickery and Deception*. HarperCollins, 2009.

Miller, Nathan. *Spying for America: The Hidden History of U.S. Intelligence*. Marlowe and Company, 1997.

Monje, Scott. *The Central Intelligence Agency: A Documentary History*. Greenwood Press, 2008.

Moore, Alex. *Fidel Castro: In His Own Words*. Racehorse, 2017.

Moynihan, Daniel Patrick. *Secrecy: The American Experience*. Yale University Press, 1998.

Neisser, Ulric, and Nicole Harsch. "Phantom Flashbulbs: False Recollections of Hearing the News About Challenger." *In Affect and Accuracy in Recall*, edited by Eugene Winograd. Cambridge University Press, 1992.

O'Brien, Cathy, and Mark Phillips. *Trance Formation of America: The True Life Story of a CIA Mind Control Slave*. Reality Marketing, 1995.

O'Brien, Cathy, and Mark Phillips. *Access Denied: For Reasons of National Security*. Reality Marketing, 2004.

Olmsted, Kathryn. *Challenging the Secret Government: The Post-Watergate Investigations of the CIA and FBI*. The University of North Carolina Press, 1996.

O'Neill, Tom. *Chaos: Charles Manson, the CIA, and the Secret History of the Sixties*. Little, Brown and Company, 2019.

Orne, Martin. "The Potential Uses of Hypnosis in Interrogation." In *The Manipulation of Human Behavior*, edited by Albert Biderman and Herbert Zimmer. Wiley, 1961.

Parrish, Michael. *Citizen Rauh: An American Liberal's Life in Law and Politics*. University of Michigan Press, 2010.

Pendergrast, Mark. *The Repressed Memory Epidemic: How It Happened and What We Need to Learn from It*. Springer, 2017.

Perisco, Joseph. *Casey: From the OSS to the CIA*. Viking, 1990.

Perisco, Joseph. *Nuremberg: Infamy on Trial*. Viking, 1994.

Polmar, Norman. *Spyplane: The U-2 History Declassified.* Zenith, 2001.

Posner, Gerald. *Case Closed: Lee Harvey Oswald and the Assassination of JFK.* Random House, 1993.

Powers, Francis. *The Trial of the U2: Exclusive Authorized Account of the Court Proceedings of the Case of Francis Gary Powers Heard before the Military Division of the Supreme Court of the USSR.* Translation World, 1960.

Powers, Thomas. *The Man Who Kept the Secrets: Richard Helms and the CIA.* Knopf, 1979.

Prothero, Donald. *Evolution: What the Fossils Say and Why It Matters.* Columbia University Press, 2007.

Ransom, Harry. *The Intelligence Establishment.* Harvard University Press, 1970.

Regis, Ed. *The Biology of Doom: The History of America's Secret Germ Warfare Project.* Henry Holt and Company, 1999.

Reid, Ed. *The Shame of New York.* Random House, 1953.

Reid, Stuart. *The Lumumba Plot: The Secret History of the CIA and a Cold War Assassination.* Knopf, 2023.

Richelson, Jeffrey. *The Wizards of Langley: Inside the CIA's Directorate of Science and Technology.* Westview, 2001.

Rid, Thomas. *Active Measures: The Secret History of Disinformation and Political Warfare.* Farrar, Straus and Giroux, 2020.

Robinson, Ben. *The Magician: John Mulholland's Secret Life.* Lybrary, 2010.

Rohde, David. *In Deep: The FBI, the CIA, and the Truth About America's "Deep State."* Norton, 2020.

Ronson, Jon. *The Men Who Stare at Goats.* Simon and Schuster, 2004.

Sagan, Carl. *The Demon-Haunted World: Science as a Candle in the Dark.* Ballantine Books, 1996.

Sargant, William. *Battle for the Mind.* Doubleday, 1957.

Scheflin, Alan, and Edward Opton. *The Mind Manipulators.* Paddington Press, 1978.

Schorr, Daniel. *Clearing the Air.* Houghton Mifflin, 1977.

Seed, David. *Brainwashing: The Fictions of Mind Control.* Kent State University Press, 2004.

Sharp, David. *The CIA's Greatest Covert Operation: Inside the Daring Mission to Recover a Nuclear-Armed Soviet Sub.* University Press of Kansas, 2012.

Shermer, Michael. *Conspiracy: Why the Rational Believe the Irrational.* Johns Hopkins University Press, 2022.

Solomon, Philip, et al. *Sensory Deprivation: A Symposium Held at Harvard Medical School.* Harvard University Press, 1965.

Spee, Friedrich. *Cautio Criminalis.* 1631.

Starrs, James, and Katherine Ramsland. *A Voice for the Dead: A Forensic Investigator's Pursuit for Truth in the Grave.* Putnam, 2005.

Streatfeild, Dominic. *Brainwash: The Secret History of Mind Control.* Picador, 2007.

Talbot, David. *The Devil's Chessboard: Allen Dulles, the CIA, and the Rise of America's Secret Government.* Harper, 2015.

Thomas, Gordon. *Journey into Madness: Medical Torture and the Mind Controllers.* Bantam Press, 1988.

Trento, Joseph. *The Secret History of the CIA.* Prima, 2001.

Troy, Gil. *Moynihan's Moment: America's Fight Against Zionism as Racism.* Oxford University Press, 2013.

Tuchman, Barbara. *A Distant Mirror: The Calamitous 14th Century.* Knopf, 1978.

Turner, Stansfield. *Secrecy and Democracy: The CIA in Transition.* Houghton Mifflin, 1985.

Valentine, Douglas. *The Strength of the Wolf: The Secret History of America's War on Drugs.* Verso, 2004.

Vogeler, Robert. *I Was Stalin's Prisoner.* Harcourt, 1952.

Wakefield, Margery. *Understanding Scientology: The Demon Cult.* Margery Wakefield, 2009.

Wall, William. *From Healing to Hell.* NewSouth Books, 2011.

Wallace, Robert, and Keith Melton. *Spycraft: The Secret History of the CIA's Spytechs, from Communism to Al-Qaeda.* Plume, 2009.

Walsh, Lawrence. *Firewall: The Iran-Contra Conspiracy and Cover-up.* Norton, 1997.

Weatherford, Jack. *Genghis Khan and the Making of the Modern World.* Random House, 2004.

Weiner, Tim. *Legacy of Ashes: The History of the CIA.* Doubleday, 2007.

Weinstein, Harvey. *Psychiatry and the CIA: Victims of Mind Control.* American Psychiatric Press, 1990.

Weisman, Steven, ed. *Daniel Patrick Moynihan: A Portrait in Letters of an American Visionary.* PublicAffairs, 2010.

Weissman, Stephen. *American Foreign Policy in the Congo 1960–1964.* Cornell University Press, 1974.

Wellerstein, Alex. *Restricted Data: The History of Nuclear Secrecy in the United States.* University of Chicago Press, 2021.

West, John. *The Last Goodnights: Assisting My Parents with Their Suicides.* Counterpoint, 2009.

Whitfield, Stephen. *The Culture of the Cold War.* Johns Hopkins University Press, 1991.

Woods, Randall. *Shadow Warrior: William Egan Colby and the CIA.* Basic Books, 2013.

Wright, Lawrence. *Remembering Satan: A Tragic Case of Recovered Memory.* Vintage Books, 1995.

DOCUMENTARIES

Koch, Egmont, and Michael Wech. *Code Name Artichoke.* WDR, 2002.

Morris, Errol. *Wormwood.* Netflix, 2017.

Roy, Richard. *Mission: Mind Control.* ABC, 1979.

Youngblood, Adrienne. *Trance: The Cathy O'Brien Story.* 8th House Productions, 2022.

Index

About the Author

Photo by Osiris Lisle

John Lisle has a PhD in history from the University of Texas, where he is now a professor of the history of science. His first book, *The Dirty Tricks Department,* tells the story of the scientists who developed secret weapons, documents, and disguises for the OSS during World War II. He has received research and writing awards from the National Academy of Sciences, the American Institute of Physics, and the National Endowment for the Humanities. His work has been published in *Skeptic, Scientific American, Smithsonian Magazine,* and elsewhere.